Financial Management for Service Companies

Financial Management for Service Companies

KEITH WARD

FINANCIAL TIMES

PITMAN PUBLISHING

Pitman Publishing
128 Long Acre, London WC2E 9AN

A Division of Longman Group UK Limited

First published in 1993

© Keith Ward 1993

A CIP catalogue record for this book can be obtained from the British Library.

ISBN 0 273 60065 6

Typeset by PanTek Arts, Maidstone, Kent.
Printed and bound in Great Britain by
Biddles Ltd, Guildford and King's Lynn

CONTENTS

Preface   xi

Part 1
Characteristics of the Service Sector

1 **Introduction and overview**   **3**
   The importance of the service sector   3
   The need for specifically tailored financial control systems   8
   Identifying specific critical success factors   11
   Key characteristics of service industries   14

Part 2
Service Companies

2 **Classifications of service companies**   **21**
   No satisfactory definition of service companies   21
   Classification by common characteristics   22
   Direct/Indirect customers   27
   Personal nature of services   30
   Risk profile of service   31
   Classification by type of competitive strategy   33

3 **Service industry competitive strategies**   **34**
   Overview   34
   Creating a sustainable competitive advantage   37
   Generic competitive strategies applied to the service sector   44
   Quality of service – a differentiation strategy   51
   Cost of service – becoming the low cost supplier   56
   Financial control systems for each type of
   competitive strategy   59

4 Key issues for financial control   **61**
  Introduction   61
  Relevance of risk profiles   64
  Planning issues for service companies   69
  Performance measures   72
  Pricing decisions   73
  Cost management   74
  Managing dynamic growth   76
  Asset and liability management   77
  Conclusion   78

5 Internal service businesses   **79**
  Introduction   79
  Available alternatives: provide internally, buy in, do without   80
  Basis of sourcing decision   81
  'Cost' of alternatives   82
  Transfer pricing system   87

Part 3
Specific financial control issues

6 The importance of a tailored financial control system   **93**
  Introduction   93
  Business risk in service companies   94
  Tailored financial controls   98
  Financial risk in service companies   103
  Segmented financial analysis   111
  Customer Account Profitability (CAP)   112
  Direct Product Profitability (DPP)   114
  Competitor accounting   116

7 Planning requirements in service companies   **118**
  Introduction: The analysis, planning and control process   118
  The planning process   120
  Long-term planning   123
  Short-term planning   128
  Conclusion   132

8 Using pricing as a competitive strategy   **133**
Introduction   133
Aligning pricing strategy and competitive position   134
Impact of cost structure on pricing strategy   136
Market development pricing strategies   138
Problems of managing complex pricing strategies   142
Summary   143

9 Cost control as a critical success factor   **144**
Introduction   144
Added value rather than cost minimisation   145
Identifying clear measurable objectives   146
Using standard costs in the service sector   147
Summary   153

10 Managing dynamic growth in service businesses   **155**
Introduction   155
Franchising   156
Acquisitions   157
Using earn-outs   160
Other innovative financial instruments   164

11 Asset and liability management for service companies   **165**
Introduction   165
Fixed assets – to buy or just use   165
Operating cash flow   168
Credit risk – is it worth it?   170
Summary   172

Part 4
Information technology in the service sector

12 The strategic use of information technology   **175**
Introduction   175
Peopleless payables   177
EPOS and EFTPOS   179
Airline reservation systems   180
Risk of failure   182
Conclusion   182

13 The operational use of information technology   **184**
Introduction   184
The right information   186
The right people   187
The right time   188
Implementation issues   190
Summary   191

Part 5
Case studies of particular service industries

Overview of Part 5   **196**
14 Retailing   197
Background to the retailing industry   197
Overseas entrants   201
Linking supermarkets and clothing   202
Other clothing retailers   203
Critical success factors   206
Financial management and control issues   207
Looking ahead   208

15 Advertising   **209**
Background   209
An alternative competitive strategy   213
Critical success factors   214
Financial management and control issues   215
The future   216

16 The software industry   **218**
Background to the industry   218
Overseas based competitors   221
Software products companies   223
Critical success factors   224
Financial management and control issues   226
Prospects for the future   227

17 The airline industry **229**
Background to the industry 229
Related industries 231
Alternative competitive strategies 232
Critical success factors 233
Financial management and control issues 235
Future developments 235

Index 238

PREFACE

While there are a large number of existing books dealing with financial management and control issues, there are no such books focusing specifically and exclusively on service companies. This book is designed to fill this significant gap for practising management accountants, financial controllers and general managers within service industries and their financial advisors, as well as being of relevance to training accountants and MBA students.

While the book is not therefore a basic accounting text, the key technical issues are clearly explained and placed in their appropriate business context. The book deals in depth with the specific problems of financial management and control in a wide range of service industries by continual reference to practical case study type examples. Indeed, not only are these examples used throughout the main body of the book, but the final part draws together the key issues relating to four separate service industries in individually focused chapters.

This practical, up-to-date approach is a key element in the style of the book, but there is also sufficient rigour in the analysis for it to be adopted as an academic text-book on appropriate courses, such as advanced accounting and finance electives on MBA and other degree programmes.

The book is divided into five parts for ease of use, with Part 1 providing a brief introduction and overview. Part 2 deals with the different competitive strategies which can be implemented by service companies and identifies their implications for the required financial management and control system. Part 3 then considers each of these implications in depth, while Part 4 discusses the impact of the dramatic development in information technology in terms of both the strategic and operational consequences for service industries. As already stated, Part 5 consists of chapters on four specific service industries, highlighting how the financial management and control system must be tailored to the particular needs of the service company in which it is to be used.

I am very grateful to my secretary, Sheila Hart, for typing the manuscript with her usual speed and accuracy, aided in part by her colleague, Marjorie Dawe. I would also like to thank Bushra Khan for her assistance in the original outline design of the book and am sorry that other commitments precluded her from being involved in the actual writing. I am, as ever, indebted to my wife, Angela, and my children, Sam and Rob, for their forbearance during the writing of the book, which has kept me locked away in my study for longer than any of them would like. I hope that you, the reader, find this effort has been worthwhile and that the book may be of use to you in managing a successful service business.

Part I

CHARACTERISTICS OF THE SERVICE SECTOR

I INTRODUCTION AND OVERVIEW

THE IMPORTANCE OF THE SERVICE SECTOR

It has been well known for a long time that as any economy develops into maturity, the relative importance of the service sector as both an employer and generator of wealth increases significantly. In the case of the earliest developing industrialised economies, this increasing importance of the service sector has been clearly evident for over 30 years. Even in Germany, which remains a highly industrialised economy when compared with most of the other major developed countries, this trend in employment can be clearly seen. Looking at total employment proportions in Western Germany (so as to avoid the distortions created by reunification), back in the early 1960s manufacturing industries accounted for approximately 60% of total employment with services contributing the bulk of the remaining 40%. By the early 1990s these proportions had become reversed with service industries taking almost a 60% share of total employment, with manufacturing declining to around 40% of the total. However, much of management theory and practice still focuses on the specific needs of manufacturing industries, with an implicit assumption that service companies can apply these ideas with, if absolutely necessary, some minor modifications. This is particularly true in the area of financial management and control where the real requirements of service companies have largely been ignored in the wealth of both theoretical and applied literature produced in this 30 year period.

This book attempts to fill what is a rather surprising gap because two recent theoretical and conceptual developments in this area, i.e. corporate financial strategy and strategic management accounting, highlight the importance of developing specifically tailored financial strategies and controls for each different type of business. As is demonstrated later in this chapter and throughout the book, the very specific needs of service businesses require that such appropriately tailored finance and accounting procedures are both conceptually developed and properly applied in practice to this sector, rather than modifying a completely inappropriate model.

This inevitable long-term shift towards service industries is accompanied by a number of other significant factors, so that this argument is worth a very brief review before commencing the in-depth consideration of the financial needs of service companies. The initial start point on the development cycle for most countries or regions is as a subsistence economy dependent on agriculture and other primary extractive industries. Almost all the resources of the economy are focused on these restricted areas. Consequently the rate of economic growth tends to be relatively slow and can be self-limiting due to the problems caused by the increasing population which often occurs in such economic conditions.

A critical change, which normally results in a dramatic increase in the rate of economic development, occurs with the transfer of some resources into the manufacturing sector. Initially manufacturing concentrates on trans forming the existing raw materials into more valuable forms of finished product. However, quite rapidly new production techniques are developed which significantly increase the productivity of the workforce and increase the ranges of goods produced. This allows the total output of an economy to grow at a much faster rate. This was obviously first illustrated on a large scale by the industrial revolution of the eighteenth century, but can be seen today being replicated in many developing economies around the world, with the rate of change being further accelerated by technology transfer from more developed economies.

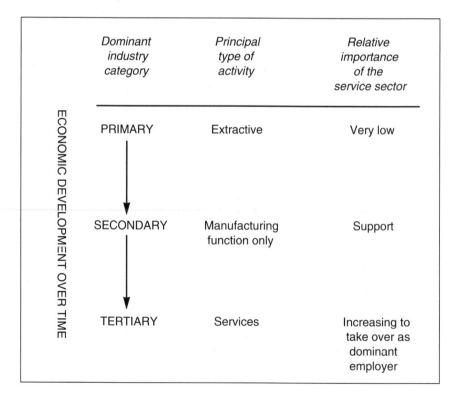

Figure 1.1 The increasing importance of the service sector

The application of improved production techniques in the existing primary industries (particularly agriculture) releases labour, without reducing the total output from these industries. This newly available workforce can then be transferred into the new manufacturing industries which are starting to develop. Thus there is the potential for a rapid increase in the total output of the economy, due to more efficient production in its core existing industries, while still enabling it to exploit the new opportunities in its infant secondary industries.

This increased total output will normally result in increased wealth, which itself leads to higher demand for manufactured goods, and hence there is a potential market for still higher outputs of existing goods. However, a demand also develops for more sophisticated products, which leads to research and development into new manufacturing technologies. Thus, this focus on the secondary industries, as manufacturing is often referred to, can create a period of very rapid economic growth, which can be still further enhanced if the potential of international trade is realised. This enables an economy to produce even greater volumes of goods, so that it achieves the maximum available economies of scale, etc., by exporting the surplus to external customers. The total wealth created is consequently increased as the extra production requires the employment of more people, whose incomes generate demand for more goods, some of which will be imported from these external economies. By applying what is known as the 'law of comparative advantage' this international trade can make both trading partners better off economically.

However, as the level of economic wealth increases, the demand for manufactured goods eventually stabilises and the major growth area becomes the service sector. From an overall economic perspective, this second transition is vitally important because manufacturing efficiencies have now developed to such an extent that this stabilised demand for manufactured goods can be produced using a much smaller proportion of the available workforce. (By this stage of development, the agricultural and other primary industries usually only employ a very small proportion of the total workforce.)   Hence there is a readily available supply of labour which can be utilised in the new burgeoning service industries (such as travel, retailing, leisure, entertainment, etc.). The good news is that not only is there a very high demand for these services from a now relatively well-off and increasingly sophisticated population, who also have an increasing proportion of leisure time, but also these services tend to be highly labour intensive during their launch and early growth years.

The contrasting bad news is that the wealth-creating potential of service industries is much lower than that of many manufacturing industries due to

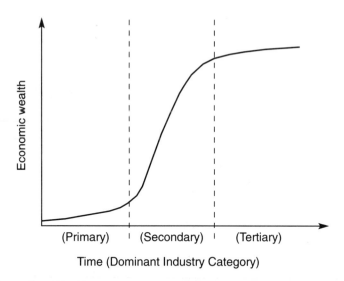

Figure 1.2 Changing rate of economic growth

their lower multiplier effect. In other words, the creation of a major new manufacturing facility creates demand for raw material and sub-component suppliers on an ongoing basis and such a plant also often requires a significant level of local service support, with a consequently further positive impact on local employment. Such a dramatic multiplier effect is less common in the service sector; although there are exceptions, such as airlines, which do generate a substantial level of associated employment in other areas such as airports, inflight catering, air traffic control, and aeroplane manufacture and maintenance.

An even more interesting aspect of this increasing importance of the service sector is that its initially high employment needs tend to reduce as these individual industries themselves mature and become more intensely competitive. This application of labour-saving technology (including, obviously, computer systems) becomes more appropriate as the scale of operations grows and the pressure to reduce labour costs increases. During the years of rapid growth, this strategy may result in a lower rate of increase in employment than would otherwise take place. However, when the industry's growth rate has fallen to a very low level, these increased operational efficiencies can lead to an absolute reduction in the level of employment, similar to that witnessed in the manufacturing sector earlier in the economy's life-cycle.

The combination of the lower wealth-creating potential and the eventual stabilisation or reduction in employment prospects of the service sector in total gives an unattractive result. It means that more mature economies inevitably face the prospect of significantly lower rates of economic growth in the future than they have experienced in the past, as is shown in Figure 1.2. This somewhat depressing overall outlook is compounded by the fact that so far no individual economy has solved the problem of what to do with the section of the workforce which is no longer needed within the service sector but which now has a high expectation of ever increasing wealth. In other words, what follows on from the tertiary stage of industrial development?

In the 1980s a fourth category was introduced, called not surprisingly 'quarternary' to try to examine the stage of development following on from the tertiary stage. Quarternary industries provide information and expertise, and therefore include the new micro-chip and micro-electronics industries. However, this 'information and expertise' sector includes many industries which have been around for quite a long time and which can be easily classified as services (such as software and consultancy). Therefore, this new category has been largely ignored for the purposes of this book, particularly as it fails to answer the question of what will produce the massive employment requirements for future generations.

If a particular economy has passed very rapidly from a manufacturing dominated position to a more substantial dependence on its services sector, severe problems can be experienced during any significant, albeit temporary, downturn in its own internal economy. When this domestic downturn, or recession, coincides with lower activity in its major trading partners the impact on domestic employment can be quite dramatic, as can be seen by examining the change in Japan between the end of 1991 and early 1993.

Even after the end of the 1980s, many economists were predicting that future growth rates in Japan would be constrained by a continuing shortage of labour. Thus, the by then well-established very low levels of unemployment within the economy and the Japanese corporate culture of life-time employment were not seen as under threat, despite the maturity and even decline of several longstanding significant manufacturing industries (such as steel, ship-building and basic engineering). These industries were being supplanted by the normal shift into services (such as banking, investment management, retailing and leisure), while the manufacture of higher added value products (such as cars and electronics) was still seen as a growth sector due to the anticipated continued growth in the major export markets.

The rapid downturn in the early 1990s, including the collapse of Japanese financial markets and property values, resulted in a significant change in these expectations. Many manufacturing companies started to reduce employment levels and they were quickly followed by a number of service sector companies, which had geared up for anticipated, but unfulfilled, higher levels of activity. The pressure to improve operating efficiencies means that these lost jobs are unlikely to be replaced, even if the previously anticipated levels of activity are eventually achieved.

THE NEED FOR SPECIFICALLY TAILORED FINANCIAL CONTROL SYSTEMS

Unfortunately, the micro-economic implications of this increasing importance of the service sector have been even less well analysed and understood than the broader macro-economic issues outlined above. Many large companies have moved into service industries in an attempt to sustain their historic growth rates once their original manufacturing businesses have clearly matured; these diversification moves are considered in more detail in Chapter 3. In even more companies, there are integral service businesses supplying internal customers, often utilising some form of internal 'transfer pricing' system in an attempt to reproduce external market conditions; these issues are specifically addressed in Chapter 5. Most of these companies have tried to apply their existing traditional financial management and control processes, albeit sometimes with a minor degree of modification, to these new ventures with, not surprisingly, a limited degree of success.

The most common method of evaluating the financial performance of either an overall business or a division of a business (the term, Strategic Business Unit [SBU] will be used for those sub-divisions of a business which have both identifiable external customers and services) is some measure of Return on Investment or ROI. As shown in Figure 1.3, ROI places the profit achieved by the business in the context of the investment needed to run the business. For many mature manufacturing businesses, this is a sensible performance measure because there is a financial trade-off between the profit achieved and the assets used in the business. Thus a plan to increase the volume of sales may require an increase in the scale of plant and machinery owned by the business and in the supporting level of raw material stocks. It will also usually result in an increased investment in outstanding receivables (debtors) if the sales are made on credit and the plan is successfully implemented.

Return on Investment (ROI)	**=**	**Profit before interest and tax** / **Net assets (i.e. capital employed)**

Note:
There is a wide variety of ways in which both the numerator and denominator are calculated. The most important factor is that consistency is applied in both calculations; e.g. if assets are included gross, i.e. before depreciation, then profit before depreciation should also be used.

Figure 1.3 Return on investment as a financial control measure

However, in the case of an independent contract catering company which runs the on-site canteen and restaurant facilities for such a manufacturing business, such a financial control measure may be of no practical relevance. It is quite common for this type of contract caterer not only to use the kitchen facilities of the client company, but also to require payment in advance for the services to be provided. Hence, there is no 'investment' as such, against which the financial return can be compared, and yet an appropriate system of financial evaluation is clearly essential. Similarly, a key element in the competitive strategy of many large supermarket chains is to ensure that they have sold their stocks, and been paid by their customers, long before they have to pay their suppliers for these goods. This results in a high level of negative working capital, which may well be represented by cash sitting on the balance sheet and earning interest income for the retailer. Alternatively, this negative working capital may have been invested in the ownership of the stores used by the retailer, rather than renting or leasing them. The overall level of investment on which the retailer's return is made may therefore differ dramatically depending on the type of competitive and financial strategy being implemented.

It is quite true that similarly dramatic changes in the investment base of a business, and hence in the reported ROI, can be seen by the selection of different competitive and financial strategies within manufacturing or extractive industries. Thus the need to design appropriately tailored financial systems for service companies is not unique to these businesses, but it is very unlikely that even a tailored version of a manufacturing based financial control system would fit any new service business, into which the manufacturing group had just diversified. Therefore the announcement by GEC in December 1992 that it intended to develop a large related services business should have severe implications for its existing ROI focused financial

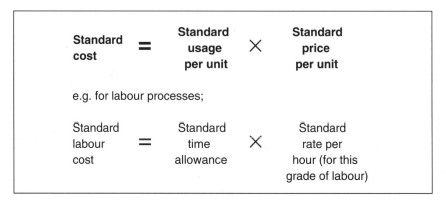

Figure 1.4 Components of a standard cost

control system. As well as supplying high technology equipment to its customers, it declared an interest in running the subsequent installation for them as well; e.g. it may deliver sophisticated road traffic control equipment and other logistics support to a privately funded toll road system and offer, in addition, a full facilities management contract for the completed project, so that the continuing operational problems are also taken away from the customer. One obvious additional benefit of such a fundamental change in competitive strategy is to cement the relationship with the customer by achieving a much more continuous level of contact and business, rather than trying to make very large individual sales which are each separated in time by several years. However, the potential benefits of such a strategy should not blind the company to the need to consider carefully the problems associated with a move into what is clearly a very different type of business from that where its existing sustainable competitive advantages have been established, even though the customers for the two businesses may be the same.

At the opposite end of the argument, it is also true that there are a number of very sound financial planning and control techniques which have become almost exclusively associated with the manufacturing sector. As a consequence they are generally underutilised in service businesses, despite the relevance of the particular approach. A good example is the standard costing technique which has, for many years, been widely used in many manufacturing industries but which can, in fact, have great value to any business which involves repetitive processes, particularly where labour is involved. This applies to many service industries and it is normally quite practical to create a 'standard cost' for almost any repetitive labour process, as this only involves establishing a standard time allowance and a standard price per unit of time, as is shown in Figure 1.4.

Therefore, as long as the average or target time for any repetitive clerical or similar process, such as order processing or other aspect of customer servicing, can be assessed, it is possible to use standard costing within a service company. It is probable that a major reason for the lack of use of this technique in such businesses is that many financial managers have forgotten the major advantages which can flow from the sensible incorporation of a suitable standard costing system. The establishment of a standard physical unit (such as the time allowance for a standard labour cost) greatly assists in the physical resources planning process, as the total required labour can be estimated from the total repetitions which are expected to be required and the time taken to process each individual event. The total expected cost for this element of the business can obviously be calculated by including the standard cost per unit, and this enables the financial planning and analysis process to be based on a more rational basis.

Even more importantly, in many companies, the comparison of the actual cost against the expected or planned cost can now be made much more useful and decision oriented. This is achieved, as part of the regular financial monitoring and control process, by producing an appropriately detailed variance analysis. Such an analysis explains whether the differences between actual and expected costs are caused by efficiency factors in the operations within the business, changes in activity volumes away from those on which the plan was based, or changes in the cost per unit from those forecast when the standard was established. Detailed, practical examples of applying standard costs in service businesses are given in Chapter 9.

IDENTIFYING SPECIFIC CRITICAL SUCCESS FACTORS

This discussion of the benefits of standard costing highlights that the fundamental objectives of financial management in the service sector are the same as for all businesses. A principal role of financial managers is to provide information which assists in the decision making process so that the company achieves its overall corporate objectives. Thus, the basic iterative financial management process of analysis, planning and control, which is diagrammatically illustrated in Figure 1.5, is totally relevant and applicable to service companies. The key issue is how this overall model needs to be tailored so that it focuses on the specific critical success factors of the service sector.

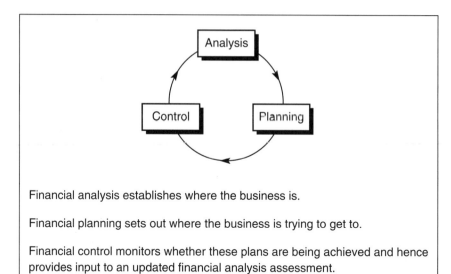

Financial analysis establishes where the business is.

Financial planning sets out where the business is trying to get to.

Financial control monitors whether these plans are being achieved and hence provides input to an updated financial analysis assessment.

Figure 1.5 Financial management as an interactive process

Critical success factors can be defined as those factors which contribute most significantly to the achievement of any particular company's overall objectives. For most commercially oriented companies, one of the key objectives will be to achieve a risk related financial return for its stakeholders. These stakeholders include, but are not limited to, the shareholders who ultimately own the business and any external financiers (such as banks and other lending institutions) who have provided funding for the business. The financial return which is demanded by any external supplier of funding (including trade creditors and customers who pay in advance) is related to their perception of the risk associated with the particular business. Hence one way in which a company can add value through its system of financial management is by raising its funding from the cheapest sources (in risk adjusted terms); this area of financial management is now often referred to as corporate financial strategy, as illustrated in Figure 1.6. However, the more common way of creating added value for these financial stakeholders is by investing these funds in business areas and specific projects, where the business has a sustainable competitive advantage over its existing and potential competitors. In other words, the company has to identify and exploit these areas of competitive advantage by developing and then maintaining the relevant critical success factors. The finance area can make a valuable contribution to this process by providing information on the competitive environment (e.g. on both customers and competitors) and by analysing the impact of prospective and actual changes in competitive strategy. As indicated in Figure 1.6, this more externally focused area of financial management is known as strategic management accounting.

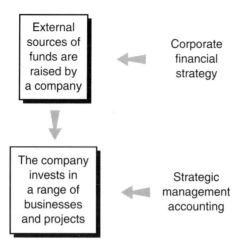

Figure 1.6 The two-stage investment process

Not surprisingly, this book uses the approaches of both corporate financial strategy and strategic management accounting, but applies them to the specific external and internal business environments facing companies in the service sector. Thus, the examples already given of contract catering and supermarket retailing illustrate the ways in which alternative sources of external funding (respectively from customers and suppliers) can be used to improve a company's financial performance. Similarly, the development of new product ranges which can be sold to the existing loyal customers of many large retailers is an example of the identification and exploitation of a critical success factor by a business (in this case, the attributes of potential new products which are likely to appeal to the current customer base). However, critical success factors should not be regarded as stable and automatically continuing in existence if the external competitive environment is itself dynamic. In the software industry, the original major method of pricing for contracts was on a 'time and materials' basis, which meant that staff were charged out to clients at a daily or hourly rate for however long the project took. Clearly, this transferred a large proportion of the overall risk to the customers. As these customers became more sophisticated and knowledgeable and computer systems became vastly more complex, the customers started to demand a fixed price quotation for a specified system. Nowadays this specified system normally includes both the hardware and software requirements, so that the prime contractor has a much higher level of risk when taking on such a contract. This has introduced two new critical success factors for software companies involved in large-scale sophisticated fixed price contracts. First, they must develop very good estimating and bidding procedures so as to ensure that the fixed price bid fully reflects all the costs which are likely to be incurred and allows for an adequate profit margin, when the associated risks of the contract are taken into account. Second, once the project has been started, the company must have a comprehensive project cost monitoring and control system; both to manage the current project and also to provide updated inputs into the estimating and bidding process for future contracts. These new critical success factors obviously require significant changes to be made to the financial information systems of these businesses; these examples are discussed in depth in Part 5, and are also referred to as appropriate in other chapters.

The different potential competitive strategies of service companies are discussed in Chapter 3 with the key issues for financial control for each type of strategy being highlighted in Chapter 4. These are then developed in more depth in Part 3, with Part 4 drawing together the information technology implications of these alternative competitive and financial strategies. However, before looking at these issues, it is important to try to distinguish any common characteristics of service industries which can assist in developing overall recommendations for financial management in this area. This is introduced briefly in the remainder of this chapter and then developed in more detail in Chapter 2.

KEY CHARACTERISTICS OF SERVICE INDUSTRIES

As a differentiating feature from manufacturing and extractive industries, it is fair to say that service products (using the term 'product' to describe both goods and services) tend to be intangible. This makes it more difficult to measure the value of the product accurately because it hinges, even more crucially than in the case of more tangible goods, on the perception of the customer as to what has been received. Difficulties with the measurement of value make the area of financial monitoring and control much more complex, as it becomes more judgemental whether any particular component of the overall service has added more value from the customer's perspective than it cost the service company to include. Hence, the use of external market research becomes even more important and yet many service businesses do very little formal questioning of their customers.

Another issue which is more significant in the case of services is that the expectations of customers may differ dramatically and may change over time or depending upon the particular circumstances surrounding the use of the service. A very simple example is the expectation of the same customer when using very different types of restaurant. For example, the quality of food, service and general ambience demanded from a special celebratory dinner at an exclusive and expensive '5 star' restaurant would be significantly higher than when 'grabbing a snack' from a takeaway fast-food restaurant.

A more complex version of the same issue has been developed to a very sophisticated level by the airline industry, because airlines have managed to produce vastly different prices for the same basic service, i.e. aeroplane transportation from one place to another. The differentiated overall levels of service, combined with a strong element of individually segmented branding, have enabled the airlines to charge customers appropriate pricing levels depending upon the style of service which they wish to purchase. This raises the issue as to whether the customer is sophisticated enough to associate the level of service received with the price being paid. If senior business executives are used to flying Concorde or first class when travelling on business, will they expect this level of service when flying off on a package holiday with their families. It is interesting to note an increase in the number of long haul holidays which now allow for an upgrade in the flights to business class, albeit for a very substantial price premium.

Another issue which is raised by this example is that in many business related services the user of the service is not actually paying any increased costs with their own money, e.g. the business travellers who are 'allowed' to fly first class or business class because of their position within the company. They receive the improved level of service but it is paid for by their companies. This means that the providers of the service have to consider both their direct and indirect customers when analysing their 'perceived value to cost of provision' equation. In some of these cases the actual decision maker regarding which company's service to purchase may not use the particular service being bought; such as in the case of business air travel when the reservations may be made by a central travel department or by the manager's secretary. This clearly adds another complication to the sales and marketing strategy of the service provider, as it now has to communicate with and convince a wider range of parties before achieving a sale.

Seats on aeroplane flights also illustrate another common characteristic of services, which is their very rapid perishability. There is no value in having a ticket for yesterday's flight, train journey, show or sporting event, and a hotel company cannot sell the occupancy of a room for *last night*; it is impossible to build up a *stock* of such products which can then be sold and used up over a period of time. Some services do contain a tangible component (such as the food element in a restaurant meal) which may have a storage potential, but even in these cases there is still a transient element to the delivery of the total service (the availability of a table in the restaurant). This characteristic means that service companies need to gather very good information on future demand for specific products and then to have a flexible, tactical promotional approach to managing this demand as the delivery date of the service approaches. This may take the form of price discounting when demand is below the expected or targeted level, which may be set at a level which is near to capacity or at least is above the break even level. It is clearly important that the financial information system aids this promotional activity by providing the required data on fixed and variable costs by the specific services which are under review; in the previous examples of scheduled airlines and hotels, the proportions of costs which are fixed in the short term are very high.

The question of lack of storage capability for services is highlighted when the production of the service and its consumption are simultaneous. This is clearly the case for many personal services, such as hairdressing, and a key part of any financial strategy is to try to optimise the utilisation of existing capacity before increasing that capacity, particularly where such an increase requires a substantial increase in fixed, committed costs. One way of achieving this is to segment the market by a variation of the method used in the airline industry, except that now the distinguishing factor is often the time of service rather than the quality of service. In other words, a hairdresser may give a discount to certain classes of customer who utilise off-peak times (e.g. pensioners). This acts as an incentive for them to avoid periods when the hairdresser cannot cope with the total demand, and consequently could lose potential customers who would be very willing to pay the full price for the service. An alternative response is to try to increase capacity, but by taking on incremental variable costs rather than incurring a large chunk of additional long-term fixed costs. For our hairdresser this may not be a practical proposition as additional part-time labour may not increase total effective capacity due to other operational constraints (e.g. availability of customer positions, chairs, etc. at peak times). However, separation of duties so that less-skilled staff provide support functions (such as washing hair prior to cutting) can increase the productivity of the skilled stylists significantly.

In retailing this concept is already widely used and is likely to become more widespread as the already intense competition increases for the relatively static total customer base. (It is widely predicted that this general trend towards an increasing use of part-time labour in many service industries will continue; representing partial replacement only for the continuing decline in total demand for labour within the manufacturing sector in most mature economies, such as the UK.) The use of part-time shop staff means that opening hours can be extended, and more staff can be made available at those times during the day when customers actually come shopping. This is instead of the current practice of having stable staff levels throughout the day, except at lunchtime when fewer staff are available in the shop because the rest are out at lunch; doing their shopping presumably! In the banking industry technology has been used to cope with much of these fluctuations in demand. Hiring large numbers of additional part-time staff may be impractical in this industry, not least due to the security and training problems involved. However, the introduction of very sophisticated automated teller machines (known as ATMs or 'hole in the wall' machines), which enable customers to transact most normal retail banking business at any time of the day or night, has effectively also extended bank opening hours as well as helping to cope with the variability of utilisation of in-bank facilities during the normal trading period.

The increasing use of technology in the service sector may reduce the impact of another common characteristic of services, which is the extent of the variability in the end product due to a high degree of involvement of people in the production process. This high labour content means that the end service is often not very standardised as it depends on the quality of the individuals involved. Also the quality of service achieved by any specific individual can vary quite significantly from day to day. In many cases, these changes cannot be removed by any post-production quality control process due to the simultaneous production and consumption of many services. Such a quality control process is also inappropriate for many services because the customer is physically present during the production and delivery of the service. This very close contact with the customer can be regarded as another significant characteristic of services in general, as it is much less common to find this in manufacturing or extractive industries.

These characteristics are used in the next chapter as part of an attempt to classify services. These classifications are then used in the later chapters when particular aspects of financial management in service companies are considered in depth.

Part 2

SERVICE COMPANIES

2 CLASSIFICATIONS OF SERVICE COMPANIES

NO SATISFACTORY DEFINITION OF SERVICE COMPANIES

The reader will have noticed that, in Chapter 1, no formal definition of a service business was given, despite the introduction of a number of common characteristics. It is very interesting that, in surveying the existing literature as part of the basic research prior to writing this book, no generally agreed specification of 'service' businesses could be found. Hence definitions tend to be made in a negative sense, that service industries are those that do not fall within the definitions of either extractive or manufacturing industries.

Fortunately these categories do, at least, have relatively clearly defined boundaries so that the concept of a service business lying outside these boundaries is not too vague as to be totally meaningless. An extractive, or primary, industry is concerned with extracting natural productions and hence includes mining and oil and gas extraction. It would also logically include agriculture, but it could be argued that the application of modern farming technology in many areas means that much agriculture now has significantly more in common with the manufacturing sector than with a traditional definition of an extractive industry. For the purposes of this book this semantics issue is irrelevant because agriculture would still remain outside the service sector, which is our area of concentration.

Manufacturing industries can be defined as being those involved in the making of tangible articles or material that did not exist before, by the use of physical labour and/or mechanical power. In other words a key element of the manufacturing sector is a *transformation process*, whereas the extractive industries may simply physically relocate the extracted material. Indeed any subsequent transformation of this basic material should normally be regarded as a manufacturing process; the refining of crude oil into its finished product formats, such as petrol, aviation spirit, etc., is a manufacturing process.

However, almost all of these modern extractive and manufacturing operations involve a large number of ancillary services which should be financially managed in an appropriately tailored manner. Unfortunately, as already mentioned in Chapter 1, it is very common to find that these internal service areas are targeted and controlled with the same type of financial measures as are used for the core part of the business. It is also important to register that certain service businesses may involve some physical transformation or processing of tangible materials, which might seem to imply that they should be reclassified under a manufacturing label. Thus restaurants and other catering businesses will process food into a prepared meal as an integral part of the *service* which they provide to the customer. Similarly, retailers receive products packaged in bulk formats, which they then split into individual items before placing them on display for sale to their customers. For the purposes of the book, the main thrust of the business is used to determine whether it should be included under our heading of 'services'. This means that restaurants and retailers are included, as are computer software companies, while processed food manufacturers (such as Heinz, Mars, Walls, etc.) and computer hardware manufacturers are excluded.

Having drawn our definition of service industries very broadly, it is important that the qualifying companies are, if possible, broken into sensible groups, so that relevant financial management issues can be discussed for each grouping in the main body of the book. Specific industry examples are then considered in detail in the case study style chapters in Part 5, when the impact of the application of different strategies within the same industry is examined.

CLASSIFICATION BY COMMON CHARACTERISTICS

An obvious first attempt at classifying service companies could be made by using the common characteristics which were introduced in Chapter 1 and are illustrated in Figure 2.1. Thus those service businesses which had a strong degree of perishability could be placed in one group, while those which had the customers present during the production process might be put into another, and so on.

This immediately raises an insurmountable problem for any comprehensive system of classification based on these individual characteristics; many service companies would fall into more than one category, indeed some would end up in almost all the classifications. For example, hairdressing is a very personal service which cannot be stored up in advance, with production and consumption taking place at the same time, and obviously the customer has to be present throughout the production process. The personal nature of the service means that the finished product will be variable in quality but the perception and expectation of the customers will also change depending upon

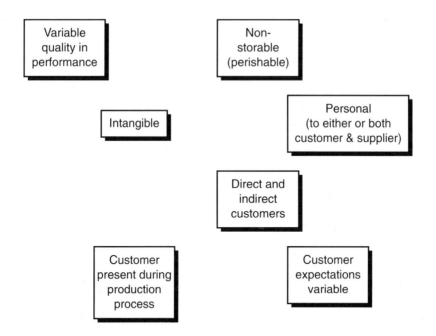

Figure 2.1 Common characteristics of services

their personal moods. Technically, the end product can be regarded as tangible, in that a physical transformation process has taken place during the provision of the service. However, the majority of the value provided by a modern hairdresser is intangible, in that it is how the customer feels as a result of the service (i.e. how *they think* that they look) which is most important.

The value of classifying service companies by these identified detailed common characteristics is not therefore in achieving a mutually exclusive set of groups, for which overall financial management systems can be specified. The benefit of such a process would be in highlighting certain issues where general financial analysis or control techniques may be of value, and can be applied to all service companies having this particular characteristic.

In fact, as the hairdressing example given above illustrates, the common characteristic analysis can be made more rigorous than that introduced in Chapter 1 by showing the interlinkages among them. When this is done it becomes relatively clear, as is shown in Figure 2.2, that some of these linkages tend to be causal, in that several of the characteristics are really the inevitable result of the fewer genuinely independent factors. Thus, it is the combination of the intangible quality, non-storability and personal nature of many services which drives many of the other characteristics. For example, the factor that the customer *has* to be present during the production of the

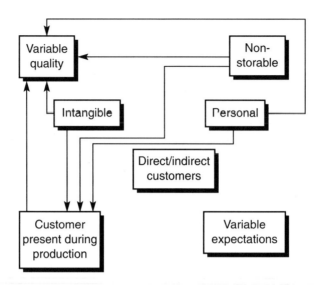

Figure 2.2 Common characteristics of services – introducing causality factors

service is caused by the combination of these three key characteristics. This customer presence, plus the original three, then contributes to the variability of the service quality when the service is carried out, because it makes it very difficult, if not impossible, to carry out any quality control on the actual performance of the service.

This causal linkage process can be taken one stage further back because it is largely the personal nature and intangible quality of services which makes them non-storable. Clearly, the tangible elements of services are storable and some business services are much less time critical in terms of their perfor- mance than most personal services, which introduces an effective element of storage potential due to the flexibility in delivery of the services. Therefore we are seemingly left with two prime, totally independent, common charac- teristics of services, but the factor of having both direct and indirect customers for certain services is also partly independent. It is to some extent caused by the personal nature of the service provided to the recipient (i.e. the indirect customer), but the second element of also having a direct customer who is paying for the service is obviously unrelated to these already identified common characteristics.

These three factors, together with the already derived 'customer presence' issue can be seen, in Figure 2.3, to combine to create the variability in customer expectations. This means that all the previously identified common characteristics have now been analysed back to the three relatively indepen- dent issues of intangible quality, personal nature and having both direct and

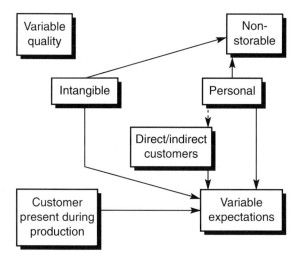

Figure 2.3 Common characteristics of services – additional causality linkages

indirect customers, as can be seen in Figure 2.4. The implications for financial management of each of these common characteristics of services are now briefly considered in turn, before examining some other interesting and useful ways of classifying service companies. However, the other common characteristics are referred to again later in the book when they are helpful in highlighting financial management issues.

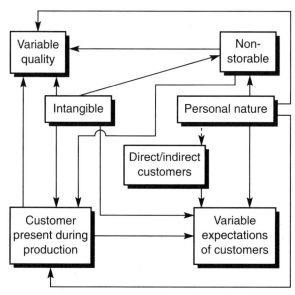

Figure 2.4 Overview of common characteristics of services and their causal linkage

All those service businesses with an intangible end product face a critical problem of measuring the value of their output in order to ensure that the overall cost level incurred is economically justified. In Chapter 1, it was mentioned that this intangibility required a greater degree of direct market research activity with both existing and potential customers. While this argument is clearly valid, it is complicated in that each customer may have a different perception of the particular aspects of the service which make it attractive enough to buy. The financial justification for carrying out such market research is therefore to try to identify a sufficient number of common aspects among the perceptions of existing customers, which can then be used to encourage new potential customers to use the service. Thus a marketing strategy can be built around these commonly perceived added-value aspects of the intangible nature of the service, so as to create a particular image which will increase the sales sufficiently to justify the overall marketing investment. In many cases this 'intangible image' is developed into a brand and for personal and intangible services, the brand is often built around an individual, even though it is well understood that this individual cannot be directly involved in the delivery of the personal service to all these new customers.

This has been achieved in the case of hairdressing, particularly for women, where leading stylists who have created a very strong personal reputation (such as Vidal Sassoon) are able to leverage off this reputation by opening a chain of branded hairdressing salons. The economic added value from this type of image related brand tends to come from an increase in the market share achieved and/or a level of premium pricing relative to the competition, which would not otherwise be sustainable. Branding issues are introduced in Chapter 3 and pricing strategies are discussed in detail in Chapter 8. A perception of good, consistent product quality can, to some extent, be developed by emphasising the training given to all the stylists before they are allowed to work in these new salons, but the real value of the brand is in the associated image of the high profile individual. In this market segment, the branding process has now gone one stage further because a range of hair care products has been launched on the back of the image of the salons, by using the same brand name and incorporating the 'salon quality' aspect into the retail brand. This idea of extending a brand into related areas, where its successful attributes can add value, is widely used in the service sector. For example, a key factor in the very profitable growth of many large retailers has been the development of their own 'retailer brands', which have enabled them both to build loyalty with their customers and to increase their negotiating power with their suppliers; this is discussed in detail in Chapter 14.

Another illustration of building a strong service brand around a particular image can be given with the dramatic growth of Body Shop, both in the UK and internationally. Body Shop has created a position as the leading 'environmentally caring' retailer due, in no small part, to the very high profile position adopted by its founder and managing director, Anita Roddick. In this case, the campaigning and lobbying on environmental issues has been almost impossible to separate from the advertising campaign to promote Body Shop as a retailer of personal care products. The use of an exclusive retailer brand strategy (i.e. everything sold in the shops is branded as Body Shop) and a highly visible move away from non-reusable packaging have been important elements in a comprehensive overall competitive strategy. The problem with such a tightly focused strategy from a financial viewpoint is that it can be very risky as it requires a significant up-front investment in what may be, at best, a short-lived fashion product (as in the case of themed pubs, which are discussed in the next chapter). If these risks can be reduced to an acceptable level, such an image based strategy can be very attractive.

The successful chains of hairdressing salons, etc., have tended to be built on the back of already well-known and high profile individuals; this makes it much easier to gain free publicity on an 'editorial' basis rather than by using 'paid for' advertising all the time. As mentioned above, Body Shop rapidly gained a reputation as an active campaigner for the environment with similar benefits for 'free' publicity. However, financing a rapidly growing retail chain can absorb massive investments in new stores, increased stockholdings and sophisticated distribution systems, in addition to the obviously very high marketing expenditure needed to create and develop the strong brand image. One way of reducing this overall investment and also to allow senior management to focus on fewer critical aspects of the business is to franchise out the new retail outlets. This has been done by Body Shop and a wide variety of other fast-growing retail based service businesses. As discussed in more depth in Chapter 10, franchising releases the main company from the need to invest capital in new shops and the associated increases in working capital. In addition, it provides an income stream to support the overall centrally controlled marketing programmes which are essential for developing the business.

DIRECT/INDIRECT CUSTOMERS

However, this strategic move into franchising as a method of growing the business changes the relationship which the company has with its end customers, who now have a more indirect linkage through the franchised retail outlet. The original company's direct customer (i.e. their paying customer) is now the franchisee operating the retail outlet, and yet the success of the business is clearly dependent upon the consumers using these retail outlets. There is therefore a need for the introduction of very strong quality and financial controls so as to ensure that the franchised businesses supply the appropriate quality of service, which is in keeping with the marketing image developed by the overall franchisor.

Thus, there is an argument that such a franchising strategy changes the nature of the company away from being a retailer (since the day-to-day control over the retail businesses has been delegated to their operators) into a marketing led business or more of a traditional wholesaler. Key elements of this role are, of course, the control over the marketing communication with the end consumer and the identification and introduction of new products. In some cases, such as Body Shop, a major focus of their attention is on the identification, design and sourcing of the new products which are essential both to keeping existing customers happy and to attracting new customers. All of these new products must meet the overall marketing attributes on which the 'brand' has been developed and, where quality is a major element of such a brand's positioning, the involvement with suppliers can become very close indeed. Consequently a company such as Marks & Spencer, which has very close and often very long-standing relationships with suppliers who send virtually all of their output to M&S, can almost be regarded as a vertically integrated manufacturing business which has merely sub-contracted out the assembly of its products. This analysis becomes even more realistic as the retailer takes ever greater control over the design and detailed specification of the product, with the result that the supplier is being told exactly how it should be made and what its manufacturing costs should be. Such a policy clearly adds in a new area of involvement for financial management, in that the service suppliers now require good cost forecasting systems for the manufacture of their retail products, even though they will not be directly involved in the manufacturing process. Even where such a 'quasi' vertical integration strategy is not followed, the franchised business also needs a good understanding of the appropriate cost structure of its franchised retailers, so that it knows very quickly when things are going wrong.

Another very good example in the service sector of having both direct and indirect customers is in the provision of services to businesses, where the actual users of the service are the employees of the direct business customer. This introduces an additional financial management complication because the objectives of these two classes of customer may be quite different and relatively incompatible. The provision of subsidised canteen facilities is an obvious illustration where the paying customer (i.e. the employer) may want to minimise the actual cost incurred whereas the indirect customer (i.e. the employee using the canteen) will desire the maximum benefit possible in the form of a high quality meal service for a very low price. The service provider has to try to balance these conflicting pressures if it is to retain the contract and make an acceptable profit for its efforts.

This can also be illustrated by business air travel where the airline industry has created a whole market segment aimed specifically at travellers who are not personally paying for their tickets. Hence, an enhanced level of service is provided but for a significantly increased price, which is paid by the employer of the actual traveller. Once again, the airline must try to justify the higher selling price to the paying customer by demonstrating that the higher quality service represents good value for money. On long distance flights, this justification is normally made by highlighting the improved performance of the executives which will be achieved if they travel in business class, with its extra leg-room and better quality of service. Any deterioration in performance which may be caused by the unlimited availability of good quality wines and other alcoholic drinks is not emphasised to the employer, but these aspects of the service quality are used when communicating directly with the traveller.

Of course a key element in the purchase decision of business travel by the company is likely to be the efficiency involved. In the case of air travel, this is largely controlled by the take-off and landing schedules of the different airlines and their relative successes in achieving these timetables. However, it may be possible for an airline to build up a degree of loyalty among regular business travellers, so that they are prepared to put up with some degree of inconvenience in order to fly on this particular airline. This loyalty may be developed through the quality of service but, if all airlines start to provide a perfectly acceptable quality product, some other factor may be necessary. Some form of 'frequent flyer' programme may be helpful if it provides an increasing level of benefit to the actual passenger as more travel is made on the particular airline. In this case the benefit is provided directly to the indirect customer, who is actually using the service, rather than to the paying customer. At certain times when cost pressure is very intense, such as during a recession, the airline may find it more cost effective to direct its promotional expenditure at reducing the selling price of the ticket, so that the benefit is received by their direct customer. Clearly the financial information system in all such third party service businesses (i.e. where the end user is not the direct customer) needs to assist decision makers in evaluating these kinds of trade-offs between the direct and indirect customers.

PERSONAL NATURE OF SERVICES

In most of the examples of third party services, the indirect customers are personal users of the service being provided. As a consequence, their evaluation of the service, particularly with respect to its intangible aspects, is likely to be even more subjective and judgemental than with direct personal services. The buyer of the service, the direct customer, will probably have a more objective set of criteria for selecting the service provider to be used, and the decision maker involved may have very limited experience of actually using the service which is being purchased. This can often be seen in the selection of hotel accommodation by companies for use by employees when travelling on business. As a reverse of the airline example, the company may decide that a particular chain of hotels should be used whenever practical, due to the ease of booking and account handling which this creates, and the potential for negotiating a bulk-buying discount.

The actual business travellers may find the service provided by any specific one of these large chains to be highly variable depending on the particular location, or even not of a style which they find attractive. If a business traveller regularly visits a particular area, a more personally suitable alternative hotel may have been identified. The problem for the local hotel company is to identify a strategy whereby it can convince the employer that it should allow its employee to stay there, and not in the usual large chain alternative. Pricing policy may be only a partial solution, because the key decision-makers within the direct potential customer (e.g. the purchasing department) may feel that the centralised billing facility already provided by their usual large hotel chain is a very attractive cost reducing feature, which justifies restricting the range of hotels used by the company.

It is certainly helpful to separate service businesses into those where the end user of the service is an individual (whether they are the direct customer or not) and where the service is primarily provided for the overall business, i.e. an inanimate customer. This focus on the type of the end customer breaks service into two categories of personal and business, where business services exclude any third party services, where the actual recipient is an employee or other indirectly related individual. In many cases it is possible, at the extreme, to argue that any business service is used by an individual, but the primary focus for the service will be used for this classification.

Thus distribution of goods for manufacturers, wholesalers and retailers would be regarded as a business service because, although the recipient of the service is clearly a manager within the customer, the primary focus of the service is on solving a business problem. Similarly, the design and development of the computer systems for business customers would be classified as a business service, as would some aspects of accountancy and legal services for corporate customers. The critical issue is the degree to which the requirements of the service can be specifically identified in a measurable way. This specification of the service enables its subsequent delivery to be monitored and evaluated in a relatively objective way, which eliminates part of the personal subjectivity associated with many services.

As a generalisation therefore, the evaluation of business services can be carried out in the normal cost/benefit manner used for most business decisions. A key aspect of financial management in this sector of service industries is the establishment of performance criteria for the specified attributes of the service, so that the cost/benefit analysis can be appropriately segmented and focused. For more personal services, such a detailed financial analysis is much more complicated and difficult. The assessment of the value added by specific component elements of the overall service then depends on gaining an understanding of the perceptions and reasons for buying of the various groupings of customers. As previously mentioned, this makes the use of externally focused analyses even more important in the financial management process for personal services.

Some businesses provide a range of services some of which can be classified as business services while others are much more personal in nature. The banking industry and other segments of financial services provide some services which can be assessed objectively by their business customers against a specific set of requirements. Thus money transmission, general transaction banking and even cash management services for businesses would fall into this category, whereas the more intangible business advisory services offered by financial institutions would tend to be more greatly influenced by the particular key decision-maker within the customer. This simple analysis also shows that certain services provided directly for individuals can, for the purposes of our classification exercise, be regarded as business services. Many individuals can objectively assess the quality and value of the simple transactional services offered by and received from their bank.

RISK PROFILE OF SERVICE

However, the introduction of financial services also indicates another useful way of classifying services and this is in regard to their impact on risk. The key selling point for many financial services is that they either eliminate risk in exchange for the payment of a fee (as in the case of the insurance industry) or that they manage the risk on behalf of the customer (as in the case of investment management), also in exchange for the payment of a fee. The customer is buying the particular risk management expertise of the service supplier; in the insurance case by transferring the risk entirely to the insurance company and with investment management by getting professional skills involved in designing and monitoring an investment portfolio, tailored to the specific needs of the customer.

These services therefore, can be grouped as risk-reducing products, which should be separated from, and contrasted with, return-enhancing services A classic example of a return-enhancing service is the advertising industry because the financial justification for buying advertising is generated by the increased contribution from the resulting higher sales revenues. The use of an external advertising agency could only be classified as risk reducing if the agency provided some form of guarantee that, if the advertising failed to produce a satisfactory return, it would refund the entire cost to the customer! As discussed in more detail at the beginning of the next chapter, it is important that all services either reduce the risk perceptions of customers or enhance their expected level of returns, but it is almost impossible for any specific service to do both at the same time.

This raises a question over the justification by many businesses for contracting out certain services, while keeping others in-house. The financial management issues for internal service businesses are considered in Chapter 5, but the company should be very clear as to whether the justification for any subsequent contracting out is based on potential cost reductions (i.e. return enhancement) or risk reductions. If the operation of in-house computer services is contracted out to an external supplier, under an increasingly common 'facilities management' contract, the total costs may, under some forms of agreement, appear to be higher. These contract costs should be regarded as including an insurance element, if the terms of the contract include specific measures which effectively guarantee the future operational integrity and performance of the company's information technology systems. Thus, for all such risk reduction evaluations, it is important that the financial comparison includes the cost (wherever possible) of acquiring a similar guarantee or its equivalent. For example, as an alternative to taking out a facilities management contract, which might specify that the contractor had to provide rapid back-up facilities in the event of a systems failure, the company might need to have spare in-house computer capacity or set up a separate emergency support facility for itself: the costs involved in such risk reductions should be included in the evaluation of the external contract.

Alternatively, where the financial justification for outsourcing is based on a cost reduction from the present in-house level, it is equally important that the potential increased return is reviewed in the context of the new risk profile of the business. It is not sufficient merely to argue that the financial return has been improved by a cost reduction, if the overall associated risk has increased at the same time. Added value is only created if either the level of return is increased more than is required to compensate for any higher risk perception, or the perceived level of risk is reduced by more than the return is reduced.

CLASSIFICATION BY TYPE OF COMPETITIVE STRATEGY

This vitally important idea of creating added value shows the most useful way of grouping together different service businesses. Added value is achieved by the successful implementation of a competitive strategy for the business. Consequently focusing on the common features of these competitive strategies highlights many more issues for financial management in service companies than is achieved by more traditional methodologies.

Most text-books talk about the financial management and control issues for a particular industry, or style of industry (such as vertically integrated process industries). While there are undoubtedly some common characteristics within industries, these are normally outweighed by the differences caused by the very different competitive strategies adopted by companies in the same industry. Thus the bulk of this book focuses on those common factors for financial management and control which have already been identified in this chapter, and which can be identified from the analysis of the alternative service company competitive strategies introduced in the next chapter. The impact within individual industries is illustrated in Part 5, when four specific industries are examined in detail to show how the selection and implementation of different competitive strategies can have a dramatic impact on the required systems of financial management and control.

3 SERVICE INDUSTRY COMPETITIVE STRATEGIES

OVERVIEW

The principal objective of any competitive strategy is to create a sustainable competitive advantage and this is exactly the case for all service companies. However, while the basic objective is the same as for manufacturing and extractive industries, many of the classification problems and common characteristics discussed in the previous chapter complicate the implementation of this simply stated competitive objective.

A 'competitive advantage' can, by definition, only be measured against the value of the services provided by competitors, i.e. it is a relative concept, and identifying the valid competition can be a major problem for some service industries. For example, are chains of cinemas competing only against each other, or against video rental shops and satellite TV stations. The newer multi-screen cinemas, which offer restaurant and snack bar facilities as well as the opportunity to watch a wide range of the latest film releases, might be placed in a much wider leisure segment of the service industry. This would bring in a much broader range of competitors who also provide a similarly regarded leisure service for the same target consumer audience; thus bowling alleys, amusement arcades, and even discotheques and clubs might be classified as competitors for those cinemas aiming particularly at the teenage market.

Another key issue is that the competitive advantage has to be 'sustainable' over time and the intangible, personal nature of many services can make this a significant problem. If the value perceptions of the customers change rapidly and without warning, what had previously been a source of very great competitive advantage may, almost overnight, become a large liability for the business. This has become a major problem for some of the large scale operators of pubs (public houses) and clubs, as they very successfully initially developed 'themes' for their pubs which focused on very specific segments of the market. Unfortunately, these focused local brands were very much a fashion item and very few have been able to sustain their attractiveness to their fashion conscious customer base. Hence, when a nearby competitor opens up with a still newer theme or branding proposition, a large proportion of the customer base might well find this a more attractive location; not least just because it was *different.*

Such a short product life-cycle creates dramatic financial management problems, particularly in the case of theming pubs and clubs. The refurbishment costs involved in totally changing the image of a public house can be very high, as are the initial launch marketing costs which are required to attract the floating, fashion conscious, customer base. All of this investment has to be recovered in the potentially short life-time when the new format will attract an increased number of customers. It must also adequately compensate for the likely loss of many of the existing customer base, who may not find the new positioning and style of the pub to their taste, and for any lost revenue caused during the period of refurbishment.

Indeed the new competitive advantage which the investment is designed to create must provide a risk adjusted rate of return for the investors and, as the money has to be spent in advance of re-opening in the new style, the risk associated with this type of fashion related strategy must be regarded as relatively high. It is a fundamental aspect of finance that, merely compensating investors for taking a higher risk does not, of itself, create any added value. This is diagrammatically illustrated in Figure 3.1, which shows a positively sloping risk/return line for investors. This simply indicates that investors demand an increased level of return if they perceive that the risk associated with any specific investment is higher than available alternatives.

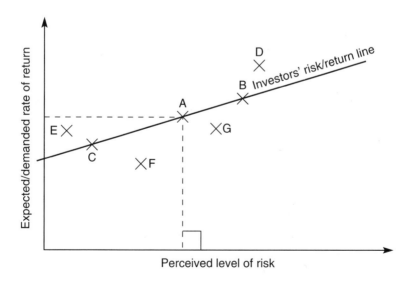

Figure 3.1 The risk/return relationship: using it to create added value

The important point about this risk/return relationship is that movements between any two points on the line are not viewed by financially rational investors as creating any economic value; the demanded return has simply changed to compensate for the change in the perceived level of risk. In other words, if investors are happily positioned initially at point A in Figure 3.1, a move to point B, which is on their risk/return line, will not be viewed as wildly attractive. Although the potential return is higher than they are currently expecting from their investment in A, this higher return only just compensates for the associated increase in risk and hence no added value is created by the move. Similarly, a move to position C where the return is lower than they are currently demanding would not be viewed as significantly unattractive, because the perception of risk associated with an investment in C is also proportionately lower.

Adherents to modern finance theory would argue that financial markets are so efficient that all potential investments now lie very close to such an investor's risk/return line, known in the theory as the 'capital market' line. This theory is not being used in this book as, even if it is true, it is only argued as working for capital markets in general and not for all specific company strategies which are being evaluated here. It is also based on an assumption of a uniform trade-off between risk and return across all potential investors. As mentioned in Chapter 1, an important part of an effective financial management strategy is to ensure that risks are borne by the party who rates them lower than everybody else, because they will charge the lowest price to bear the risk.

Hence there are two moves shown in Figure 3.1 which would create added value (i.e. increase their wealth) for existing investors. The move from point A to position D increases the return more than it increases the perception of risk, and thus would make investors better off. Similarly the move to point E would achieve this because, although the return is reduced, the associated risk is reduced to a greater extent. In other words, any strategic move to a point which is above the investor's risk/return line can be seen to add economic value. The theoretical argument is that such a position is unsustainable because all investors would try to move to this position from where they were initially on the risk/return line. The buying pressure on the price of the attractive investment proposition would increase its price until its effective 'rate of return' was reduced to that expected by its risk profile; in other words, it was pulled back on to the line.

There is a similar theoretical argument relating to positions F and G on Figure 3.1. As they are currently shown, both of these investment opportunities show unattractive rates of return for their risk profiles, so that a move from A to either F or G would reduce the wealth of our investor. Because they are unattractive, the theory argues that the prices of all the investment opportunities positioned below the line would fall, through lack of investor demand, until their rates of return increased sufficiently to move them back up to the line. This highlights two other essential assumptions underlying the theory, which are that all investors not only know about all these other potential investment opportunities but also can switch from one investment position to another without incurring any significant investment costs.

However, this discussion does have very important implications for the financial management and evaluation of different competitive strategies. The financial evaluation must take into account any changes in the risk profile of the business which will occur as a result of any competitive move or due to any change in the external business environment. This change in risk can then be compared to the predicted change in financial return to see if the new strategy is economically worthwhile. Many companies do not include an explicit risk assessment process in their competitive strategy analysis, concentrating exclusively on trying to increase the financial return. Many very attractive strategic moves may actually reduce the overall rate of return but still increase the value of the business (i.e. by moving from A to E). As discussed in Chapter 2, these strategies are often financially focused as they involve some form of insurance being taken out such as through hedging foreign currency exposures, interest rate risks, etc. Paying an insurance premium is a classic example of reducing return but removing the financial consequences of a higher perception of risk by transferring it to the insurance company. The problem with many of these financially focused risk reduction strategies is that they do not create 'sustainable competitive advantages' because they can easily be copied by competitors once they find out about them and yet it is difficult to keep them a secret!

CREATING A SUSTAINABLE COMPETITIVE ADVANTAGE

A critical element in developing a successful competitive strategy is, therefore, identifying how any potential competitive advantage can be sustained, once the company starts to exploit it. As explained above, any market which demonstrates above normal levels of return will attract potential new entrants, with the common end result that the attractive levels of return rapidly disappear. Hence, the sustainability of any competitive advantage depends on creating and maintaining 'barriers to entry' which stop or delay these potential new competitors. The existing companies within the industry are consequently able to continue to earn a high financial return, without new entrants driving down selling prices. This idea is diagrammatically illustrated in Figure 3.2 but this does not indicate what actually constitutes an effective barrier to entry in service industries.

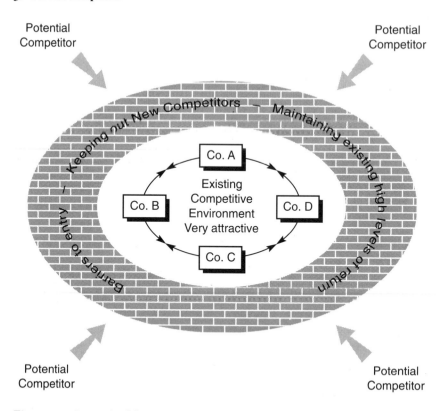

Potential
Competitor

Potential
Competitor

Potential
Competitor

Potential
Competitor

Figure 3.2 A sustainable competitive advantage – developing an entry barrier

In some industries, there are legal barriers to entry such as can be created by exclusive distribution agreements. In the UK, the car manufacturers have granted their retail dealers the exclusive right to their franchise in a specified area, normally a particular town. This clearly creates an entry barrier and should enable the dealer to make an improved rate of profit due to the absence of direct, local competitors. Of course, any car dealer faces very severe local competition from other dealers selling other makes of car and from numerous second-hand car dealers. Also, in the case of such a very large scale purchase, potential customers may be willing to travel to the nearest alternative distributorship if they believe a sizeable saving or significant improvement in service quality can be obtained.

In exchange for this exclusive agreement, the car manufacturers normally insist that their dealers invest heavily in car servicing and repair facilities, as well as the essential showrooms and stock of new cars. These high standard service and repair facilities enable the car manufacturer to offer a consistently high quality of service to their end customers, albeit indirectly through the dealership network. It can also be a significant source of profitable sales revenue for the dealers provided that they can retain the service business after they have sold the car. Most car companies now assist significantly in this area by the requirement that the new car must be regularly serviced by an officially authorised dealer if the extended warranty granted by the manufacturer is not to be voided. Thus, this lock-in of the service business for at least the first three years (for many cars) creates another effective barrier to entry for other car service companies, which do not possess a main-line new car dealership.

Clearly, the many other types of retail franchise agreements discussed already in the book are also illustrations of effective barriers to entry. However it is the control over the barrier to entry which creates the ability to earn a 'super-profit' (i.e. an above normal rate of return), and the real control is normally held by the companies granting the franchise. Thus they will require a higher than normal level of investment by the franchisee, e.g. by specifying a particular style of building and staffing policy, and they may require the franchisee to buy the right to the franchise. In these cases therefore, there is a very clear cost involved in acquiring the entry barrier which gives the franchisee the ability to earn its super profit.

Indeed, as it is normally necessary to invest to create any effective entry barrier, the abnormally high return can be regarded as being, in part at least, a return on this additional investment. Of course, if the entry barrier is intangible it will probably not be recorded as an asset in the financial statements of the company, but this does not affect the economic logic of this intangible asset as the source of the enhanced rate of return which is being achieved.

There are many other potential types of entry barrier which can be built up by service companies, and illustrations of these are given throughout the rest of this chapter. However, it is important to highlight immediately that many types of barriers to entry not only require an initial investment to fund their development but they also need maintaining if they are not to crumble and decay rapidly. The expectations of customers change rapidly in many service industries and potential competitors are continually looking for ways to attack existing entry barriers. This means that an initially very strong entry barrier can disappear very quickly due to a combined assault by customers and new competitors.

In the early years of development of the computer industry, the computer manufacturers supplied their customers with a complete package comprising all the hardware, the software operating system to make the hardware work, the application software packages and maintenance for both the hardware and software. Some dominant companies in the industry would not supply the hardware unless all these other elements were purchased from them as well. However, the lack of knowledge about computers on the part of customers, and their consequently high perceptions of risk in this area, meant that most customers were prepared to pay a premium to have their entire computer installation under the control of a single, very large, specialised supplier. The result was an initially effective barrier to entry against stand-alone software companies and computer maintenance companies. However, over time, these customers became much more knowledgeable about what computers could and could not do effectively in their businesses. Consequently customers started to demand tailored software solutions for their particular requirements and they also started to mix hardware products from different suppliers in their overall computer configurations. This meant that they had several maintenance engineers from these different suppliers visiting each site, which opened up a new competitive opportunity for third party independent companies. These service businesses were able to offer a complete computer maintenance service to the customer, irrespective of which manufacturers had supplied which bits of hardware. This cost-effective service was attractive to this now sophisticated buyer, because the perceived insurance value of the all-encompassing service of the computer manufacturer had now reduced significantly.

Similarly, independent software companies became able to sell directly to the computer user, rather than to the supplier of the computer system. As a result of these changes the computer industry spawned a range of rapidly growing service companies providing specialised services to the end

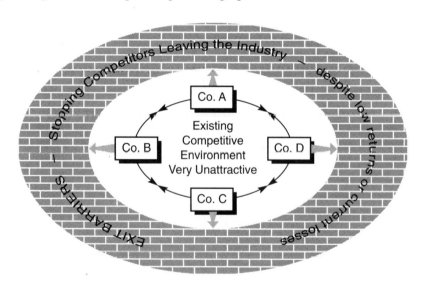

Figure 3.3 Maintaining the unattractive status quo – exit barriers

customer, missing out to an ever increasing extent the actual supplier of the hardware. For many of the original computer manufacturers, this has been a very painful learning experience because it has happened during a period when the proportionate share of the industry value chain held by computer hardware has been declining dramatically. This has forced several of the major computer companies to re-emphasise the importance of the service elements of their business, but this is being done well after their original entry barriers have been dismantled by competitors who are now well established. It is probable that the loss of these initial entry barriers was inevitable as the industry matured, but their real strategic error was in failing to invest in erecting a replacement barrier before they were fighting a rearguard action against very aggressive new competitors.

The opposite end of this argument is how do companies develop competitive strategies for the situation where there are too many existing companies in the industry, with the unsurprising result that none of the companies is making an acceptable rate of return. A key question here is what is it that is stopping the weaker companies from leaving this currently very unattractive industry; these constraints are normally described as exit barriers, as is shown in Figure 3.3. As with barriers to entry, exit barriers can take many forms but a very simple example is where the companies in the industry have invested heavily in very specialised assets. If these assets have potentially very low realisable values, e.g. if they cannot readily be used in any other way, the existing company may prefer to remain in the industry as the current rate of return may be the best available, when compared against the salvage value of this specialised asset (i.e. using the genuine opportunity cost argument rather than assessing the return against the cost or net book value of the original investment).

This argument can be applied to the airline industry during the early 1990s, particularly in North America where it has been calculated that in total the airlines lost more money in a three-year period than they had made in the previous 30 years! The problem for many of the airlines is that their significant investments in aeroplanes represent a sunk cost, which has a very low realisable value when the industry is in a position of significant over-capacity. Even worse, in the case of scheduled airlines, much of their cost-base is of a fixed nature so that they cannot rapidly respond to sudden downturns in sales volumes (such as those caused in 1991 by the Gulf War) by reducing their operating costs. Having a high level of long-term committed fixed costs often represents a very significant exit barrier from an industry, because it reduces any potential saving in the short and medium term which can be achieved even by completely ceasing activity in this area of business. This highlights the risks associated with taking on long-term leasing commitments, either for property or for equipment, which is often done by service companies under the mistaken argument that leasing represents a significantly lower risk than buying the asset outright. The airline industry is discussed in more detail in Part 5, as is the retailing industry which can be used to illustrate an example of an increasing barrier to exit.

A major element of the capital investment of most retailers is in the retail premises which they occupy; indeed in the case of supermarket retailers, this property often represents the only net investment in the business as the strategy is to operate with negative net working capital (i.e. outstanding trade payables exceeding the total of inventories and outstanding receivables). When retailers were primarily based in the high street, it was possible to argue that most retail premises had quite high resale values, which were also relatively easy to realise if necessary. If a particular type of retail business was not doing well, the site might be usable for a different form of retail or could be converted into a restaurant, photo-copying shop, or even office accommodation.

Obviously this argument was less applicable to the much larger retail locations situated in the normal high street, but the accelerating trend for large retailers to move out of the high street into custom-designed 'off-centre' retail parks has made the alternative use value of the premises much more debatable. This is particularly true for the very large and specifically tailored superstores, which have been developed in many parts of the country for the leading chains of supermarkets. These increasingly specialised fixed assets create a much larger barrier to exit from the industry even if, as many forecasters now predict, excess capacity has been created by the dramatic rise in construction of new retail space in the late 1980s.

One way of trying to minimise this impact is by developing the new retail space on a very uniform basis (what can be described as the large retail 'shed' concept), so that it is possible for the space to be utilised by other retailers/other businesses if necessary, even if this involves breaking the total area into several separate pieces. An extreme example of this idea of building in alternative asset uses as a way of reducing risk can be seen in the way several sports centres have been built.

Indoor tennis centres (providing, say six indoor tennis courts, car parking, and the required changing and restaurant facilities) would appear, at first sight, to be a very specialised asset with very limited alternative uses. However, if this issue of an alternative use was highlighted during the design phase of the tennis centre, it becomes possible to develop a building which comprises a large high-ceilinged open area plus an attached reception area with potential offices and canteen facilities. If roller shutter doors are built into the sides and end of the large area, this becomes a perfectly viable distribution warehouse for a wide range of uses; of course, sets of roller shutter doors are not exactly essential to the originally specified use as a tennis centre. Such ideas have been incorporated into the design of several leisure centres, thus significantly improving the value of the alternative use of the asset and hence reducing the exit barrier. There is an offsetting argument to this strategy, which is that the incorporation of these additional requirements to facilitate the transition to an alternative use means that the building is less well suited to its original purpose. Hence it makes the alternative use somewhat of a self-fulfilling prophecy; the fact that several of these indoor tennis centres have failed financially supports this argument to some degree, but they may well have failed anyway.

In certain industries, the assets are so specialised that it is virtually impossible to conceive of any alternative use. Where the value of these single-use assets is very significant as a proportion of the total investments, the exit barrier is equally significant. Thus Eurotunnel plc (the fixed rail link between France and England) has invested vast sums of money in a unique asset; therefore, as long as the operation of the tunnel generates sufficient revenue to cover all its operating costs, it is likely to stay open, irrespective of whether the profit represents an acceptable rate of return on the original investment. In some cases, the scale of this type of investment and the lack of economic logic in at least duplicating the investment in order to create an acceptable degree of competition has resulted in the creation of a monopoly position. (Eurotunnel plc has been granted the first option to build a second set of tunnels, should the additional capacity become required.)

A monopoly position, particularly if supported legally, is the best possible 'sustainable competitive advantage', as it may create an insurmountable barrier to entry. Hence, as a means of combating the fear of the exit barrier, it must be used with extreme caution. One common method of attempting to stop any abuse of such a monopoly has been for such monopolies to be government owned, as used to be the case in the UK for the major public utilities where this type of argument can be applied. However, during the 1980s and continuing into the 1990s, the British government 'privatised' many of these businesses by selling them to private owners, who would of course have the normal commercial objectives of maximising the value from their investment. This required the establishment of quite complex rules for each such privatised monopoly to safeguard its customers, who were the general public and the locally based business community. At the same time, the government attempted to encourage competition but, in areas where both the entry barriers and exit barriers are massive, potential new entrants need a lot of encouragement. One such industry, the electricity generating industry, illustrates two aspects of exit barriers quite nicely. There are very limited alternative uses for outdated, inefficient power stations, but there has been an attempt to transform Battersea Power Station (located in London on the banks of the River Thames) into a theme park! At the other extreme, the nuclear industry faces a massive bill when it tries to decommission its power plants; illustrating that exit barriers can represent new real expenditures as well as lower realisable values. As with entry barriers, more examples of exit barriers are given in the remainder of this chapter.

GENERIC COMPETITIVE STRATEGIES APPLIED TO THE SERVICE SECTOR

Given that the key objective of any competitive strategy is to create a sustainable competitive advantage and that this can be achieved by developing a barrier to entry, it would be useful to have a simple model for classifying the various ways in which this can be achieved. There are many such models which have been developed in the field of business strategy but, given our focus on service industries, we will consider one general model developed by Michael Porter in his books *Competitive Strategy* (Free Press, 1980) and *Competitive Advantage* (Free Press, 1984). This model of generic competitive strategies is illustrated in Figure 3.4, which highlights its very attractive simplicity. Porter's argument is that companies can achieve a competitive advantage by becoming the *lowest* cost supplier in their industry, but this position must be sustained over time if the competitive advantage is to be retained. If this position cannot be achieved, then the company must develop some unique attributes for its service which mean that its customers are prepared to pay a premium for its products or will buy them at the same price in preference to competitors' offerings. This differentiation of the service can be achieved in a variety of ways such as by offering a higher quality of service or branding the service in some way. These industry-wide strategies of differentiation and cost leadership are examined in detail in the following two sections of this chapter, but Porter's analysis also identifies a third alternative which requires explanation.

If a company cannot develop either competitive advantage across the whole of its industry, it may be successful if it concentrates its efforts on a more restricted area of competitive activity. Thus, this type of competitive strategy is referred to as a focus strategy as it focuses on parts, or segments, of the industry. A focus strategy does not introduce any new ways of competing because the company still has to develop a competitive advantage in its chosen segment (or niche) by either differentiation or cost leadership. However, for many personal services there is the potential for a focused

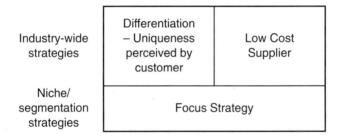

Figure 3.4 Generic competitive strategies – Michael Porter's analysis

strategy based on location, where the targeted area of supply is deliberately restricted so that a competitive advantage can be maintained. The problem with this geographically focused strategy is that it is difficult to erect any significant barriers to entry, which prevent new competitors from opening up for business within this area and dramatically changing the competitive environment. A local hairdressing salon or dry-cleaning business can find its effective monopoly position destroyed by a direct competitor opening up nearby. When this new competitor itself has a significant advantage through being a branch of a much larger chain, the competitive position of the local business can be seen to deteriorate dramatically. It is therefore very important for focused businesses to consider the impact that new competitors entering their segment of the industry would have and plan accordingly. One way of doing this is to develop a competitive strategy which establishes the business in a unique position within its segment of the industry and then to continue to develop that positioning to keep ahead of any potential competitors. In other words, the objective of the competitive strategy is to eliminate all competition from the particular area in which the company operates. This can only normally be done by a differentiation strategy in a tightly focused area of the industry, with a very clearly defined target group of customers. If allied to a strong brand image, an emphasis on providing extremely high quality can create such a positioning, but the challenge is on staying ahead of the competition as they try to attack this extremely attractive market segment. Successful examples are difficult to cite but the Orient Express could be regarded as a unique travel experience with the result that it is able to charge a significant premium price and still cannot realistically be attacked by any other form of travel between the same destinations, whether by train, road or air. In the past, the major liners, such as the *QEII*, might have claimed a similar uniqueness but newer competitors with improved facilities have made it difficult to maintain such a positioning over time; any positioning which is exclusively, or largely, dependent on image will inevitably decay over time.

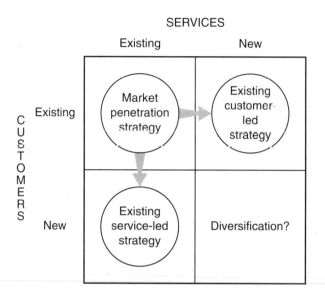

Figure 3.5 Potential strategic thrusts of service businesses (based on Ansoff matrix)

Some companies have now identified ways of increasing their level of sustainable competitive advantage and this is achieved by very deliberately focusing their strategic thrusts so as to build on current areas of advantage. A very common marketing planning technique is known as 'gap analysis', because it establishes the gap between where the overall objectives want the business to get to and where an extrapolation of the current business performance indicates it will arrive. The strategic plans of the business are then supposed to identify how this gap will be filled and this indicates the strategic thrusts of the business. In essence there are only four ways in which a business can grow and develop, and these are neatly encapsulated in the Ansoff matrix, a variant of which is illustrated in Figure 3.5. The simplest way to grow is to sell more of the current services to existing customers but, unless the total size of the market is growing, this requires an increase in overall market share. Such a market penetration type of strategy is most appropriate when the market is growing rapidly, because existing competitors are less likely to respond aggressively if they are themselves still growing at what they regard as an acceptable rate. Trying to increase market share in a stable, no growth market may trigger very rapid competitive reactions, because this growth can only be achieved by taking volume directly away from these competitors.

There are two alternative strategic thrusts which can provide significant growth opportunities for a business, but successful implementation depends upon building on an existing competitive strength. In addition to the existing range of services, the company may decide to develop new services which it can offer to its existing customer base. Marketeers tend to refer to this as a 'product development' strategy, but from a financial viewpoint it should be regarded as an 'existing customer led' strategy, as is shown in Figure 3.5. This is because it is vitally important that any new products launched have attributes which will appeal to the existing range of customers, at whom they are aimed.

Such a customer led strategy has been implemented in many service industries, including retailing. Many major retailers have decided, some after very expensive experiments, that it is financially preferable to try to expand the range of products sold to their existing customers rather than to take their retailing expertise into other international markets (illustrations of UK retailers attempting to expand into the USA are discussed in Chapter 14). There are a number of important impacts from selecting such a strategic thrust. It is based upon a premise that the company has a loyal existing customer base, which is willing to purchase an increased range of services from this supplier. This has very great implications for the financial analysis required within the business, because the relative profitability of different customer groupings needs to be assessed. It could be financially disastrous to implement a growth strategy, focused on a particular group of customers, if increasing sales in this area of the business would lead to increased losses! Yet it is often the case that the most loyal customers are the least profitable; they are loyal because they are getting such an attractive deal from the company.

Another industry which has attempted a customer led strategy of launching new products has been financial services. In the personal retail area, clearing banks and building societies have been developing a wide range of new products in an attempt to provide a comprehensive service to their individual customers. At the same time, insurance companies and investment fund managers have also been developing new products aimed at the same customer base. Inevitably many of the new products introduced by one business are in direct competition with existing products offered by other financial service companies. Indeed, in an attempt to gain access to potential customers at an even earlier stage, several large financial service groups invested very heavily, during the late 1980s, in acquiring large chains of estate agents spread all over the country. Historically estate agents had been run as relatively localised businesses, building competitive advantage out of local knowledge and local contacts. The business rationale of the financial services companies was very different; they saw these chains of estate agents as introducing a steady supply of customers for their range of finan-cial products. As buying a house is the major investment decision for most individuals, they are also in the market at this time for mortgages, endow-ment insurance, temporary life cover, buildings insurance and other savings/investment products such as self-employed pension schemes, etc. Unfortunately for these acquiring groups, the sharp decline in activity in the UK housing market at the end of 1989 meant that the immediate return on their substantial investments was disastrously low; several have, in fact, reversed their strategy by selling off, rationalising or closing down the busi-nesses which they had purchased only a few years earlier.

Indeed, this whole strategy of developing new products for existing customers can be seen to hinge on this issue of customer loyalty. Retailers have worked very hard at this aspect of the strategy, in that the development of retailer brands (what were originally known as 'own-labels' or 'private-label' products) is a good way of increasing the loyalty of the customer to the particular retailer. If the customer is visiting the retail store in order to purchase a range of manufacturers' branded goods, their loyalty is likely to be stronger to the manufacturer than to the retailer. Thus, if the retailer fails to hold stock of a particular brand, the customers may not accept the alterna-tive offered by the retailer and may take their custom elsewhere. Similarly, if a competing retailer offers these specific branded products at lower selling prices, the customers may quite rapidly transfer their transient loyalty to this cheaper supplier. A certain degree of customer loyalty may be created by the pleasant ambience of the store, the consistent design and layout, the friendli-ness and helpfulness of the staff, and particularly by the location of the store, but these may not build a very strong sustainable competitive advantage. The critical success factors in this kind of retail industry are likely to be price and stock availability.

However, if the reliance on manufacturers' brands can be transferred to the retailer's own brands, a much greater degree of loyalty can be devel-oped. This loyalty to the retailer reduces the negotiating power of the manu-facturers supplying the retailer, and enables the retailer to increase its share of the total value chain. In fact, the total value chain may be increased slightly because the end customers become less focused on price as they are now taking into account the total offering of the retailer. The objective of the retailer's strategy is to develop a sustainable competitive advantage by creat-ing a much greater degree of loyalty on the part of the customer. One way of exploiting this loyalty is by expanding the range of products which are sold to these customers, but this must be very carefully done if the new products are introduced under the umbrella of the retailer's brand. The customer will have developed a clear picture of the attributes of the retailer's brand, such as reasonable quality and good value for money, and the new products must clearly fit with these existing brand attributes. If they do not, the retailer runs the risk of damaging the existing competitive advantage which had been developed. It is important that the financial evaluations of all such competitive strategies, which leverage off a current advantage, include the risk of damage which may be caused to the existing business.

Also this discussion should have highlighted that the super-profit being made by a business really does represent the return on the investment made in creating the sustainable competitive advantage. Retailers have invested vast amounts of money in developing their own corporate image and their retailer brands; indeed, it is a sign of their success that several major branded f.m.c.g. (fast-moving consumer goods) companies (including Kelloggs, Nestlé and Heinz) have responded by actively advertising that they do not manufacture retailer branded products.

The other directional strategic thrust of the growing business could be in finding new markets (or customer groups) in which to sell its existing services. As before, marketing texts tend to refer to this as a 'market development' strategy, but it is more appropriate to think of it as an 'existing service led' strategy. There are similar implications for the focus of the required supporting financial analysis, in that it would be most logical to extend the marketing reach of existing profitable services. Hence, direct product profitability analysis (or DPP, as it is commonly known) is an important pre-requisite before selecting the products around which such a strategic thrust should be built. It is also important to understand which particular attributes of this service make it successful in its existing markets, so that the potential new markets can be tested for similar requirements and customer expectations. Such an analysis may have indicated that the competitive advantages possessed by successful British retailers in their domestic market were less than adequate for survival, let alone similar success, in the more developed retail market of the USA.

In many cases the 'existing service led' strategy is based on a brand which is believed to have international appeal and, not surprisingly therefore, the majority of the successful examples both are personal consumer services and have originated in the most developed consumer market in the world, the USA. Thus the fast food restaurant chain, McDonalds, has established itself all over the world using a consistent package of service attributes, even if the actual product may have been modified very slightly to suit local market conditions. The belief in the strength of this type of strategy is very great as can be attested by the major acquisitions made (and the very high prices paid) by companies to buy brands, which they believe have underdeveloped international potential. In the fast food restaurant market, Grand Metropolitan acquired Burger King in 1989 when its business was dominated by outlets in the USA and it was loss-making. The growth objective was to transform Burger King into a viable worldwide competitor to McDonalds. In order to accelerate the growth towards this goal, Grand Metropolitan subsequently acquired several smaller localised chains of restaurants and transformed the suitable locations into Burger King outlets. The residual unsuitable locations were sold off in some cases as they did not fit Grand Metropolitan's strategic view of only being in globally based businesses (for example, it sold off the rest of the Wimpy restaurant chain to its management after having converted the suitable fast-food outlets into Burger Kings).

In the business services sector, the development of global accountancy firms can be regarded as similar, in that the accountancy profession is now dominated by a few very large firms with operations in all major countries around the world. The logistics of this exercise are complicated by the partnership structures legally required by such firms, which result in a complex web of interlocking international partnerships for some firms. However, this is irrelevant to the customer, who can deal with the same firm all around the world and, of course, this is the objective of the strategy. As their customers became more global, the accountancy firms felt the need to develop internationally as well so that they could provide financial advisory services to these important customers wherever they were required. At the same time, these firms also adopted the 'existing customer led' strategy of developing new services (such as management consultancy) which they could offer to their existing 'loyal' customers.

A very similar strategy has been followed in the advertising industry, which has also developed a limited number of global agencies offering a much wider range of marketing and business advisory services to their clients. This illustrates the dangers of such a strategy if it goes wrong, because some of these very large advertising groups are now in severe financial difficulties. These difficulties have undoubtedly been exacerbated by the very rapid growth of these companies during the 1980s which included a vast array of both acquisitions and new service ideas.

The apparently risk-reducing strategy of moving internationally in response to the development of existing loyal customers can be illustrated by examining the development patterns of many Japanese and German banks. As US and British banks had done earlier, these companies set up operations overseas to service in the first instance, the banking requirements of its local customers which had already started on an international development strategy. From this base in the overseas market, most companies then attempt to develop a more localised customer base. However, such a transition to servicing the needs of local customers is only likely to be successful if the previously discussed analysis, which matches profitable domestic services with the requirements of these locally based potential customers, is properly carried out. Far too often, companies try to expand the scope of the international operations simply by offering their existing services to new locally based potential customers. Unfortunately the needs are likely to be different as one is interested in services appropriate to its new operations in an overseas market away from its head office and in an area where it may lack expertise; to the other customers, this same market may be home.

QUALITY OF SERVICE – A DIFFERENTIATION STRATEGY

As stated earlier, one of the generic competitive strategies depends upon creating a service which is differentiated from competing offerings and is perceived to have added value by customers. This perceived differentiation may be achieved across the whole industry or may be restricted to a particular segment of the market. The primary role of any branding involved is therefore to encapsulate the key attributes of the differentiation so as to enable it to be communicated consistently to as wide an audience of existing and potential customers as possible. Obviously if a high level of repeat purchase is to be achieved, the actual service provided must live up to the expectations created by the brand's image and its associated attributes.

In the service sector, a major element of many successful differentiation strategies is the quality of service which is offered. This can clearly be incorporated in a brand image and may vary across a particular industry in that differing levels of quality may be used to create equally successful competitive advantages. For example, the fast-food end of the restaurant industry requires the rapid service of a limited range of consistent quality products to be provided in a relaxed, friendly manner in clean pleasant surroundings. At the other extreme, the extremely high quality of food and service expected in a Michelin two or three star restaurant would, to its customers, justify the enormous premium charged for this type of meal. Arguing that these two service offerings are directly comparable and competitive is obviously ludicrous, even though the same individual may, on very different occasions, eat in each type of restaurant. By its focus on its particular style of service within one industry, each business has differentiated itself away from competing with many of the other companies in its industry.

It is perfectly possible to achieve this level of differentiation through quality of service in the business-to-business sector as well. Insurance broking is a service where the broker acts as an intermediary between the company requiring insurance and the insurance market supplying the cover.

As with most forms of brokerage, the traditional way for the broker to be paid is by commission on the premium paid by the insured party. This has the potentially absurd result that the more successful the broker is in reducing the level of premiums, the less it is paid for its effort. However, this position also pre-supposes that the only important issue for the buyers of insurance is the level of premium paid. They are likely to be very interested in being sure that any subsequent claims will be settled in full, without undue delay and excessive argument on the part of the insurer. Therefore, it is perfectly possible for an insurance broker to create a successful strategy based on their professional excellence and totally objective advice in obtaining the 'best' insurance cover for their clients.

Developing a quality position in this market does dictate that a number of consequent steps must be taken by the insurance broker. The cost-base associated with such a level of service will almost certainly be high relative to the competitor providing an average level of service. However, much of the cost-base is relatively fixed, because it is invested in the very high quality technical people who know their particular area of the market in great depth. Hence, if the reputation for excellence achieves a sufficiently high market share, the volume of business generated may produce an adequate level of contribution not only to cover these costs but also to leave a more than satisfactory profit margin. Also once gained, the quality of service should create a higher degree of loyalty among the customer base so that the volatility of profits for such a company should be below the average for the industry.

The critical issue in successfully implementing such a strategy is in identifying which customers are likely to place a high value on such a high quality service and who will, therefore, be loyal to a broker producing such excellent advice. An alternative, and more revolutionary, way of implementing this type of strategy would be to attempt to transform the pricing strategy of the industry. Instead of receiving commissions based on premiums paid by their clients, the insurance broker could charge a fee to the clients for its advisory and administration work, but rebate to the clients all commissions received from the insurance market. The argument is that this pricing structure would ensure that the broker was completely objective in its advice, rather than being 'tempted' to recommend one particular insurance company which paid a higher rate of brokerage commission. Interestingly, this approach has always been used by professional accountants when providing insurance and investment advice for their clients; they charge the client for the time spent on providing the advice but deduct any commissions received from the company with which they eventually place the business.

However, this objectivity is only a small part of the benefit, because the introduction of a fee structure should highlight the costs actually incurred by the broker, and subsequently paid for by the client, in each area of services provided. This would enable the client to analyse whether it would be more cost effective for it to carry out internally some of the administrative workload, which is currently done by the broker. In other words, it enables the service provider to focus on those areas of activity where it adds most value to the customer, rather than providing an all embracing service where parts may be of almost no added value. Such an analysis may also indicate, if the insurance broker is efficiently organised, that it makes economic sense for it to take over a much greater proportion of the risk management role for the client. A closer focus on the cost involved has, over recent years, led to significant changes in the way audit firms carry out their work. Instead of producing all their own working paper schedules, which to a large extent either duplicate or restate existing records of the client, auditors now utilise a large proportion of base schedules prepared by the client's own staff. The reduction in duplication of effort represents a real saving to the client, and a similar potential would appear to exist in other types of service industries, including insurance broking.

The insurance sector can also be used to illustrate the use of branding of a service, as a means of focusing and differentiating the product. The buyer of most insurance policies has no sensible method of assessing the relative merits of the competing products; the financial benefit of a whole life insurance policy is, after all, only felt after the buyer has died! Even in the case of an endowment or pension policy, the value is in the future benefits which will be received, either on death or maturity of the policy, and past history may not be a good guide to this future performance of the insurance company. However, if an insurance company can create a very strong brand image of security, trust, permanence and a sound track record, the consumer is likely to favour that company over its competitors. It is very difficult in this industry to create a sustainable competitive advantage through launching innovative products because, by the rapid application of reverse engineering techniques, competitors will be able to copy the product very soon after it is made publicly available. Even the level of service for most investment type insurance products is difficult to differentiate, although various companies have tried this by creating their own dedicated sales-forces and by offering financial health checks to potential customers. Obviously each of these is relatively easy for competitors to copy.

In fact, private health insurance is another interesting example of differentiation by focusing on a tightly defined niche. These companies have developed brand images based on the customer's perception of them providing a high level of specialised health care, which can be rapidly accessed whenever necessary. If the operation is not urgently required, its timing can be made to suit the business and personal commitments of the customer, rather than the efficient operation of the health-care insurer's hospital. However, although they may operate a few hospitals of their own, the insurance companies are really only providing the financing for the insured party to buy their own private health-care. As with car repairs which are carried out under warranty or will be the subject of an insurance claim, the customer receiving the treatment can become indifferent to its actual cost, and may not even ask the price in advance of requesting the work to be carried out. The service has been sold on the basis of removing the risk and the worry about paying for it, even though the health insurance company is not actually providing the health-care.

Another way of differentiating the product and providing what is perceived as a high quality service is by increasing the speed of response to the customer. This can be a pizza delivery service, which promises delivery within 30 minutes or the customer receives a discount, but it can also involve the use of sophisticated telecommunications and computer technology. Some new services have been developed on the back of the new breakthroughs in technology, such as home banking and home shopping using television and telecommunications facilities. Other existing services have received new potential sources of competitive advantage by harnessing what is now available. Travel agents can now be linked into the computer facilities of the major tour companies and airlines, so that checking availability and making bookings can be done while the customer is present. In the case of business travel particularly this has developed into a major issue for the airlines due to the buying process used by the average customer. Many business travellers would set as their first priority the departure time and/or the arrival time of the required flight; thus three busy individuals may not want to leave London before 11.00 a.m. but need to be at a meeting in New York by 5.00 p.m. that day. The choice of flight therefore has to fit that schedule but they may be indifferent as to which airline they travel with. They will take the first flight suggested by their travel agent which meets those parameters and it is therefore important to an airline that their flight schedules are considered first, particularly if several airlines could comply with the customers' requirements. This can be achieved if the airline invests heavily in providing the travel agents with a sophisticated computerised timetable viewing and booking system. The travel agent would simply specify London to New York flights on the appropriate day and these would appear on the computer screen in a pre-determined order, i.e. the airline supplying the system would ensure that its flights appeared first so that it increased its share of the market. The cost of developing and operating such a comprehensive computer network is clearly immense and it would be logical for airlines to group together to share the cost. This is what has happened in the industry with two major European reservations systems being developed by different groups of airlines. Clearly it is difficult to get the travel agent to utilise a vast range of these type of systems if they have been designed to be mutually incompatible; therefore, gaining distribution within the travel agents is a critical success factor.

The use of technology as a source of competitive advantage is here being used in conjunction with the idea of taking control over the channel of distribution of the service (in this case, the computerised reservation system used by travel agents). In other service industries, access to the channel of distribution can also be critical to developing a successful competitive position. This can be very difficult if it is owned by a competitor and the replacement cost investment is massive, such as in the case of the major utilities. In order to encourage competition in the post-privatisation environment, the UK government has tackled this problem in slightly differing ways. The national grid, through which electricity is supplied by the generating companies to the regional electricity distribution companies and then on to the end customers, was set up as a separate business owned by the regional distribution companies. This enables potential new generating companies to gain access to the market without having to invest in developing their own infrastructure. The similarly vital national telephone network was retained by British Telecom and British Gas kept the gas pipeline network. The regulations under which these privatised companies operate forces them to make available their networks to competitive suppliers but only at a price which reflects a return on the investment made in the infrastructure. Not surprisingly, there are very heated arguments over whether this return should be based on the historic cost of the investment or its current replacement cost.

These types of issues can be handled by regulation but it becomes more difficult as technology develops in ways which blur the divisions among industries and, particularly, across channels of distribution. The increasing use of fibre-optic cables and the capability of mobile telephones using radio signals to transmit data electronically means that it is technically perfectly possible for television companies to carry person-to-person voice communications (i.e. a computer information type network), while telephone companies could transmit television signals in the same way as cable television companies do but on a national network. Thus barriers to entry can suddenly be transformed by technology, particularly if radio and microwave communication ever make the need for the massive infrastructure networks effectively redundant.

COST OF SERVICE – BECOMING THE LOW COST SUPPLIER

Of course, using Porter's model differentiation is only one source of a sustainable competitive advantage; the other potential route to success is to become the low cost supplier within the industry. Interestingly, advances in technology are being used as major ways of achieving this type of competitive advantage in many service industries, including some where technology is also a potential source of differentiation.

The use of real-time computer networking over vast distances has enabled several industries to relocate their volume driven clerical processes to regions where labour and occupancy costs are as low as possible. For example, some North American airlines have now located all their ticketing and reservations operations offshore, relying on information technology linkages to maintain the required speed of transactions. Similarly, many financial services companies have moved their clerical support functions away from their main operations areas. In the UK, this means that banks have moved cheque processing, customer accounting, and credit card functions out of London, while insurance broking have similarly relocated policy documentation, accounting and claims processing; in the USA the relocation of these functions out of the main New York business districts has been at least as marked. This practice is also being used in the administration and accounting areas of many non-service businesses. The strategic use of information technology is discussed in more detail in Chapter 12.

As has already been mentioned in Chapter 1, technology has enabled banks and building societies to improve their efficiency through the introduction of automated teller machines (ATMs). These can be used to reduce labour costs for processing routine transactions and allow staff to concentrate on selling more added value services to existing customers. The benefit to the customers is that the core services are available over a much extended period (i.e. potentially 24 hours a day, seven days a week), and from a much wider range of locations (due to the sharing of ATMs by different organisations).

In order to take advantage of these technology driven cost reductions, the businesses must be able to justify the sizeable investments required. Hence technology can be used to create an effective entry barrier because smaller competitors would be unable to realise what are, in practice, economies of scale. Economies of scale can be regarded as anything whereby increased size or volume of transactions results in a reduced cost per unit. Thus, if a large proportion of an industry's costs are fixed, the per unit cost can be reduced significantly by spreading these fixed costs over an increased volume of business. This enables a competitive advantage to be developed by gaining a dominant market share and ensuring that the company's fixed costs are fully utilised and/or that any potential scale economies, which can be realised by employing different operating methods, are achieved. In many cases, these economies of scale are found in the indirect support areas of the business but, of course, increased volumes may enable the business to utilise its increased buying power and thus reduce its direct cost base below that of its smaller competitors.

However, there is a potential negative aspect to these strategies of reducing total costs through economies of scale and that is in respect of the risk associated with the business. If the fixed cost base of the business is increased, as indicated above, there is correspondingly increased risk, since relatively small changes in volumes of activity will lead to a much greater degree of volatility in the profitability of the company. Therefore, it would be sensible for the business to try to guarantee a substantial proportion of its sales revenue; if possible, it should guarantee sufficient sales revenue to cover its increased fixed cost base (i.e. so that it will, at least, break even). Where new technology developments introduce opportunities for major economies of scale which can only be realised with the commitment of sizeable investments in fixed or sunk costs, there is the possibility for a new type of competitive strategy, and even the creation of a new service industry.

A clear example of this can be given using the car industry. Technological developments during the 1970s increased the dependence upon automated production techniques in many areas of the car industry. This had the impact of changing the role of much of the labour employed in the industry from that of direct production employees to indirect or support functions, such as monitoring or maintaining the new automated machinery. These changes significantly increased the fixed cost bases of the major companies in the industry, with the result that, during the sharp North American recession of the early 1980s, these companies reported very high financial losses due to the downturn in volumes. A common managerial reaction was to try to reduce the cost-base as quickly as possible, but one of the features of investments in specialised fixed assets is, as has already been mentioned, that they represent a sunk, committed fixed cost to the business which cannot subsequently be recovered.

Therefore attention was focused on the labour element of the cost-base. Labour had, for accounting purposes, been largely treated as a variable cost, but decades of negotiations with the strong United Auto Workers Union had meant that, in reality, much of the shop-floor and office based labour was a fixed cost. The companies learned this very expensively as they reduced their labour forces during this recession. This experience made them very reluctant to re-hire these workers on a similar basis when sales demand returned after the recession. Several new service companies took advantage of this opportunity to build very large employment agencies, which acted as intermediaries between the very large companies and their workers.

The logic of using an employment agency was that the labour cost was kept as a variable expense by the employer, whereas had the employees been hired directly they would have acquired all the normal contractual benefits and job security of permanent employees (i.e. fixed costs). As these temporary employees are forgoing these advantages, it is only fair that their rate of pay should be slightly higher to compensate. In essence, the employer is paying a premium to the employees and to the employment bureau for the increased flexibility of turning a fixed cost into a variable cost. It is therefore somewhat ironic that some employees (e.g. secretarial staff) have been constantly employed on this week-to-week temporary basis for ten years. Their employment was not even stopped in the early 1990s recession even though General Motors, in 1992, reported the world's greatest ever annual financial loss.

This example is a very specific case of a more general trend in many industries of an increasing use of outsourcing (i.e. buying in services from external suppliers rather than providing such services internally). A major argument, which is used to justify this trend, is that it can transform internal fixed costs into external variable costs, but this clearly depends on the type of contractual agreement entered into with the external supplier. The issue of internal service businesses is considered in more detail in Chapter 5, but there are several other arguments in favour of outsourcing certain services.

If the chosen competitive strategy is to be the lowest cost supplier in the industry, this often requires a great deal of specialisation and focus within the business. It is quite probable that the company will not be the cheapest at everything it does because it may not achieve the maximum economies of scale. However, by sub-contracting this function to an external supplier which specialises in this area, it may be able to gain access to this more economic scale of operation. The outside supplier may be able to provide the required service more efficiently than the in-house department and therefore, despite the suppliers' need to make a profit over and above its own costs, the bought-in cost may be less than the internal equivalent. Some large companies, such as BET plc, have used this as their own business strategy in that they provide a range of services such as cleaning, laundry and temporary staff for other large business customers.

However, they would argue that they bring at least one other major advantage to their customers. In addition to providing a cost-efficient level of service, they also allow the senior managers within their customers to concentrate on running their businesses, without worrying about a lot of relatively peripheral but necessary services. This freedom for managers to focus on the critical success factors in their own industry can be financially evaluated using a variant of the opportunity cost argument; what business opportunities could be lost because managerial attention was preoccupied with resolving an operational problem in an internal support service department? When these arguments are used, the change in the cost structure from fixed to variable becomes less significant, which is just as well because, in the long term, all costs are variable. Hence, a justification to continue, in the long term, using an external supplier merely because its charges are a variable cost is not very strong.

FINANCIAL CONTROL SYSTEMS FOR EACH TYPE OF COMPETITIVE STRATEGY

This chapter has indicated that there are a variety of alternative competitive strategies which can be implemented in service industries, and several different strategies may be in use in a particular industry at the same time. Therefore it is not logical to try to specify a single financial control system for a given service industry, as the control system needs to be appropriate to the competitive strategy being used. It is clearly vitally important, at its simplest level, to monitor the level of costs very closely if the company is trying to become the lowest cost supplier. This cost monitoring is much less significant if the company has achieved a position of delivering a very high quality level of service for which its customers are prepared to pay a significant premium price.

What is important for all businesses is that the critical success factors associated with the specific competitive strategy are identified by the business and incorporated within the financial monitoring and control system. This requires specifying meaningful measures which will rapidly indicate whether the strategy is being successfully implemented. These measures should also highlight, as far as possible, why the objectives of the business are not being achieved so that appropriate modifications to the strategy can be made before the position becomes irreversible.

Consequently, a simple comparison of actual sales revenue to the budgeted level on a monthly basis may not be adequate because this does not indicate the reason for any variance. The total market for the service may be dramatically different to that on which the budget was based. Therefore, if the market is expanding much more rapidly than predicted, the fact that actual sales are slightly above budget may hide a decline in market share. For many fast-growing businesses, a critical success factor is achieving an adequate market share during the growth stage so as to ensure a high level of profitability when the industry matures; this critical success factor must be identified and monitored by the financial control system.

Similarly, it has been emphasised throughout this chapter that a sustainable competitive advantage is, by definition, a relative concept and must be measured in comparison either to competitors or to the perceptions of customers, or both. It is consequently also critically important that the financial measures used to evaluate this competitive strategy attempt to take some account of these external factors, rather than focusing exclusively on internal comparisons. No business can realistically claim to be the lowest cost supplier in its industry unless it has compared its costs against those of its competitors which are trying to implement a similar strategy. Most systems of financial management do not include this essential element of externally focused financial analysis.

Another aspect of competitive strategy which has been referred to several times already is that the required level of return must be related to the degree of risk associated with the particular strategy. The true financial measure of success of any competitive strategy is the extent to which the actual return exceeds the risk adjusted rate of return which would be expected by investors in this type of company. Hence, the financial control system must be tailored to take account of the risk profiles of the business, both now and as it changes in response to alterations in its business environment. As has been discussed, existing competitive advantages can be destroyed by sudden changes in the external business environment and new potential competitive advantages can be created equally dramatically or evolve gradually over time. Thus, the ideal financial control system must be able to cope with these changes in competitive strategy and strategic thrust. These changes may result in significant modifications to the critical success factors of the business and, correspondingly, can require considerable flexibility in the way the financial analysis and reporting is carried out.

The implications of these issues for financial control in service companies are considered in the next chapter and the key issues are then dealt with in more detail in Part 3 of the book.

4 KEY ISSUES FOR FINANCIAL CONTROL

INTRODUCTION

In the previous chapter, the main objective of any competitive strategy was clearly stated to be the development and maintenance of a sustainable competitive advantage. It was also established that sustainable competitive advantages can take very different forms through the implementation of alternative strategies in the same industry, and that they can change significantly over time.

Within this framework of alternative competitive strategies, it is important to establish a clear role and set of objectives for financial management. It has also been argued that sustainable competitive advantages do not simply occur, they are usually the result of a development process requiring the investment of considerable time and money by the company. The results of this effort are normally far from guaranteed because, even if the process is successful, competitors may launch a better, cheaper, more attractive service either before, at the same time, or just after the introduction by our company, thus destroying any prospect of a 'sustainable' advantage for the business. Consequently, this expenditure must be seen as being risky to some degree, although the level of risk clearly depends on the type of advantage being developed and the existing competitive position of the company. The key role of financial management in any service company is, therefore, to ensure that *all* actual sustainable competitive advantages result in an enhanced rate of return to the stakeholders in the business. This means that the initial and ongoing investment to be made in developing and maintaining any sustainable competitive advantage must be objectively evaluated to ensure that the potential financial return justifies the required expenditure. In this context, 'investment' simply means 'expenditure made on the assumption of receiving a financial return in the future', and should not be limited to that expenditure which is capitalised on the balance sheet. Many service businesses do not need to invest heavily in tangible fixed assets but they do spend heavily on creating intangible assets (such as brands, dedicated distribution channels, technical know-how, etc.), which can represent significant sustainable competitive advantages. These investments in intangible assets should also be subjected to rigorous financial evaluation, in the same way that most investment in more tangible assets are.

However, this financial evaluation does not ensure that the predicted return is actually achieved by the business and, just as importantly, is delivered back to the investor. As illustrated in Chapter 1, investment in large companies is a two-stage process with shareholders and other investors injecting funds into the business, which then invests in a range of businesses (such as divisions or SBUs) and projects.

The competitive strategies discussed in Chapter 3 are implemented at the second stage of this process (i.e. in the market place where the services are actually delivered to specific customers in competition against other identifiable suppliers). It is at this lower detailed level that sustainable competitive advantages are developed, but the enhanced financial returns should be received eventually by the investors at the first stage of the process. The importance of financial management in ensuring that these abnormal returns are not wasted by the business units should not be underestimated.

This wastage or 'slippage' factor, as it is often called, can occur because the divisional managers want to continue either new investment on the development of a potential new competitive advantage, or maintenance expenditure on an existing competitive advantage, beyond the level where it is economically justified. Such dysfunctional behaviour can be apparently encouraged by the overall group if the wrong set of financial measures is used to judge the performance of the business unit and the managers running it. For example, if the business unit is judged on the growth in either sales revenue or its market share, there will be an emphasis on increasing or continuing marketing expenditure, even if the predicted financial return on this expenditure is no longer attractive. Thus the design of financial performance measures is very important in ensuring that business units seek to *optimise* the use of their sustainable competitive advantages.

However, the concern with achieving a super-profit (i.e. an above normal rate of return) is even more fundamental than this. Several academics and researchers have questioned Porter's generic competitive strategies, because it is not immediately obvious as to how these strategies lead to the achievement of above normal returns by the businesses implementing them. If a company becomes the lowest cost supplier in its industry, it could earn a super-profit if it sells its services at the same price as its competitors. However, this does not pass on any of its cost advantage to its customers and will not lead to an increased market share or to a higher level of customer loyalty. These objectives could be achieved by reducing the selling price to customers but this could remove the super-profit, which its competitive advantage makes achievable. The most logical strategy is to pass on part of the cost advantage to customers and to retain part for the shareholders of the company. A sensible financial management system would ensure that all the stakeholders share in the potential benefit to be generated by the low cost base; customers through a reduced selling price, employees through increased job opportunities and job security as the market share of the company grows, and the shareholders through a higher rate of return over the life time of the competitive advantage.

The evaluation of this shared benefit should take account of the probable decay over time of the competitive advantage, as competitors reduce their costs, unless additional investment (or reinvestment of some of the initial super-profit) is made to sustain the current cost advantage, or enhance it. As with the initial investment to create the lowest cost base, any reinvestments to sustain or enhance the competitive advantage should be financially evaluated. It is not inevitable that it is financially worthwhile to spend new money to preserve a cost advantage; the market may have changed significantly so that costs are now less important, or the required new investment may be too great given the available size of market for the still lower cost service.

A similar issue exists with a differentiated strategy in that the financial management system should focus on how the differentiated service can actually produce an enhanced level of return to the investors and other stakeholders in the business. A brand can create customer loyalty, as can a very high quality of service, but both will result in higher costs than an almost equivalent competitive product (e.g. an unbranded service). Thus the differentiation must either allow the company to charge a premium price which more than recovers the higher cost-base, or a much greater market share at competitive pricing levels must be attained so that the total return achieved is again enhanced (e.g. through economies of scale in spreading the marketing expenditure over a much greater sales volume). As before, the most logical and sustainable solution is that the benefits of the competitive advantage are shared among the key stakeholders involved in the business; the financial management system should assist in evaluating the optimum way in which this can be done.

It is therefore clear that the emphasis of the fundamental financial analysis, planning and control process illustrated in Chapter 1 cannot be either exclusively internal or standardised for all service businesses. There is a need to look outside the business both to establish the sources of potential and actual competitive advantage and to evaluate the optimum way of exploiting them. The ongoing financial monitoring and control process must also take into account changes in the external environment, as internal comparisons may lead to completely disastrous strategic moves by the company. This external orientation of the finance function is probably the greatest difference between traditional management accounting and the

(a)

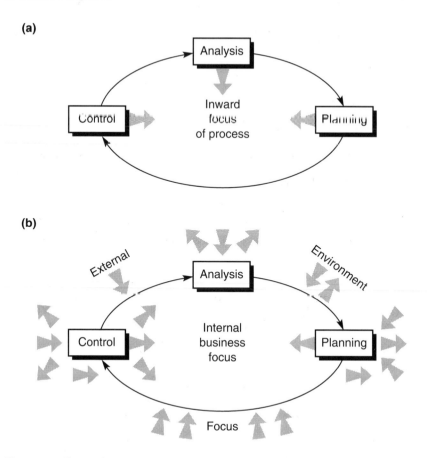

Figure 4.1 Strategic management accounting: (a) traditional management accounting process; (b) strategic management accounting process.

increasingly important area of finance known as *strategic management accounting*, as is illustrated in Figure 4.1.

RELEVANCE OF RISK PROFILES

The required rate of return by investors is positively correlated with risk, as was established in Chapters 1 and 2. Therefore the risk profile of any business and the particular competitive strategy being implemented must be taken into account by the financial management system when setting the targeted rates of return, but risk analysis can be used to give much more specific guidelines to the financial strategy of the business. Risk can be separated into two component elements, business risk and financial risk.

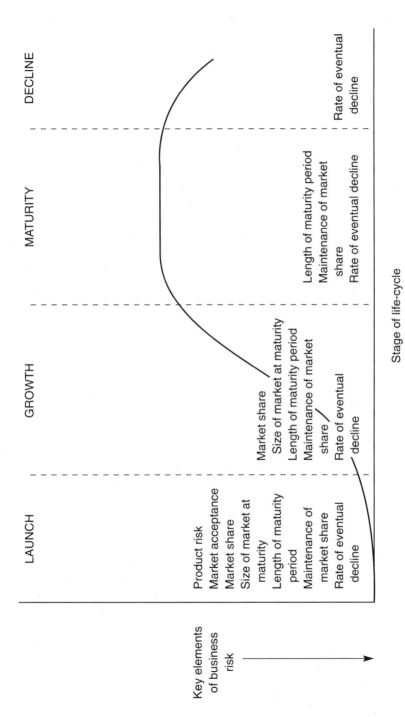

Figure 4.2 Changing business risk profile over the product life-cycle

Business risk represents the risk associated with the nature of the business and its particular competitive strategy, whereas financial risk takes account of the way in which the business is financed, and what type of cost structure the business has selected in terms of the mix of fixed and variable costs. Consequently, there is a greater degree of choice with respect to the level of financial risk undertaken by a business, because the business risk is largely dictated by the dynamics of the particular industry in which the company operates. However, the level of business risk also varies quite significantly over time and with changes in the external environment; for example, the level of business risk can be seen to reduce as the product moves through its life-cycle. As illustrated in Figure 4.2, the risk associated with a brand new service, particularly one based on a yet unproven technology, is very high during the launch stage as the product may not work, and even if it does the market may not want to buy it. After these risks have been overcome, there remains the significant risk that the particular company may not achieve a viable market share in this new growing market or the market may not grow to a sufficient size to justify the initial investment made in developing and launching the new service. Even when these are no longer perceived as risks, there is still the challenge of retaining the high market share during the maturity stage of the business, and this maturity stage may be cut off prematurely due to competitive moves or changes in the external environment. Any significant shortening of the expected maturity stage, which is when the product is highly profitable and strongly cash positive, may make the total return inadequate to justify the original investment. When the product eventually passes into its final stage of decline, the only remaining risk relates to the rate of this decline.

As can be seen in Figure 4.2, the remaining elements of the associated business risk reduce as the product passes through the stages of its life-cycle, because each risk has to be overcome if the next stage is to be reached. Thus, it is possible to redraw a summarised matrix representation of Figure 4.2 showing the reducing trend of business risk, as is done in Figure 4.3. The required relationship between business risk and financial risk, over which there is a much greater degree of control, must now be examined. Both types of risk affect the overall risk of the business and like all such compounding factors, the effect of putting together two very high risk factors results in a very, very high risk company. Thus, using debt financing and taking on mainly long-term committed fixed costs (such as long-term leases on property and specialised fixed assets) in a new start-up high risk service company (such as a computer software business, a telecommunications company, or a new airline) is not a sensible combined strategy. If the business grows very rapidly without any significant fluctuations in sales revenues, which is very

Figure 4.3 Business risk over the product life-cycle

unlikely, the company may be able to service the interest payments and principal repayments on the outstanding debt. However, should the business suffer any significant degree of volatility in its early period of trading, its unsuitable financial structure is likely to lead to its rapid collapse. Therefore, as shown in Figure 4.4, there should be an inverse correlation between the level of business risk and financial risk. As the company can exercise a much greater degree of control over its level of financial risk, this means that the sources of funding and relative mix of costs used by the company must be tailored to its current and projected degree of business risk.

The combination of high business risk and high financial risk is shown as incompatible, because high business risk companies should utilise low risk sources of funding (such as equity) and keep their costs as short term and variable as possible. Therefore, the top left-hand box is an appropriate mix of risk profile. Similarly, companies which have a low degree of business risk can afford to take on a higher level of financial risk, without making the total combined risk of the company unacceptably high. As already discussed, the business risk reduces as an industry matures, because its sales revenues become less volatile. Due to its high level of profits and positive cash generation, it can now afford to pay interest on any outstanding debts and to repay the principal as it falls due.

The irony is that, if such a business was originally funded with equity (as it should have been when it was launched due to its high business risk), it has no automatic need of debt financing when it has become mature due to its high level of positive operating cash generation. Therefore, there is a

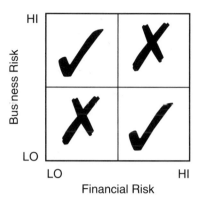

Figure 4.4 The inverse correlation of business and financial risk

tendency for many companies to move down the vertical axis of Figure 4.4 on the left-hand side as they mature; this moves them from a logical mixture of high business risk and low financial risk to an incompatible combination of low levels in both business and financial risk areas. Companies falling into this bottom left-hand box have been the most common target of corporate raiders and other acquisition experts. These financially focused businesses know that they can increase the overall value of the target company, not by changing its existing business strategy but by making its financial strategy more appropriate to this existing business strategy; in this case, by increasing the proportion of debt funding within the business, which can be achieved by structuring a highly leveraged acquisition of the company. Therefore, these specialised corporate raiders do not look for weak companies

GROWTH	LAUNCH
B. Risk – High	B. Risk – V.High
Financial Risk – Low	Financial Risk – Very Low
MATURITY	DECLINE
B. Risk – Med	B. Risk – Low
Financial Risk – Medium	Financial Risk – High

Figure 4.5 Financial risk – as it should change over the product life-cycle

as their targets, they try to identify businesses which have developed good sustainable competitive advantages in relatively mature, low risk industries, but where a much higher level of debt financing can be utilised than is being employed at present.

This inverse correlation can be shown diagrammatically, as is done in Figure 4.5, and this shows how the financial risk of the business should be changed as the business matures. It also highlights the essential need to develop specifically tailored financial control systems, which take account of the risk profile and the stage of maturity of the industry. These issues are discussed in more detail in Chapter 6.

PLANNING ISSUES FOR SERVICE COMPANIES

The underlying iterative financial management process of analysis, planning and control has already been discussed, and the necessity of expanding this general model to include the relevant external issues (such as the business environment, competitor repositionings, changes in customer expectations) has been introduced. However, there are several major issues for financial control relating to the design and operation of a meaningful planning system. Most companies now operate a two-tier planning process which involves the development of a long-term (normally five or seven years) strategic plan followed by the more detailed short-term (i.e. the next financial year) budget for the business. However, it is important that this two-stage planning process is properly understood, as there are fundamental differences between the long-term strategic plan and the short-term budget.

As shown in Figure 4.6, the overall business model starts by establishing the mission or goals for the organisation. This mission should be expressed reasonably generally as it should not need to be changed every year. In other words, 'goals' are the statement of what the organisation is (i.e. the area of business in which it operates) and what it wants to be. Thus a mission statement might be 'to be the best fast-food consumer oriented restaurant chain in the world'; this focuses attention on the specific area of operations (fast food restaurants) and restricts the market by stating 'consumer oriented', which can be taken to exclude canteen services and other business-to-business service operations. However, the aspirations of the company are both global and 'to be the best', and neither the range of products to be offered nor the marketing positioning (low cost or differentiated) are specified in this mission statement.

The role of the corporate objectives is to translate these general goals into more measurable objectives, which the organisation will try to achieve over

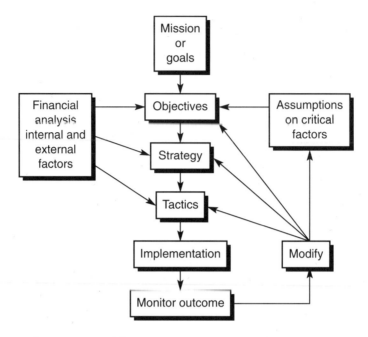

Figure 4.6 Business model

the long-term planning time horizon. Thus, as part of its planning process, the business must define what it means by 'the best' and establish how this will be measured (e.g. by market share or by market research to monitor consumer preferences). These objectives must be set in the context of the existing, and predicted future, internal and external environments. This requires a large amount of data collection and analysis, which must be given a clear sense of direction and focus. A major purpose of this internal and external analysis is to identify constraints and inhibiting factors, which may stop the company achieving its overall goals. Therefore, a realistic assess-ment of the current relative competitive positioning is very important, and any internal constraints (such as lack of spare capacity or availability of financing) must be highlighted.

However, this process indicates one of the major differences between long-term planning and operational budgeting. One of the justifications for long-term planning is, having identified a key inhibiting factor, to plan either to remove the constraint or to minimise its impact on the future development of the business. As such, a plan may take time to implement, it is often the case that short-term budgets have to recognise the existing constraints on the business. Short-term plans may have to be made to live within these bound-aries, but this restriction does not apply to the same extent to long-range planning. An obvious illustration of this, following on from the discussion in Chapter 3, is that, whereas a long-term plan can include the idea of creating a new competitive advantage with the objective of changing the existing balance of power in the market place, the sales revenue budget for the next year will mainly reflect the current market level under the impact of the existing competitive positions, as any changes will take time to feed through into market shares.

Of course, the strategy and tactics parts of the business model are the selected methods of trying to achieve the agreed objectives, and must be established in the light of the internal and external analysis. However, this analysis can only show up the current positioning and indicate likely future trends based on the historic analysis. The planning process requires the establishment of a wide range of assumptions on critical external issues (e.g. the rate of inflation, movements in exchange rates, wage and other supplier costs, competitive moves, customer expectations). The strategy and tactics are implemented based on the best available set of these assumptions, but it is inevitable that some of these assumptions about the future will turn out to be wrong. Therefore, there is a vital need for a good monitoring and feed-back process to enable the business to modify, as soon as practical, its strat-egy and tactics. If the actual situation is dramatically different to that assumed during the planning process, the objectives may need to be modi-fied, as it is pointless continuing to aim at a target which has been rendered irrelevant by a change in the business environment.

These planning issues are considered in detail in Chapter 7, but this process also has relevance for the organisational structure of the company. The organisational structure needs to be tailored to the needs of the business and this tailored structure must be incorporated into the planning process. Thus very large international businesses would tend to be organised on a fairly formal divisional basis but, if a critical success factor is the delivery of a non-standard service on a face-to-face basis with the end customer, a different organisational structure is necessary. The business has a need for flexibility and responsiveness to cope with the individual demands of each customer, and a flat decentralised organisation may be the best way of achieving this need. Alternatively, most franchised services have very delib-erately standardised the overall product offerings in order to maintain quality control in a very decentralised environment. In the retail and airline sectors, these organisational issues may be tackled very differently by the various competing companies. These organisational structure choices must be built into the planning process and the competitor analysis, but they also have implications for the performance measures used within the business.

PERFORMANCE MEASURES

Most businesses try to incorporate within both their planning and financial monitoring processes, measures of relative performance. Indeed one of the major benefits of any planning system is to evaluate whether the planned performance of the business is acceptable. However, there is a very great danger of misusing these performance measures if they are not properly understood and carefully applied.

Financial performance measures must be separated between economic measures and managerial performance measures. The economic measures of performance can, and should, be applied to the business as a whole and to its relevant separate SBUs. The objective is to assess how well the business either planned to perform or actually did perform so that, among other things, decisions relating to expanding, maintaining or contracting the scale of operations can be made. These economic decisions normally relate to the allocation of resources, and hence should be based on the opportunity cost logic of what would be the return from the next best available use of resources. Thus, if one area of the business is generating a sizeable loss, which is not expected to improve in the foreseeable future, the economic decision may be to close down these operations and reinvest any disposal proceeds in a more attractive area of operations.

However, this rational economic closure decision does not automatically translate into a poor managerial performance by the manager running this loss-making operation. Equally, a highly profitable business does not necessarily have a brilliant management team; economic results include the impact of non-controllable, externally driven events. Therefore, it is very important that managerial performance measures concentrate on those areas where managers genuinely exercise control; hence the linkages between the organisation structure and the way the business plans are segmented are very significant.

It is also critically important that the performance measures used reflect the effectiveness of the business as well as its efficiency. Efficiency is a measure of the level of inputs required to generate any given level of output and can be characterised as 'doing things right'! Effectiveness, however, reflects how well the business is achieving its objectives and therefore can be depicted as 'doing the right things'! Most simple financial measures are measures of efficiency rather than effectiveness, and therefore the business must incorporate key measures of effectiveness within its system of financial control. In many companies, the basic departmental financial control measure is the comparison of actual expenditure against the budgeted level. This creates a very strong culture of not overspending on any account and reporting a small underspend over the period is often looked on as a good performance. Unless the over-or under-achievement of the key objectives of the department is measured and reported on, this emphasis on 'efficiency' can be immensely counter-productive. Thus spending only 95% of the total budget but failing to achieve most of the key objectives could be counted as a good performance, while spending 105% of the total budget in order to achieve all of the key objectives might be looked as a failure due to the slight overspend.

This area of financial performance measures is considered again in Chapters 6 and 13, which deals with the operational use of information technology. There is a need to consider the type of financial information which is needed for both economic decisions and management performance evaluations, and the trade-offs which must be made between the speed with which the information can be supplied and its cost and accuracy. Clearly the type of information must be tailored to the competitive strategy of the business and its importance to the decision will dictate the priority which it is given in terms of both speed and accuracy. The next two sections look at some of the key information needs for a differentiated service business and for a low cost service respectively.

PRICING DECISIONS

The decision as to how to price any particular product in a given market is obviously of great importance to almost all companies but, in the case of most services, the issue is much more critical. As discussed in Chapter 2, it is impossible to build up a stock of many services as can be done with most tangible products. This makes pricing a key way of trying to control demand so that it matches available supply, and this can lead to a very flexible approach where prices are changed by time, day, weather or any other factors which significantly affect the level of demand.

Indeed, some service businesses almost deliberately try to create a level of demand slightly above their ability to supply so that a 'queue' develops (obviously in the case of many personal services, there is literally a queue formed in these circumstances). The logic of building a queue is to avoid having spare resources sitting around waiting for a customer to arrive; thus the balancing decision is between discounting pricing levels slightly to create this excess demand and incurring costs which cannot be recovered in the future due to the inability to hold 'stock' of the service. As discussed in depth in Chapter 8, this trade-off depends on the cost structure of the service business but can lead to dramatic changes in pricing levels in the case of highly perishable services, such as airline seats, hotel rooms and fresh fruit and vegetables.

Pricing decisions must also be related to the objectives of the company because, if major objectives are both to increase market share and to grow the total size of the market, much lower prices may be established in order to encourage new customers to try the service and to build loyalty to the company's own service among existing users. The alternative to this 'penetration pricing' strategy is to implement a 'skimming pricing' strategy which charges a premium price for the service. Clearly such a premium pricing policy should be supported by very strong barriers to entry by potential competitors, or the high prices being charged will serve to attract new competitors.

If new competitors did start to enter the industry, the existing companies may need to modify their pricing policy and hence information regarding the threat of new entrants is necessary. In many personal service industries it is difficult to erect significant barriers in the form of economies of scale or size of investment and hence, if the original company wants to avoid having to reduce its selling price in the face of new competitors, a strongly differentiated competitive strategy is to be recommended. However, changes in the overall competitive environment can result in dramatic changes in pricing strategy within an industry.

The development of increased customer loyalty in retailing through the growth of retailer brands and the achievement of economies of scale and consolidation of buying power has led to the largest supermarket chains implementing a sophisticated mixed pricing strategy. In this strategy some branded and commodity products are sold at relatively low prices, almost as loss leaders, while better profit margins are achieved on the retailer's own branded products. The computer software industry is a good illustration of how pricing strategies can change over time as, originally, most projects were charged for on a time and materials basis. However, as customers became more sophisticated, they expected the software company to guarantee the total cost by offering a fixed price at the outset of the contract; the dramatic implications for financial control are considered in Chapter 8.

COST MANAGEMENT

If a cost leadership competitive strategy has been chosen, it is obviously vital that the company produces very good, up-to-date financial information on the cost of its services. As already discussed, this cost information should not be exclusively internally focused because a competitive advantage means having *lower* costs than competing companies. However, there are several key issues regarding the way in which this important cost information should be produced, and these are of great significance to the design of the financial management system.

The major reason for developing accurate relative cost information is to provide inputs for the strategic and tactical decisions regarding the competitive positioning of the business; it is very important to confirm that the main sustainable competitive advantage really exists before implementing a major strategic initiative based on this assumption. Hence, all the cost analysis should be focused on providing decision support information. This means that the costing system can concentrate on those areas of difference from competitors and on those items of cost which will change as a result of future decisions.

Thus cost management must focus on the commitment of expenditure because it is prior to the commitment stage that managers can exercise real control over the organisation's cost levels. Once committed, the expenditure will inevitably take place and the discretion, or choice, which can be exercised is very limited. This concentration on decision making also means that the cost management system should be much more than a neat reconciliation system, which is achieved by spreading all costs to a product and a customer. Such a detailed full costing system does not generally aid decision making, because at least some of the shared cost will not change if decisions affecting individual products and customers are taken and implemented by the business. Costs should be allocated to the area of the business which causes this specific cost to be incurred; what is now generally referred to as the 'cost driver'. The future behaviour of the cost can now be predicted by understanding the relationship of this cost driver to the particular decision under consideration. This emphasis on identifying the relevant cost drivers within the organisation is the major contribution of new costing techniques such as Activity Based Costing (ABC); the application of cost management to segment profitability analysis is discussed in Chapter 6.

The idea of deriving relationships between the movements in cost levels and business decisions is fundamental to a sensible, practical system of cost management. One of the most direct ways of achieving this is to identify a physical input to output relationship, which can be used predictively to determine either the level of outputs which *should* be achieved from a given level of input, or the level of inputs which *should* be needed to produce a required level of output. These physical cost relationships are usually described, not surprisingly, as engineering costs, but this title may have acted as a deterrent to the widespread use of this process in many service industries. In manufacturing industries, these input–output relationships have been developed into quite sophisticated standard costing systems but, despite the existence of many similar physical relationships, relatively few service companies have made use of standard costs.

Standard costs can be developed for any repetitive process which has a predictive input to output relationship, and this clearly applies to many functions in many service companies. The advantages of using standard costing in the service sector, which are illustrated in Chapter 9, include an ability to monitor the efficiency of operations by eliminating changes in price from the assessment of performance. It should be remembered that this type of efficiency measure does not indicate the effectiveness of the performance, in terms of achieving the objectives of the business. However, if cost price movements are sensibly incorporated into the analysis, the standard costing system can be used to provide a very early indication of the impact on total costs of any changes in the costs of bought-in goods and services.

MANAGING DYNAMIC GROWTH

In many industries, a key element of the selected competitive strategy is a period of rapid growth. This may be desirable in order to achieve the maximum level of economies of scale or to increase market share to a dominant level before the market reaches maturity. There is a limit on the rate of growth which any company can sustain organically in terms of its ability both to finance and manage the growth. If the desired rate of growth exceeds this internal sustainable rate, the company may decide to accelerate its overall rate of growth by making acquisitions; this is normally described as dynamic growth, in order to distinguish an acquisition led strategy from the internally oriented organic growth strategies. Many service industries have been the subject of dramatic changes in ownership and competitive structure due to the implementation of a large number of acquisitions.

There are always potential problems of integrating and assimilating any acquired businesses into the existing group structure but, in the case of many service companies, these problems are once again amplified due to the personal nature of the services and the critical nature of the people working in the acquired business. This has resulted in the development of some very sophisticated methods of structuring acquisitions of people based service companies, where it is vitally important to retain the motivation of the key employees. If the target company is owner-managed prior to the acquisition by a larger group, it is quite possible to tie the final purchase price to the future performance of the business over a specified period. Such a deal should act as an incentive to the sellers to achieve rapid growth in profitability during the earn-out period (as these deals are normally known), whereas the receipt of a large sum of money immediately at the time of sale would remove all further financial interest on the part of the original owner-manager. Earn-out deals have been widely used in the advertising, computer software, and employment bureaux industries.

Another way of achieving a very rapid rate of growth over a considerable period is through the use of franchising, which has already been mentioned. Franchising reduces the financial investment required by the original company, and also allows the managers to focus on fewer critical areas of activity, because the direct interface with the end customer has been delegated to the franchisee. However, this strategy normally requires a standardisation of the service, if control over the quality delivered by the franchisee is to be a practical proposition. These ways of managing rapid dynamic growth in service businesses are considered in detail in Chapter 10.

ASSET AND LIABILITY MANAGEMENT

Many discussions on financial control tend to focus exclusively on the profit performance of the business and how this can be managed using a variety of financial measures. However, financial management is much broader in its scope as a sensibly managed business must control its cash flow if it is to survive and prosper. Cash flow management involves understanding both the sources and uses of funds for the particular business and, in addition to generating funds from profitable trading, this requires a clear analysis of the assets and liabilities of the company.

In many service industries, this management of assets and liabilities can be absolutely critical to the development of a successful competitive strategy; indeed, it can almost be regarded as a key sustainable competitive advantage when allied to a dynamic acquisition strategy. For example, advertising agencies, like many service businesses, act as the agent for their clients for the booking of advertisements with the media companies, such as commercial radio and television, newspapers, magazines, etc. This means that the advertising agency receives payments from its clients, from which it deducts its commission and then it pays the media company for the advertising which it has booked on behalf of its clients. The sales revenue of the advertising agency is the commission, etc., which it earns for the service it performs but, if these represent say 15 per cent of the value of the advertising booked for clients, it is clear that the cash flow passing through the agency's bank account is nearly seven times the value of its sales revenue.

This multiplier effect, which also applies to many other service businesses which act in an agency capacity, highlights the critical importance of managing the assets and liabilities of this type of business. If the advertising agency is not very good at collecting its outstanding debtor balances, it could find itself needing to pay the media companies before it has received the necessary funds from its clients. The impact of such a financing requirement can be dramatic, not only on the profitability of the business but also on its financial viability in the medium term. In this industry, the original strategic thrust of most advertising agencies was concentrated on the creative side of the business, with a limited focus on financial management.

It is possible, as a result, to change the financial performance of these companies by introducing very sound financial controls which restore a sound balance in the asset and liability mix. If the company can accelerate the cash inflows from clients sufficiently, it may be able to generate a continuous positive net cash position as it can hold on to these receipts until the corresponding payments have to be made to the media companies. This type of strategy has been implemented with great success in the advertising industry and other significant asset management strategies have been implemented in retailing and computer software as is explained in Chapter 11.

CONCLUSION

The specific characteristics of service businesses and the alternative competitive strategies available to these companies combine to create a number of key issues, which must be addressed in the financial management system of each business. These specific financial control issues are addressed in detail in Part 3 of the book. However, before moving on to consider these issues in depth, it is necessary to consider how the decision whether to outsource a particular service, or to provide the service internally, is taken; this is done in Chapter 5.

5 INTERNAL SERVICE BUSINESSES

INTRODUCTION

Several examples have already been given of relatively new, but large and growing businesses which have based their strategy on supplying services to other businesses. Their growth indicates an increasing trend towards outsourcing, i.e. buying in, many of the services required by the modern corporation. It is therefore instructive to consider what specific circumstances would encourage companies to look for an external supplier or to decide to continue to supply the service internally. It is also important to examine the differences in financial controls which are necessary depending upon which alternative is selected.

To some extent, the decision to opt for outsourcing is dependent upon the availability of external suppliers as an alternative to having an internal service department. Therefore, in the very early periods of any industry, the innovative new companies may have very little choice but to be relatively vertically integrated because the external suppliers may not yet exist. However, all such new industries have some requirements for fairly standard services such as secretarial support, accounting and administrative assistance, cleaning, office equipment, etc. These services could be outsourced relatively easily even though the more specialised support services may not yet have developed as stand-alone service businesses. As the industry develops (this argument can be applied to the car industry, the oil industry and the computer industry), more and more of the required services will become available from external suppliers.

Indeed, if these suppliers specialise in a particular service area and supply more than one customer in the industry they may well develop a sustainable cost advantage, due to economies of scale, over the in-house service department. Thus, it is not surprising to see an increasing degree of outsourcing used as industries mature and their service needs become more well known. It is quite possible to argue that a degree of vertical disintegration is an inevitable consequence of a maturing industry, as can be evidenced by the three industries mentioned above.

AVAILABLE ALTERNATIVES: PROVIDE INTERNALLY, BUY IN, DO WITHOUT

Most services sourcing decisions are based on a choice among a range of external suppliers and an existing or potential internal source of supply, and this type of decision forms the major focus of this chapter. However, it is important to remember that the cheapest alternative may be to do without the service completely. In many cases, this will not be a viable option but such a drastic suggestion can force managers to review what it is that they really need from this particular service. It may be that the current level of service is not really necessary or that the results can be achieved in a completely different, but much more cost effective manner. For example, before comparing the costs of an internal versus external maintenance operation, the required response time should be assessed carefully as this will clearly have a significant impact on the cost of either type of service. Some companies, which operate a large number of similar machines in one location, have found it more cost effective to build in a certain level of spare capacity (such as having one spare machine) which enables them to avoid the high premium cost required to guarantee same-day servicing.

In some areas it is now considered by several companies to make sound financial sense completely to do without any maintenance service at all, even though this means that the machine may have to be thrown away if it does break down. This is normally a combination of high reliability of the machine and the high cost of servicing relative to the replacement cost of the machine. Where the replacement cost is steadily decreasing even in nominal values, while the labour element of the service cost is rising in real terms, as is the case with personal computers, the economic case for doing without the service becomes more attractive over time.

This example also introduces one of the other criteria used to decide whether and how to source a particular service. If a personal computer system fails, the user may find it impossible to access a large amount of important company information and this may necessitate that some form of service contract is undertaken, even if this only ensures the safe transfer of key data from the old machine to the new. In the case of computer systems it is, of course, possible to insist that all important files are copied onto floppy disks as a back-up, which should minimise the disruption from any specific machine failure. Where the individual machines are networked through a 'controller' computer, the required back-up storage can often be achieved automatically via the file maintenance routines within the overall system.

BASIS OF SOURCING DECISION

However, there is a very important, more general point regarding the use of external sources of supply. Many companies believe that there are certain areas of their business which are so critical to their overall success that they cannot be entrusted to outsiders. This is irrespective of the level of guarantee of performance provided by the external supplier. In order for this argument to be valid, it is clear that these areas should really be sources of competitive advantage to the business. If this is not true, the business should select the most cost effective source of supply, having built in any essential requirements regarding the level of performance and quality of service.

This careful specification of the required service is vital if a valid comparison is to be made between the competing potential internal and external sources. It avoids the apparently cheapest source of supply being selected when the actual quality of service makes it completely unacceptable for the needs of the business. In the case of many technically complex or rapidly changing services, it is quite possible that an external supplier may be able to deliver a much better and more up-to-date service than an exclusively internal service. It is important that the value of this improved level of service is assessed before the decision is made, because it may appear that the external service is more expensive than its outdated internal alternative. The continued use of such a poor quality internal service may eventually translate into a competitive disadvantage for the company, if its major competitors adopt the alternative strategy.

Thus, while it is true that an externally sourced service is unlikely to provide a source of sustainable competitive advantage, it is quite possible that an uneconomic reliance on internal services may create a competitive disadvantage. This highlights that it is very important for a company to examine carefully old arguments seeking to justify the retention of an in-house service purely on the grounds of the strategic significance of that service. An interesting example of this type of problem is the provision of the computer services which are an ever increasing requirement of most businesses.

One of the fastest growing areas of business-to-business services is facilities management, under which a specialist outside computer systems company takes over the operational management of a company's computers and the related software systems. A major reason given by many companies for sub-contracting this important support area of their business to an external supplier is that they do not possess the required in-house expertise and scale of operation to keep up with the rapidly changing technology in this area. However, at the same time, several service industries, as is illustrated in Chapter 12, see information technology as a major potential source of competitive advantage and consequently wish to maintain direct control over their computer systems. The challenge for the facilities management service companies is to try to convince these companies that they can preserve their perceived competitive advantages and yet realise cost savings and/or service quality improvement by bringing in outside specialist management. It is quite possible to achieve this if the sustainable competitive advantage is actually created by the specific application of the information technology as an integral part of the competitive strategy, rather than by the technology itself.

In the airline industry, the information system which models the expected load factors by class of passenger for all forthcoming scheduled flights, based on the current booking position and the historical trend for past flights, might be regarded as very strategic. Such a system would enable the airline to modify its pricing strategy for any specific flight if its predicted load factor was too low, and any such promotional activity could be very tightly focused. However, the operation of such a system need not necessarily be compromised by introducing an outside facilities management company to control the airline's very sophisticated computer systems.

This type of argument regarding the use of external service suppliers can be extended to many other areas of strategic importance to airlines. Thus aircraft servicing between flights can be a critical efficiency factor in terms of improving the utilisation of aircraft achieved by the airline. However this does not mean that the airline must internally do all of its own refuelling, technical checking, cleaning and catering in order to achieve the greatest level of efficiency. This could be achieved by specifying the exact level of service required by the specialist outside suppliers and by establishing appropriate performance measurements and financial incentives or sanctions in the agreed service contracts.

'COST' OF ALTERNATIVES

Once it has been established that it is potentially perfectly possible for a specific service to be sourced from an outside supplier if it is economically attractive to do so (i.e. there is no strategic or other reason for keeping the service in-house), the financial comparison must be carried out. The key issue is to ensure that the comparison is genuinely comparing like with like, not just in terms of the quality of service but that the cost comparisons are conducted on a fair basis.

In the case of a potential decision to cease an existing internal service and switch to an outsider supplier, the costs associated with the outside supplier are normally quite easy to establish. These will represent the cash payments to be made by the company to the supplier under the terms of their proposed supply agreement; although any cancellation terms and terms of payment may need to be carefully evaluated. This establishes the cost of the externally sourced alternative, but calculating the 'cost' of the existing internal service department, which may well be closed as a result of this decision, is by no means so straightforward.

Many companies operate very detailed costing systems which spread the costs of support or indirect departments to the more direct areas of operation within the company. This means that the reported total costs of any specific department within the business, as disclosed in its internal management accounts, include a significant proportion of these indirect, or apportioned, costs. Equally importantly, these reported costs represent the historic costs which *have been* incurred in the past in operating the service department, while the external cost estimates will usually be based on the forecast of the costs which *will be* incurred if a decision is made to change to the outside supplier. Logically the economic decision should be based on a comparison of the cost which will be incurred with the costs which will be saved if the in-house department is closed down.

In this context, savings mean exactly that, i.e. that funds currently being spent will no longer be spent by the company. This means that any costs which will be incurred in closing down the in-house department, such as redundancy pay, must be taken into account to reduce the gross savings to their true net value. However, the greater impact is that only those costs which can actually be saved should be taken into the evaluation; not surprisingly, those costs are usually described as the avoidable costs. If only avoidable costs should be considered, many of the indirect apportioned costs charged to the internal service department will be excluded from the financial comparison, and this could clearly make a significant difference to the final decision.

This problem can most clearly be illustrated with a very simplified numerical example using a large service company which currently has three internal service departments, namely, maintenance, computer systems and distribution, each of which it is considering changing to an outsourced basis. As shown in Figure 5.1, the company has a costing system which spreads the cost of certain support departments to other areas of the business; for simplicity, these other costs have been grouped together under the title of Head Office costs and it is also assumed that all these costs are correctly charged to these three departments.

	Internal Service Departments			
	Maintenance £000s	Computer Systems £000s	Distribution £000s	Total £000s
Annual Direct Operating Costs	2,000	3,000	5,000	10,000
Annual Head Office Costs	4,000	6,000	10,000	20,000
Total Costs (as per internal management forecasts)	6,000	9,000	15,000	30,000
External Supplier Quotations (Annual contract basis)	8,000	16,000	12,000	36,000

Figure 5.1 Service company – outsourcing example

If it is assumed that the cost comparisons are made on a similar forward looking basis, the comparison of the overall totals indicates that the performance of the in-house departments is, in total, better than could be achieved by outsourcing the three services; a total annual internal cost of £30 million against a bought-in combined total of £36 million. However, a closer inspection appears to reveal an opportunity to generate substantial savings. By transferring the distribution operation to the outside supplier an apparent saving of £3 million could be generated; comparing the £12 million external quotation to the total internal cost of £15 million. Unfortunately, two-thirds of this cost is the distribution department's apportioned share of the total annual Head Office costs (the £20 million has been spread to the three departments in proportion to their own direct costs; this is a very arbitrary but also very common method of apportioning this type of cost).

The financial impact of the proposed decision to close the internal distribution department and use outside suppliers depends upon what is likely to happen to these Head Office costs in the absence of one of the three original departments. At the extreme, it is possible that virtually no savings are made at Head Office. This means that the total costs must now be apportioned between the remaining two internal departments, with the result shown in

	Maintenance £000s	Computer Systems £000s	Distribution £000s	Total £000s
Internal Service Departments				
Annual Direct Operating Costs	2,000	3,000	Closed	5,000
Annual Head Office Costs - original share	4,000	6,000	10,000	20,000
- reapportionment of distribution share	4,000	6,000	(10,000)	–
Sub-Total	10,000	15,000	–	25,000
External Supplier taken on	–	–	12,000	12,000
Total Costs	10,000	15,000	12,000	37,000
Remaining Supplier Quotations	8,000	16,000	N/A	

Figure 5.2 Service company – analysis of outsourcing decision

Figure 5.2. The total costs incurred by the company have now increased to £37 million, because the avoidable costs actually saved by closing the internal distribution are £7 million less than the incremental costs incurred by taking on the outside contract.

However, if this logic is continued, worse is yet to come! Figure 5.2 highlights that the reapportionment of the Head Office costs makes the maintenance department appear to be more expensive than the outside supplier's quotation. Therefore, it is quite possible that the company would decide to save still more money by outsourcing this service operation as well. This would leave only the computer systems department, which would have to bear all the costs of Head Office unless these could now be reduced. Figure 5.3 assumes that no real cost savings can yet be achieved with the not surprising results that total costs have increased again, and the computer systems department now appears more expensive than the external supplier's quotation.

	Internal Service Departments			
	Maintenance £000s	Computer Systems £000s	Distribution £000s	Total £000s
Annual Direct Operating Costs	Closed	3,000	Closed	3,000
Annual Head Office Costs - previous appt	8,000	12,000	–	20,000
- reapportionment of maintenance share	(8,000)	8,000	–	–
Sub-Total	–	23,000	–	23,000
External Suppliers taken on	8,000	–	12,000	20,000
Total Costs	8,000	23,000	12,000	43,000
Remaining Supplier Quotations	N/A	16,000	N/A	

Figure 5.3 Outsourcing example – two down, one to go!

The ultimate decision would, of course, now be to close the computer systems department in a further attempt to save money. Interestingly, if the company had actually arrived at this point, this decision might actually achieve this objective because, with all the internal service departments closed, the company might be able to get rid of its £20 million Head Office costs (however, such a result is by no means guaranteed!). The obvious point of this very simplified example is how dangerous it is to use apportioned or shared costs as the basis for financial decision making, particularly when there is no sound logical basis for the apportionment process (such as would be achieved by identifying the principal cost driver for the overall cost level incurred).

This does not mean that outsourcing decisions should ignore all internal fixed costs or all indirect costs, but the evaluation should only take into account those internal costs which can genuinely be saved as a result of the change to an external source of supply. As most sourcing decisions, especially those involving the closure of an internal department, are made on a long-term basis, the distinction between fixed and variable costs is of limited interest; remember that, in the long term, all costs are variable. The key issue is to focus on the avoidable nature of the internal costs over the time period of the decision.

Conversely, if the decision required the evaluation of the opposite change, i.e. from an existing external supplier to an internal service department, the relevant level of costs would be the incremental costs which would be incurred in running the internal department. Any existing overheads which would simply be reapportioned to this new service department are as irrelevant as the Head Office expenses were in the previous example. Financial decisions are always based on the future cash flows which change as a result of the decision, and this excludes unchanging indirect apportioned costs from the financial evaluation.

TRANSFER PRICING SYSTEM

If the final decision indicates the establishment or continuation of an internal service department, the financial control issues are by no means finished. This internal service will, by definition, be used by other areas of the business and it is very important that their level of usage is economically justified. The fundamental problem with anything that appears to be free is that people will usually demand a lot of it; it is only by associating a 'price' with its usage that the level of demand becomes dictated by the relative perception of its price to value relationship. Thus if the price charged for a service bears no relationship to the true cost associated with the production of the service, the level of demand may still not be economically rational. With an externally provided service, this rational behaviour should be quite easy to ensure through the introduction of an appropriate pricing mechanism; thus, a price per unit can normally easily be derived from the vendor's total charges, even if it is not explicitly stated in the supply agreement. In the case of an internal service department, the problem of defining the relevant level of 'cost' which should be used is once again a problem.

However, the issue is more complex than this because the objective is not simply to apportion costs around the organisation but to encourage economically rational behaviour.

This means that the resources allocated within the business to the production of this service should be justified by the value added by the service. For an externally sold product, the selling price and the resulting level of demand can be used to control the resource allocation process as long as each product is given the long-term objective of, at least, covering its costs. A similar resource allocation control function is needed for internally concerned services. This is most easily created by an appropriate internal pricing mechanism and therefore any internal pricing, or 'transfer' pricing, system should be regarded as a means of 'allocating resources in an economic fashion', rather than merely recovering the 'costs' of an internal service department. Any pricing system requires the presence of a buyer and a seller, and this implies the ability to exercise choice as to whether to buy at the quoted price or not. These issues are critical to the implementation of a sensible transfer pricing system because if there is no alternative, there is no choice and hence no need for a transfer pricing system.

Unfortunately in many companies, transfer pricing systems *are* imposed in situations where the 'internal customers' of the internal service department have no choice about using the service and no ability to negotiate on the transfer price. This type of system assists neither the economic allocation of resources nor the assessment of the performance of the two internal departments (i.e. buyer and seller) involved. It is actually worse than a waste of time, because it can have a dramatically demotivating effect on the externally focused managers who are *forced* to buy from these internal service departments; particularly if they are then held accountable for the subsequent recovery of these arbitrary, non-negotiable transfer prices in their own external sales revenues. Also, there is no effective incentive for the internal service departments to improve their own financial performance, if they know that their total costs, whatever they are, will be charged out, through the transfer prices, to their customers who must buy their services.

The most logical basis of a transfer pricing system is the external market price for the equivalent service (i.e. adjusting the external price to reflect the actual contractual relationship between the supplier and the customer, such as any guaranteed level of purchase or volume discount which should be obtainable). This pricing system should also include the ability for the buyer to purchase the service from the external market, but this can lead to significant problems if this is not carefully managed by the group. Certain external suppliers may be willing to quote short-term prices which are below their full cost levels; this may be due to excess capacity in a service industry which has high levels of fixed costs, so that a short-term marginal pricing policy may be logical. However, this low level pricing strategy may be an attempt to attract away internal customers so that the company closes its internal service department as no longer being economically viable. Once this has happened, the external supplier may significantly increase its selling prices. Consequently, any use of external prices must ensure that these prices are fairly representative of the long-term sustainable levels in the industry, before major strategic changes are implemented. Given this proviso regarding the use of external market prices, a sensible transfer pricing system for internal service businesses can normally be established.

Transfer prices are also required in vertically integrated service businesses, in order to establish whether it would be more beneficial to focus on a more limited section of the total industry value chain by outsourcing some areas of activity which are currently carried out internally. Another use of transfer prices in this context is in multi-product companies where many of the end services make use of a common input higher up the value chain. The primary rationale for transfer pricing should still be supporting economic decisions regarding the allocation of internal resources (which clearly includes the internal versus external sourcing decision). As a consequence, transfer pricing systems, which cannot be directly based on external market prices, should incorporate the appropriate level of costs, which means either avoidable or incremental costs rather than the apportionment of total costs. The business will want to concentrate its resources on those areas of activity which will generate the greatest level of contribution to overall profits. Where a critical limiting factor can be identified, this can be achieved by focusing the transfer pricing process on the contribution per unit of this limiting factor in addition to the appropriate measure of attributable cost.

In some cases, the impact of an internal market, which can be created by the introduction of a transfer pricing system for the purchase and sale of certain specialised services, can create a dramatic change in the allocation of resources within the business. For example, the introduction of this process within parts of the National Health Service has led to the expansion of certain specialised facilities in some hospitals and their closure in other areas, as the 'internal market' creates a significant reallocation of resources. Unfortunately, as in all cases of transfer pricing, if the basis of establishing the underlying transfer prices is flawed, the subsequent decisions regarding the reallocation of resources are also likely to be flawed, leading to some efficient units being closed while less efficient operations are expanded.

Part 3

SPECIFIC FINANCIAL
CONTROL ISSUES

6 THE IMPORTANCE OF A TAILORED FINANCIAL CONTROL SYSTEM

INTRODUCTION

This chapter considers the financial control systems which are appropriate to service businesses at various stages of development and employing different types of competitive strategy. The discussion is equally applicable at the overall corporate level and at the business unit (e.g. SBU) level. However, as is made clear throughout the chapter, the key requirement of specific tailoring of the selected financial controls means that different financial control systems may be needed in each of the individual business units within any large organisation, if the circumstances of the business units differ.

As discussed in Part 2, it is helpful to separate risk into two component elements, namely, business risk and financial risk. A logical sustainable overall corporate strategy requires an inverse correlation between these two component elements, so that an organisation with a high level of business risk should adopt a financial strategy that has a correspondingly low level of risk. However, in Chapter 4, the significant changes in business risk that occur during the product life-cycle were discussed.

A major objective of any good financial control system must be to assist managers in making financially based decisions; there is no statutory obligation on companies to produce management accounting information and all such information must itself be justified on a cost/benefit basis. Many financial decisions relate to the management of risks, as was discussed in Chapter 2, and it is therefore important that the financial control system takes account of the major risks faced by the organisation. As these change over time, it will be necessary for the focus of the financial control system to be adjusted appropriately. This chapter examines how, in practice, this tailored system of financial controls can be designed and operated.

However, the inter-relationship of risk and return is also important in the development of the key strategic thrust of the competitive strategy of the business. As illustrated in Chapter 3, the main objective of any competitive strategy is to develop and then maintain a sustainable competitive advantage, which will enable the business to earn an above normal rate of return for its associated level of risk. If financial management is to make a positive contribution in this area, it is also important that the financial control system highlights these strategically important areas of competitive advantage, rather than reporting equally on all areas of the business. This means that more frequent or more detailed reports may be needed in some specific areas, but more generally it means that the most important role of financial management should be seen as 'accounting for competitive advantage'.

By definition competitive advantage is a relative concept and is normally achieved in specific product/market interfaces. This indicates that a vital element of the financial control system should be to report on the performance of important segments of the business. This chapter also considers the way in which this segmented analysis should be carried out, by discussing accounting and analysis for customers, products and competitors.

BUSINESS RISK IN SERVICE COMPANIES

Business risk is influenced by the industry in which the company operates, its stage of development and the particular competitive strategy which is being implemented. A key indicator of the level of risk in financial terms is the degree of volatility in the actual return generated by the business, as an absolutely guaranteed level of return would be regarded as having a zero risk. One factor which clearly helps to reduce this volatility in financial return is the strength of the sustainable competitive advantage which can be developed by the business.

As discussed in Chapter 3 sustainable competitive advantages are mainly created by erecting entry barriers which stop or delay new competitors from entering what is, by definition, a financially attractive market. Unfortunately, for many service companies their ability to erect strong barriers to entry is very limited, and hence many such industries are still dominated by a vast number of small competitors. This high level of competition increases the level of business risk in these industries. Also, an absence of significant entry barriers even makes it difficult for an organisation to develop a competitive advantage by implementing a very tightly focused strategy, such as might be achieved by concentrating activities on a very localised basis. As soon as a super-profit is being earned, new competitors are likely to be attracted to this focused area of activity.

This does indicate one way of maintaining such a localised competitive advantage and this is to try to avoid communicating that an abnormally high level of return is being achieved. Imperfect knowledge is obviously a deterrent to new competitors entering a particular market, but the need for better comparative information is a major reason behind the increasing emphasis being placed on competitor accounting and analysis. However, this sophisticated analysis of competitors' strategies and the returns being achieved in different market segments is only really being done by larger companies. Hence, in several personal service industries (such as painters and decorators, kitchen fitters, plumbers, gardeners, window cleaning, etc.), which are still dominated by small suppliers, it can be possible to retain a localised competitive advantage based on the lack of competition in a very focused market segment.

Another factor, which affects the level of return in some of these service industries with low entry barriers, is the presence of exit barriers which may stop existing competitors leaving the industry. Fortunately, the exit barriers are very small for most of these personal service industries, because there is almost no significant investment in highly specialised assets for the multitude of small companies operating in these areas. Consequently, these industries typically have a large, but quite rapidly changing, population of small companies operating on a very localised basis. Franchising has been tried as a method of developing a more sustainable competitive advantage (e.g. plumbing services), where the franchisor's role is to create awareness of both the brand name and the 'guaranteed' quality of service provided by their local, semi-independent franchisees. As with all such strategies, this increased up-front marketing investment, which is used in attempting to create an intangible asset, increases the overall associated business risk. It must be financially justified by the expected enhanced financial return which will be produced either from charging a premium price or by achieving a larger share of the market. Many franchisors attempt to transfer much of this increased business risk to their franchisees, who have to pay a franchise fee based on a percentage of their sales revenue but must make a specified minimum level of monthly or annual payment.

The low level of entry barriers also affects some high technology industries, such as computer software, because it may be possible to start a new business with a very low level of investment. Thus, an individual skilled computer specialist can, with the aid of a personal computer, set up as a software house either selling tailored development services direct to business customers or attempting to develop a packaged software product for future volume sales. If either strategy proves unsuccessful the 'company' may rapidly leave the market place due to the low levels of any exit barriers, which again creates a fluctuating population of small software houses.

However, in this industry, the large software companies have been able to create significant barriers to entry to their segment of the market. By concentrating on large scale projects, these companies have effectively excluded a large number of the very small, single person software consultancies, which simply do not have the resources to compete at this end of the market. The effectiveness of this entry barrier was enhanced by also changing the role and risk profile undertaken by the leading software house in these complex development projects. If the client acts as the main project manager, it would be quite practical for very small specialised software businesses to be utilised in their particular areas of expertise, wherever this was appropriate within the context of the overall project. This possibility is effectively removed if the large software house takes over the role of project manager for the client because, even if the smaller specialist supplier can gain a share of the project, it will now be as a sub-contractor to the overall project manager. The ability to develop any loyalty from the final customer is greatly diminished. The large company can also make the risk profile of the large project unacceptably high from the perspective of a smaller competitor. This can be done by bidding on a fixed price basis for a specified set of performance characteristics to be delivered to the customer; if it costs more to develop the pre-agreed system, the loss is wholly attributable to the software company. For many small suppliers, the sheer scale of these contracts would place their entire business at risk if only one such fixed price quotation was to go badly wrong. Thus, an apparently effective entry barrier has been created around one very important segment of the computer software industry.

Unfortunately, this industry faces another factor which not only highlights a high business risk but also can, very rapidly, demolish what appear to be very strong entry barriers. All products follow life-cycles but some life cycles can be very unpredictable and may be dramatically cut short by new technological innovations. Where the innovation is particularly great, it may destroy the effectiveness of the existing entry barriers, thus allowing a mass of new entrants into the previously very attractive industry. Undoubtedly some of the major breakthroughs in computer technology have had this impact on the existing companies within the industry, thus making it very important both to exploit any current competitive advantage as rapidly as possible, and to develop replacement entry barriers before the current ones have been made obsolete.

In some cases, the source of the change in life-cycle may be completely unexpected, or an expected adverse impact may turn out to be favourable, and vice versa. All such instances of rapid volatility must be seen as increasing the risk profile of the business, and consequently the level of financial return which is required from the business should be increased. Also the financial control system must focus on these key areas of risk, and financial managers should try to find some early warning indicators that significant changes are *about* to take place. These warnings could enable alternative strategies to be implemented so as to minimise the adverse consequences or to take full advantage of a new opportunity; an historically focused financial management reporting system which merely reports how badly the business *has* performed is of very little value.

The business-to-business courier services, which provided a very rapid document delivery service on a worldwide basis, have seen a period of dramatic growth over the last ten to fifteen years. However, the development of international computer networks with instant electronic mail capabilities, and the widespread use of facsimile machines to transmit hard copies of documents electronically might have been expected to restrict the development of the industry. In fact, it is almost as if the impact has been as a positive stimulus because, far from being viewed as a directly competitive service, the result appears to have been to create an increased expectation of an even faster document delivery service. This has enabled some of the courier businesses to offer premium services at, of course, premium prices.

Another specific characteristic of many services can have an impact by increasing the unpredictability of product life-cycles. This is the personal nature of many intangible services, which means that the customer's perception of the value of this 'intangible, personal' service is critical. Clearly, if customers change their minds suddenly, the service suppliers can find their market disappear almost overnight, which indicates that they are in a very high risk business. Obviously, the service company must do as much as possible to manage this risk down to acceptable levels, but the required rate of return for a highly fashion conscious personal service should be set at a suitably high, risk adjusted level. The risk could be reduced by providing a range of services or products so that, if customers suddenly stop buying one specific offering, they may switch to another part of the company's portfolio. This strategy can be used to some extent by fashion clothing retailers, because they may stock a range of different styles at the beginning of the season until it becomes clear which is this year's 'winner'. If these stocks could be held on a 'sale or return' basis, the associated risk would be much lower still.

This transfer of risk by not fully committing external purchases too far in advance is well developed by package tour operators, who can face very sudden dramatic switches in customer preferences. The most popular overseas holiday destination from Britain during the 1980s was Spain and, based on this consistent demand, tour operators might have tried to reduce their costs by committing to buy, for much of the 1990s, vast numbers of hotel rooms, villas and apartments in Spain and chartered flights to and from Spain. If, possibly for no well-understood reason, a large proportion of their customers decided that they wanted in future to go further afield (e.g. to the

USA, Greece, or the Far East), these fully committed tour operators would face a major problem. However, if they reduced *their* risk profile, both by not committing to buy in advance of demand (i.e. keeping their cost base very variable), and by offering a range of holiday destinations to their customers, they might not be adversely affected by this dramatic change; of course, the same would not be true for hotel and holiday property owners in Spain! Indeed, if the change in customer preferences meant that total expenditure on holidays abroad actually increased, the tour operators could find that their financial performance improves, despite the dramatic volatility in product life-cycles. As mentioned very early in the book, any personal service business which delivers a high fashion service must put a strong emphasis on good market research information, to help it to predict these dramatic changes in demand.

TAILORED FINANCIAL CONTROLS

The analysis introduced in Chapter 4 can be developed to indicate a range of tailored financial control measures which can be applied to businesses at different stages of development; the specific financial control issues relating to the alternative competitive strategies of differentiation and cost leadership are dealt with in Chapters 8 and 9 respectively.

As any product progresses through the life-cycle, the associated business risk reduces but more importantly the critical success factors of its competitive strategy change, as shown in Figure 6.1. During the launch phase, the critical issue for the business is to develop the product successfully and

GROWTH	LAUNCH
B. Risk – High	B. Risk – Very High
CSF – Growth in Market Share and Development of Total Market	CSF – Development and Launch of New Product
MATURITY	DECLINE
B. Risk – Medium	B. Risk – Low
CSF – Maintenance of Market Share at Minimum Cost	CSF – Cost Minimisation and Asset Realisations

Figure 6.1 Changing critical success factors (CSF) over the product life-cycle

launch it onto the market before competitors are able to respond. The emphasis of the business is therefore on this research and development effort, but it is during this initial stage that many companies make a catastrophic error in the design of their financial control system. The control measure used for the critical area of R&D is often to compare actual expenditure against the budgeted level, i.e. to run the R&D department as a cost centre or expense centre. As mentioned in Part 2, there should be an emphasis in financial control systems on measures of effectiveness not simply efficiency. Any comparison of budget and actual expenditure measures, at best, the efficiency of the department; its effectiveness must be assessed by how well it achieves the objectives set for it by the business.

During the launch stage, the key objective is obviously to develop the new product successfully and on time, with the cost level being an important consideration but by no means the main driver of the R&D department's actions. Thus, it may be preferable to overspend slightly against budget, in order to deliver a well-developed new service product to the market six months ahead of schedule, compared to a slight underspend against budget but with no new product launches at all.

The financial control system during the launch stage should therefore focus on monitoring how the development process is going, so as to indicate whether the business needs to make any changes, either to increase the probability of success or to accelerate the launch of the new product. At this stage, there is no single financial measure which will give a meaningful indication of performance and greater reliance needs to be placed on physical measures (such as decision milestones within the R&D process and updated probability assessments of ultimate success), as indicated in Figure 6.2.

Once the service has been successfully launched, the critical success factors change significantly. The focus of attention is now on the total growth of the market and particularly the growth in market share of this company's service. It has been well established by research that it is financially more attractive to increase market share while the market is itself growing rapidly. If this strategy is attempted once the market has matured, the competitive response is likely to be much more aggressive, leading to less sustainable and much less cost effective gains in market share. As shown in Figures 6.1 and 6.2, these new critical success factors should form the focus of the financial control system during this stage of development. The growth stage is clearly a period of substantial investment in the business, even though much of it may be in the form of marketing expenditure in an attempt to grow both the total market and market share; the lack of tangible net assets in many service businesses has already been emphasised.

GROWTH	LAUNCH
FCM – DCF Evaluation of Investments in Growth in Market and Market Share	FCM – R & D Milestones, Decision- focused Reviews Probability Assessments
MATURITY	DECLINE
FCM – Accounting Return on Investment or Residual Income	FCM – Free Cash Flow from Operations

Figure 6.2 Tailored financial control measures (FCM) over the product life-cycle

The financial return on this investment will be received when the market eventually matures and the business can exploit its dominant market share, or other competitive advantage, to generate higher profits than its competitors. This means that the short-term financial performance of a rapidly growing business may not appear very good, especially in terms of profit generation, due to the accounting convention of expensing all marketing expenditure in the period in which it is incurred. A sound financial control system must assist in the proper assessment of performance. This means that long-term methods of evaluation may be more appropriate than those which focus on the short-term, during these periods of rapid growth and high net investment in the business. The most common long-term method of financial evaluation and control is the technique known as discounted cash flow (DCF). By applying an appropriate negative interest rate to the future expected cash flows, DCF can take into account both the time value of money and the risk associated with any specific investment. This enables a valid financial evaluation of the expected net return from the investment to be made but, by updating the expected future returns, this technique can also be used to control the business after these investments are actually made.

If a short-term accounting based financial control measure is used during these early stages of development, the short-term performance may be improved, but to the detriment of the longer term development and overall financial return of the business. For example, the most common financial control measure is some form of Return on Investment (ROI), which consists of some measure of profit divided by some assessment of the investment made in the business. If the main performance measure of the managers in the business is ROI, this can be improved in the short term by reducing R&D expenditure or development marketing activity. As both are treated as expenses for accounting purposes, any reductions in expenditures will show immediately as an increase in the bottom line profitability of the business. The benefits from this expenditure would have been felt in the future accounting periods, which are not considered under normal ROI based financial control measures.

Hence, this type of short-term accounting based measure is only appropriate when the business wants to continue in the future at much the same level of activity that it has at present. This becomes much more relevant once the market moves into its maturity stage, when the critical success factors become maintaining the existing market share as long as this is economically attractive, and achieving a high level of financial return by exploiting the competitive advantages which have been developed during the earlier stages of development. These objectives of maintenance and immediate return are not inevitably in conflict as the requirement to maintain the competitive advantage acts as a control on the rate of return which is targeted for the business. As long as this balancing requirement is remembered, it now becomes possible to use an accounting ratio-based measure of performance as the main financial control measure.

The most common form of divisional accounting performance ratio is, as already described, the Return on Investment ratio, which is normally used in its percentage form. The actual ROI percentage is often compared against the budgeted ratio, and/or last year's actual performance, or less frequently against external yardsticks such as competitors. The problem is in assessing the reported or predicted financial performance in terms of the risk profile of the business (i.e. does a 30 per cent ROI represent a good performance). A large part of this problem is that the use of a percentage measure can induce a high level of *game playing* by managers, in that perceived 'performance' can be improved either by increasing the profits or by reducing the level of investment. If a major objective is to maintain the scale of the business during this mature stage, this may not be a sensible strategy, and this behaviour could be avoided by using a modified financial control measure.

Instead of calculating financial performance as a percentage measure, the profit of the business unit is reduced by a charge based on the net investment made in the business unit. This charge should reflect the perceived risk associated with the business unit and the assets employed in it. (However, many large groups use a standard rate of charge for all their businesses and this is often equal to the group's cost of capital.) The deduction of this money value charge leaves the business with a lower net income (which could now

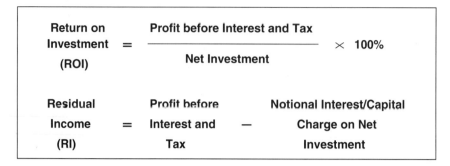

Figure 6.3 Comparison of residual income with ROI

be negative depending on the size of the charge levied on the net investment) which, as shown in Figure 6.3, is known as the Residual Income.

Using Residual Income as a financial control measure for mature, stable
businesses has a number of advantages over ROI. It is a money value rather
than a percentage, which enables the absolute scale of the return to be easily
established (a £1 profit on a £0 investment is an infinite ROI percentage, but
it is still only a £1 profit). Also, it is in the interests of the managers of the
business unit to increase the scale of their investment as long as the incremental return is expected to be greater than the increase in the charge on the
larger investment, i.e. the Residual Income will increase. As long as the
basis of the charge is logically developed so as to cover the cost of funding
the investment, this increased investment is also in the interests of the
overall business. When ROI is being used it is not unusual to find business
units not wanting to invest if the new investment will reduce the overall
reported ROI for the business. This may be against the interests of the group
because successful business units, which are currently achieving a high ROI,
will reject attractive projects from a group perspective. Conversely, business
units, which are now achieving a very low ROI, will submit much less
attractive projects if they will increase the existing level of ROI. A key
objective of a sensible financial control system is that it helps the business to
focus its new investment on the most financially attractive area *for the group*
as a whole.

Also, as mentioned briefly above, the Residual Income (RI) measure
allows companies to vary the notional rate of interest charged on the unit's
investment base depending on its risk profile. For example, different classifications of asset types could be established and the overall volatility of the
returns for the business unit could be used. As the correlation between risk
and required return is another major objective of a good financial control
system, Residual Income seems significantly more attractive than ROI in
this respect.

It is therefore somewhat surprising to find that most companies still use ROI as their principal financial control measure (this is irrespective of their stage of development) and that relatively few have adopted the conceptually more attractive RI in its place. It would, of course, be very reassuring to write that those which have done so have been significantly more successful than their competitors, but this research has not yet been completed. (It is also interesting to note, in passing, that a similar phenomenon exists with respect to the alternative ways of applying DCF analysis. There are some conceptual problems with using Internal Rate of Return as the base project evaluation measure and these flaws are not present when using the Net Present Value measure and its derivative the Profitability Index. Despite this, most companies still use the Internal Rate of Return form of calculation.)

Eventually the particular service will pass through its maturity stage into the final stage of decline. The critical success factor now becomes the rationalisation of costs so as to keep the product alive as long as it is economically sensible; once a declining product becomes a net consumer of cash, it should be closed down. It is no longer logical to assume that the existing scale of operations should be maintained and therefore using an accounting based measure such as ROI is not sensible. If the depreciation expense is not automatically reinvested any more to maintain this current level of activity, the most appropriate financial measure of performance becomes the cash generation capability of the business. This is normally described as the 'free cash flow' of the business, as shown in Figure 6.2, which represents the cash generated by the business which is not required to be reinvested in the business. During the decline stage this free cash flow can include any operating profits still produced by the business, plus any depreciation expense which is not being reinvested in the business, plus the cash proceeds from the sale of any assets which are no longer required by the business. When the level of activity reduces in many declining service companies, it may be quite possible to generate sizeable amounts of money from the ensuing reductions in the level of working capital that is tied up in the business.

FINANCIAL RISK IN SERVICE COMPANIES

The use of free cash flow as the main financial control measure during the decline stage of the life-cycle indicates the need to include both profits and cash flow when considering financial management. This is particularly true in the assessment of the financial risk of the business, where a key element is in the source of the funding used within the business. A fundamental tenet of sound financial management is that the sources of funding used by a company must be appropriately matched to the uses of that funding.

This matching should be in terms of the timescale of the funding in that a long-term investment in fixed assets should be funded by using a long-term source, while a temporary seasonal increase in the working capital tied up in the business can be financed by a similarly short-term funding facility, such as a bank overdraft. (UK companies are almost unique in that they tend to use overdraft lines of credit as an ongoing, almost permanent part of the company's capital structure. An overdraft is instantly repayable at the behest of the lending bank and therefore, if it has been used to finance long-term investments which are not readily realisable, such a request can create at best serious embarrassment and at worst the total financial collapse of the borrowing company.)

In addition, the matching should include the inverse correlation between business risk and financial risk which was discussed in Chapter 4. Thus a high business risk should be funded by low risk financing such as equity supplied by the owners of the business. The key differences in terms of risk profile between debt and equity financing relate to the control over their return and eventual repayment. If a company borrows money it *must* pay interest on the outstanding balance, whether or not the company is generating profits and positive net cash flows, and it must repay the principal in accordance with the terms of the loan agreement. Should the company fail to meet these obligations, the loan agreement will normally give the lender significant powers to enable it to try to recover the unpaid money, including taking possession of specific assets and/or assuming overall effective control of the business through the appointment of a receiver. Conversely if these funding needs had been raised by selling shares, i.e. giving the shareholders a proportionate share in the ownership of the company, the company has much greater flexibility and control regarding future cash flows leaving the business. Thus dividends are paid at the *discretion* of the directors of the company and, even if they are not receiving any dividends, the shareholders cannot demand the repayment of their investment from the company.

This highlights why only businesses with relatively stable positive net cash flows should use debt funding, as it increases the associated financial risk due to the loss of flexibility and control. At the same time, the additional security and operational sanctions available to lenders decrease their perceived level of risk and, consequently, these lenders should be willing to accept a lower rate of return than is required by the shareholders in the company. It is important to remember that financial risk must be viewed from the perspective of both the provider and user; hence, as shown in Figure 6.4, financial risk can be regarded as two sides of the same coin.

Figure 6.4 also indicates that there are an infinite number of potentially compatible ways of combining these differing perceptions of financial risk,

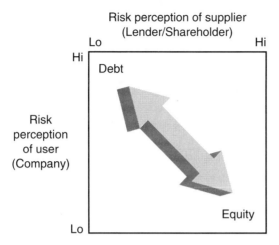

Figure 6.4 Financial risk: two sides of the same coin

e.g. with a financial product which is viewed as being medium risk by both supplier and user. Not surprisingly, the financial services industry has responded to this product development opportunity and a massive array of subtly different sources of finance now exist. However, there are a few very basic rules, the breaking of which can have very significant consequences for the companies involved.

The myriad of sophisticated financial products have incredibly compli-cated sounding titles (most of which do actually explain the characteristics of the product), but the really important factor is the underlying nature of the source of funding. In other words, is it a form of debt which is repayable and on which interest *must* be paid, or is it more like a permanent equity invest-ment which receives a *discretionary* and variable dividend. Irrespective of what it is called by the issuer, the expected return on the product will be conditioned by its underlying nature and the associated risk profile. A debt-type financial instrument has a lower risk profile (and hence a lower cost to the borrower) because lenders have some degree of control over the recov-ery of their money. Indeed this control factor can be used as a good working definition of what funding really is of a debt nature.

If the borrower does not produce the anticipated profit and cash flows, the lender should still be able to recover its money by exercising its security or other operational sanctions. Where this is not the case, the lender is taking on the underlying *business* risk of the company and the demanded return should reflect this level of risk. It is clearly unacceptable, given the discus-sion in Chapter 2, to take on an equity type risk in exchange for a debt based return. Therefore, before accepting the lower level of financial return, lenders should ensure that they have an alternative way out, if the business venture they are lending to turns out to be unsuccessful.

The alternative way out could be in the form of a financial guarantee from an outside party, but normally it relies on the underlying value of the assets which are being financed by the company. This immediately raises a problem for many service companies because they do not invest in many tangible assets, which could be sold by lenders in order to recover their outstanding loans. Even where funds are invested in such assets their resale second-hand value is so low as to make them of no interest as security in a loan agreement, this is the case for office furniture and equipment, and most modern computer systems.

One of the most attractive tangible assets to a lender is freehold land and buildings as this asset *may* actually increase in value over the life of the loan. Some service businesses do invest heavily in these assets and may therefore look to debt financing as a major potential source of funds. Careful analysis of the resulting risk profile is still required, as this may indicate a radically different and potentially more attractive combination of competitive and financial strategies.

New hotel companies require a significant investment to be made in land and buildings but, as security for a loan, the specialised nature of the asset should make it less attractive to a potential lender. The resale value of the hotel will be primarily driven by the expected future cash flow which it will generate as a hotel; there are relatively few alternative uses for most modern hotels, although the particular location may make the land very valuable, without the hotel. Clearly this value is influenced by the relative success of the hotel but, if the hotel is trading successfully, the lender has no need of its security. It is only when the borrower fails to repay the principal or interest that the lender needs to exercise its security. If the value of that security is directly linked to the success of the underlying business, it becomes much less attractive to the lender. The lender may try to overcome this problem by building in a substantial buffer between the expected resale value of the asset and the amount advanced as a loan; unfortunately, many property based companies and their lenders learnt how volatile underlying asset values can be during the UK recession of the early 1990s.

There may also be an alternative if the underlying needs of the hotel business are examined in more detail. The hotel industry is really a combination of two businesses; there is a business concerned with operating the hotel and a separate business to do with owning the property. The return on the property owning business comes partly in the form of a rental income but mainly through the anticipated appreciation in the value of the underlying assets. If this rental income could be 'guaranteed' in some way, it would provide a matched source of funds to allow a relatively high proportion of debt finance to be used in acquiring the property.

The financial return from the hotel operating business is generated by selling the rooms, meals in the restaurant, drinks in the bar, etc. Consequently, the success of this business is largely dependent upon the level of occupancy which is achieved. If the hotel buildings were rented rather than owned, the total investment required would be dramatically lower but the fixed cost base of the operating company would be increased. Several very large hotel groups, such as Holiday Inn, have now effectively separated these two parts of the business, because the hotel chain acts purely in the guise of an operator. The individual hotels in the chain are often owned by local property companies, which are primarily interested in the capital gain potential from their investment. They reduce their perceived risk by bringing in a large professional hotel operator to run the business on a contract basis. A further advantage to these owners is that they can gain access to the marketing power and distribution channels of a multi-national hotel operator, even though the property company may only own *one* hotel. The advantages of managerial focus and specialisation can also be considerable from this type of business segmentation.

This concept has developed in a different way in the case of supermarket retailing and the increased reliance on very large superstores. The sophisticated use of sale and leaseback deals is explained in Chapter 11. The segmentation of the hotel business also introduces another element of financial risk, which is the cost structure of the business. A high proportionate use of borrowing creates a correspondingly high level of interest expense and this is a committed, fixed cost of the business. In order to reduce the risk profile, the company should try to generate an appropriately guaranteed level of income to cover this type of fixed expense. It may be possible to do this for the hotel owning company by arranging that the hotel management contract guarantees an income stream (e.g. the rental payments) which is sufficient to pay the interest on any debt financing used to fund the construction or acquisition of the hotel.

More generally, it is clear that a high proportion of fixed costs will create a much greater degree of volatility in profits for any given change in the level of activity. This is diagrammatically illustrated in Figure 6.5 for two very similar companies with the same break-even point but dramatically different cost structures. The higher fixed cost business will show a much higher rate of contribution per unit of activity, and this means that if volumes increase it will report much higher profits. Of course, there can be a correspondingly rapid move into significant losses if the volume falls by a relatively small proportion. For the company with the low fixed cost structure, the higher

(a)

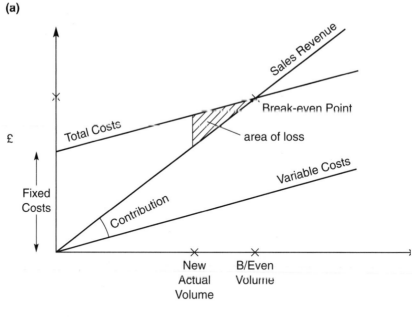

Volume of Activity

(b)

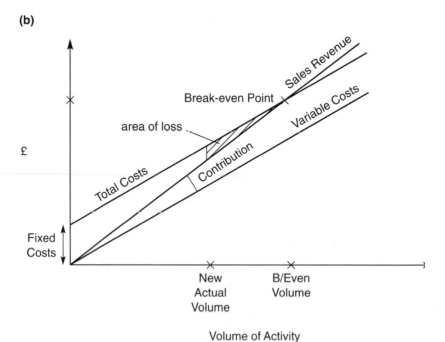

Volume of Activity

Figure 6.5 Comparison of cost structures: (a) high fixed costs and high contribution; (b) low fixed costs and low contribution

proportion of costs which vary with the level of activity means that the impact on profitability is greatly reduced for similar volume changes.

Some service industries have relatively little control over much of their cost structure because it is dictated by the nature of the industry. For example, the utility companies providing electricity, gas and even telecommunications have a high fixed cost base due to the basic infrastructure needed to provide the service to their customers. The impact of changes in demand is therefore rapidly and significantly seen in their reported profits; e.g. if the UK winter is very mild, consumers use less gas for central heating and the profits of British Gas are reduced due to its inability to reduce its fixed costs. The fixed cost structure of the water companies, providing both water and sewage services, is even more dominant as its costs principally comprise collection, treatment and distribution through fixed facilities. This can be highlighted by examining the published financial statements of the privatised water companies, which show a very high profit margin when expressed as a percentage of sales revenues; but this still represents a very low return on assets, due to the very high long-term, specialised assets employed in the industry. Therefore a similarly fixed charge to its customers may seem a sensible way to match its sales revenues to its cost structure, and so reduce its risk profile. However, it seems unrealistic not to give customers an incentive to reduce their usage of a natural resource, and hence metering is an increasingly popular alternative. The fact that installing the meters creates a significant additional fixed cost, which must be paid for by the customers through a new variable charge, is ignored. The main problem facing the industry is really how to control an effective monopoly, which is now run for profit, and to provide *it*, not its customers, with a significant financial incentive to improve the efficiency of its operations.

Many other service companies which regard people as a critical resource can also be considered to have a very high fixed cost base. Thus most consultancies, accountancy practices and legal firms would regard their professional staff as a key resource, and consequently as a fixed cost. This means that staff utilisation ratios will have a significant impact on the overall profitability of the business. Indeed managing the trade-off between utilisation levels and prices charged for the staff members is a major issue in this type of firm. This is particularly true if giving a discount to one particular type of customer, in order to increase an unacceptably low utilisation rate, may create pressure to reduce general price levels across the firm. It can be very useful to operate in relatively discrete market segments as this can avoid this problem; thus discounting the price in one segment is very unlikely to lead to a need to reduce prices in the other unconnected markets. Software companies have been quite good at this because many of their staff have skills which can be utilised in almost any of their markets. Yet the charge out rates achieved in these markets can differ considerably and can also change dramatically over time. Therefore, the ability to reallocate staff across these segments can help to keep up utilisation levels and maximise profitability. During the boom years of the mid-1980s, the daily rates chargeable for skilled software specialists in the financial services sector greatly exceeded the levels which could be obtained in the commercial, scientific or defence markets. The situation changed dramatically in the early 1990s with the decline in demand and price from financial services, making it advisable to switch staff back to the more stable areas of business.

The large accountancy firms can also be used to illustrate this issue with the state of the economy being a good indicator of the most profitable area of the business. Thus the deep UK recession which started at the end of the 1980s meant that staff who were no longer needed to do business feasibility studies, etc., could be transferred to the administration, receivership and liquidation departments, which were unable to cope with their increased workloads. These issues highlight the need for a segmented system of financial reporting which indicates the relative profit contributions of the different business areas, and this is considered in the remainder of this chapter.

However, it is first useful to examine one industry which shows how the cost structure can be dramatically transformed depending on the competitive strategy which is implemented. The airline industry can be divided into two broad segments; scheduled services and chartered flights. The cost structure of a scheduled airline is almost exclusively fixed, once the flight schedule has been established. The aeroplane will take off and land whether it is full, half-full, or virtually empty, and very few of the other costs change depending on the volume of passengers. The food and drink consumed on board can be regarded as variable costs, and the amount of fuel used is supposed to vary somewhat depending on the total weight of the aeroplane (which, of course, includes the passengers and their luggage). Thus a critical factor in the profitability of scheduled airlines is the proportion of available seats which are actually sold. This was very clearly illustrated during the 1991 Gulf War when the number of airline passengers dropped dramatically, with disastrous financial consequences for many of the world's airlines. When this type of cost structure is allied to the very high perishability of the product, it is not surprising that the scheduled airline industry has become very sophisticated in using information technology to help it predict the level of demand and a wide variety of pricing levels to try to maximise the level of demand for any particular flight. These issues are considered in Chapters 12 and 8 respectively.

The chartered segment of the industry has a potentially very different cost structure. The principal difference is caused by the ability of the chartered flight operator to cancel any specific flight if insufficient seats have been sold. This clearly makes a larger proportion of the operating costs truly variable, but this variable proportion can be still further increased if the chartered airline does not itself own any aeroplanes. Many chartered airlines rent the aeroplanes they require on a very short-term basis, possibly even for a specific flight. This dramatically reduces the level of long-term, fixed committed costs which such an operator has, and enables it to guarantee that any flights that actually take off do make a positive contribution towards its remaining level of fixed costs.

SEGMENTED FINANCIAL ANALYSIS

It is very unusual for all the various segments of any large business to make a uniform contribution towards the overall profit. If the financial management system is to assist in the optimum future allocation of resources, it is important that the financial analysis indicates the relative profitability of these various sub-divisions of the overall business. The first task, therefore, is to decide on the type of segmented analysis which should be carried out. The alternatives are fairly clear; profits are made by selling specific services to identified customers in competition with known competitors. Therefore segmented analyses could be carried out on a product basis, a customer basis or by comparison with specific competitors. In an ideal world, the financial management system would provide all of these analyses on a regularly updated and forward looking basis. However, no company has such a totally comprehensive financial analysis system and it is necessary, in the real world, to set some priorities for this type of segmented analysis.

The highest priority should be set according to the strategic thrust of the business. If the main strategy of the business is to sell more products to its existing customers, it is clearly important to ensure that the customers on which this strategy is focused are generating a good level of profit contribution from their existing level of sales. Consequently, Customer Account Profitability (or CAP, as it is known) becomes the main emphasis of the segmented financial analysis. Alternatively, the competitive strategy may concentrate on taking existing services into new markets, which requires that the segmented analysis provides meaningful information on the profit contribution produced by existing services in their current markets. It could be disastrous to attempt to build a global business around a set of loss-making services.

This issue indicates a critical element in designing any segmented financial information system, which is that it must assist in the decision-making process. The objective is not to produce a neat accounting reconciliation of the net profits of the overall business apportioned across all the current products or customers. The aim is to provide comparative financial information which shows which areas of the business are significantly *more* profitable than the rest, so as to enable managers to invest productively in the future by building on existing competitive advantages. Apportioning shared costs which will not change as a result of future decisions destroys the validity of this type of analysis and can lead to completely erroneous strategic moves by the company. Consequently, the analysis should be based on a relative comparison and can stop at the level of contribution to common general overheads without restricting the decision-making support. This is particularly true when competitor analyses are being undertaken, because it is the *relative* costs of competitors which are important. Thus, this type of financial analysis should focus on the differences from the company's own costs, both better and worse, rather than trying to develop from scratch a detailed cost statement for each competitor. It must always be remembered that a competitive advantage is a relative concept.

CUSTOMER ACCOUNT PROFITABILITY (CAP)

CAP has been widely used by a number of service companies for a number of years with quite dramatic results on their competitive strategies. At its simplest level, it may indicate how the relative profitability of different customers can be dramatically affected by the mix of products which they buy. For example, in the distribution industry or the wholesale trade (such as cash-and-carry warehouses), these changes in sales mix can be significant due to the wide differences in gross margin obtained on various ranges of products.

The use of CAP can be much more sophisticated due to material differences in the way groups of customers are serviced. A sensibly structured CAP analysis can highlight the cost implications of these differences and consequently indicate any pricing movements which may be required to restore comparable levels of net contribution. Many wholesalers and distribution companies have needed this type of segmented financial analysis to cope with the changing delivery requirements of the major retailer chains; some retailers have been changing from store delivery to regional or central warehouse delivery, while others have gone in the opposite direction and are requiring more frequent deliveries to individual stores. Without a sensibly structured CAP analysis, the level of discount and price increases offered in response to these demands would have been based on guesswork.

Another sensible application of CAP analysis is where the overall service is itself segmented to target several levels of potential customer. A clear example of this is in the travel industry where even train services provide first class, standard, off-peak and reduced ticket prices. However, the airline industry has segmented the level of service much more and also has more flexibility as to how it arranges the accommodation within the fixed total available space in the aeroplane. Consequently, the basis of this analysis is initially by class of passenger; first class, business level and economy or standard passengers. The obvious objective of the analysis is to maximise the total contribution achieved from the particular product, which can be regarded as the route because the potential mix of passengers changes according to the route being flown. Thus, the revenue from selling a first class seat is much greater than a business seat, which is itself greater than a full-fare economy seat, etc. However, the direct costs involved are higher and particularly the space occupied is much greater, resulting in fewer passengers being carried. This analysis of the segmented contributions to the shared fixed costs of the flight, let alone those of the airline, can provide very useful information, when allied to the potential market for each category of travel, to support the decision on the configuration of the aeroplane; i.e. how many first class seats, etc., should there be.

Airlines can also use CAP analysis to highlight groups of passengers who are particularly profitable and who therefore should be targeted by the airline in the future. Frequent business flyers would be one such category and the analysis could also be used to evaluate the relative success of alternative loyalty building marketing programmes aimed at such a category. However, one of the most common uses of the technique is to identify profitable groups of customers, and then to try to expand the range of products sold to these groups. In addition to the segmented profitability analysis, the company needs information on the key common characteristics of such groups, in order to identify the type of new products which would appeal to them.

This has been done by several major retail chains on a reasonably systematic basis. Increased customer loyalty has been developed by the creation of retailer brands. Financial information on the buying habits of frequent loyal customers has been collected, particularly where an in-store charge card has been introduced. This has given information on those groups of customers who buy the higher profit margin items and personal characteristics of these groups can be accessed from the data-base created from the charge card applications. Their perceptions of the retailer can be learned from tightly focused market research. This means that the new products which are developed can be designed to have attributes which match the perceptions of these targeted loyal, profitable customers. This shows how a good system of financial management is completely integrated within the strategic management process of the business.

Some of the other examples of customer led strategies were less closely integrated and were much less successful. In the financial services industry, many financial institutions decided to expand the range of products sold to their existing customers, e.g. individuals, and therefore introduced a wide range of new financial services. Unfortunately, the rest of the required analysis was not done in many cases, with the result that the services were inappropriate, did not match with the existing attributes of the institution, or were aimed at an unprofitable segment of their existing customer base. The most successful examples of this type of strategy were where the financial institution started by identifying a highly profitable segment of its customers (e.g. high net worth individuals) and then designed new products specifically to fit their needs.

In the advertising industry, there are similar examples of major agencies which decided that they could offer a much broader range of 'consultancy and advisory' services to their existing major corporate clients. Hence, they acquired or developed new ranges of products which they tried to sell to these existing customers. Again, it appears that their strategic analysis may have missed identifying a key attribute of why these sophisticated clients bought advertising services from them; they were perceived as the best in the industry. If this was the principal reason, these clients would only be likely to buy new services which were also regarded as 'the best in their industry'. The objective of a 'customer led strategy' is to leverage off an existing competitive advantage, which makes it vitally important to understand what the current advantage really is (i.e. what has created the existing degree of customer loyalty and profitability). Also, as buying decisions are made by the key decision-maker within the customer, the advertising agency strategy may be further flawed if the new services would be 'bought' by a different key decision-maker, who is not yet an existing loyal customer of the agency.

DIRECT PRODUCT PROFITABILITY (DPP)

The alternative major emphasis of segmented financial analysis is product based and is designed to show the relative profitability of the different products sold by the customer. This was initially developed as a sales tool by the major f.m.c.g. manufacturers (Procter and Gamble is normally credited as being the initiator) in order to indicate to their retail customers why they should continue, or start, to buy particular products. Thus the idea was to go well beyond the earlier logic of looking at the gross contribution per unit and to incorporate all the major differences affecting the net contributions of the products. This included rate of sale, selling space occupied by each product, relative ease of storage and handling, payment terms granted by the supplier, frequency of delivery, sales support and indirect promotional allowances.

The concept was so successful that the retailers rapidly adopted it and substantially improved it, because they obviously had better information on the relative costs associated with different products. DPP analysis is now a major part of the decision-making process for most large retailers, and selling space allocations and stocking decisions are made using the supporting financial analysis. Some degree of DPP analysis is now used by most businesses which sell a range of services, but it is still carried out to varying levels of relevance. For example, in retailing it is most commonly used in conjunction with the limiting factor on the store, which is available shelf space. Hence DPP analysis tends to be calculated in terms of the net contribution per unit of cubic capacity (cubes are used where the heights between shelves can be altered, alternatively area occupied is used) per week, per month, or per year. The analysis usually takes into consideration all the significant differences affecting the contribution of the product groupings but does not attempt to apportion the shared costs at either the store level or the head office of the retailer. Thus it is focused on supporting the short-term reallocation of resources decisions for which it is ideally suited.

The analysis can be similarly used in other industries as long as the limiting factor can be identified and applied to the product contributions. Thus in the legal and accounting professions, the limiting factor is likely to be the skilled personnel available within the firm. To some degree they can be allocated across the services offered by the firms and therefore an analysis of the relative net contributions per hour or per day may be a useful aid in resource allocation decisions. It may be necessary in this case to make allowances for varying levels of productivity when staff are being transferred across areas of specialisation. A more sophisticated version of this approach can be applied when the cost structure of the various products is substantially different.

This is done in the hotel industry if the basic accommodation, restaurants, bars, and leisure facilities are regarded as separate products. The cost structure of the overnight accommodation is highly fixed. Therefore, if the hotel has spare capacity, the accommodation can almost be given away free in order to encourage additional guests who may buy some of the available additional services; thus increasing the overall contribution made by the hotel. Of course there are many alternative ways of implementing this type of strategy (some of which are considered in Chapter 8), but they all hinge on the segmented financial analysis which indicates the differing rates of net contribution available from the range of services sold by the company.

COMPETITOR ACCOUNTING

There has been a significant increase, in recent years, in the emphasis placed on external comparisons of financial performance. Many of these initiatives have concentrated on creating some type of competitor accounting analysis, to see how well the business is doing in comparison to its competitors. Given the earlier discussions on competitive advantages, their development in financial management is clearly to be applauded. Unfortunately, the quality of the decision making which has resulted has generally been less impressive than it might have been due to the way in which the analytical process has been carried out.

As already mentioned, some companies have attempted to develop, from scratch, detailed costings for competitive services, which is both difficult and largely unnecessary. The key objective is to establish the relative positionings of the company and its key competitors, and yet most companies go into very detailed comparative studies without any serious consideration of the information which they really need. The detailed analysis can be very specifically focused if there is an initial overview analysis of each competitor and how it relates to the company undertaking the analysis.

Some companies are only competitors in certain products and certain markets. The importance of these segments to their overall business must be assessed, as this will affect their response to any new competitive moves. For example, if this area is only peripheral to their mainstream business and there are very low exit barriers, it may be possible to force them out by an aggressive price discounting policy.

Thus the degree of the competitor's commitment to any product/market segment must be assessed. This requires an understanding of the strategic objectives and the financial performance measures used by the competitor. For example, if a competitor emphasises market share as its main performance measure, it may be prepared to continue a heavy level of marketing support even though price levels have been driven down by competitive pressure. Differences in strategic objectives, including the timescale of achieving an acceptable financial return, are of vital importance to any competitor analysis; this analysis forms a fundamental element of the planning process discussed in the next chapter.

The direction of the strategic thrust of the competitor in this area is also important. Our company may be attempting to launch a new service to our existing customers, whereas this service may be a mainstream current product of the competitor, for which it is trying to find new market segments. The relative competitive strengths of these two companies are likely to be very different, as are their detailed competitive strategies. Indeed, the type of competitive strategy being implemented is also clearly fundamental to the focus of the detailed competitor analysis. If both companies are following highly differentiated, brand led strategies, a detailed comparison of cost levels may be completely irrelevant. However, in a fiercely cost competitive market, the identification of even small relative cost differences may indicate a significant potential competitive advantage, or disadvantage. It is only once this strategic overview is properly carried out that a sensible competitor analysis can be undertaken. These issues are considered in the next three chapters, with the planning requirements being dealt with in Chapter 7 while the main alternative competitive strategies are considered in Chapters 8 and 9.

7 PLANNING REQUIREMENTS IN SERVICE COMPANIES

INTRODUCTION: THE ANALYSIS, PLANNING AND CONTROL PROCESS

Complete books have been written exclusively on the role and operation of planning within modern business corporations. Consequently, there is no attempt to reproduce such a comprehensive coverage in one brief chapter within our overall focus on financial management and control in service companies. Instead, the objective of this chapter is to highlight the key areas within the financial planning process where managers can add value to the business and consequently where most of their attention and resources should be focused.

Chapter 4 introduced the key issues relating to the planning requirements in service companies, including the essential nature of the underlying financial management process of analysis, planning and control. Financial analysis is clearly the basis for any forward looking planning system, but even the most comprehensive level of financial analysis is unable to provide any guarantee of accurate forecasts of the future. Indeed, almost the only certain statement that can be made about any financial plan is that 'it will be wrong', due to the essential assumptions which have to be made about both the external business environment and the internal performance of the business.

Given this virtual certainty of being wrong, it is important to consider the fundamental reasons for planning. Financial planning enables the business to evaluate the financial outcome of any proposed strategy, so that only strategies likely to produce acceptable financial results are implemented. Also the financial planning process highlights the resources required for the successful implementation of the proposed strategy. This should ensure that all these necessary resources are made available; if this cannot be achieved, the plan must be modified in some way to ensure that it is internally consistent. Thus the basic business model illustrated in Chapter 4 can be expanded, as shown in Figure 7.1.

Figure 7.1 also indicates the other major benefit of a sound, financial planning process because, in addition to quantifying the expected financial implications of the company's intended actions, the financial plan provides a

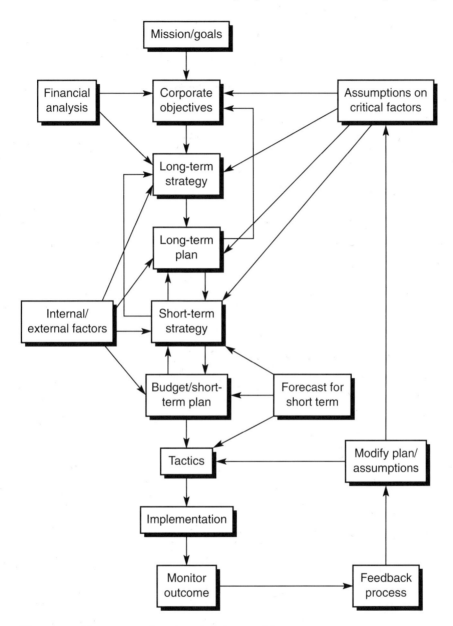

Figure 7.1 More comprehensive planning model

reference base against which the actual financial outcome can be compared. This monitoring procedure can indicate the need for modifications to either the competitive strategy or the objectives of the business in the light of the actual business environment and level of competitive activity. Therefore, the monitoring and control part of the iterative financial management process must not be seen as a simple reconciliation between the actual financial results and those expected in the financial plan. The idea is to highlight areas where the objectives will not be achieved unless changes are made, or where subsequent, unpredicted events have made the existing objectives inappropriate. This may indicate a problem or an opportunity but, in either case, it is essential that the business responds as quickly as possible to the new competitive environment. During the Gulf War in 1991 concerns about international air travel had created a significantly worse business environment for all airlines and holiday tour operators. However, the dramatic collapse of Air Europe and its related tour operating companies (the other parts of the ILG Group) completely transformed the prospects for other UK based airlines and package tour operators, as it suddenly removed the second largest company from the market place. It is most unlikely that such an event was included in the short-term business plans of the competing businesses, but its occurrence certainly required rapid responses which included significant modifications to their business plans. Subsequently, both industries have seen further sizeable alterations to their competitive structures, through both financial collapse (such as happened to Dan-Air) and actual (British Airways acquisition of Dan-Air) and proposed acquisitions (Airtours and Owners Abroad).

These examples indicate the challenges of planning in a rapidly changing environment, but such dramatic external changes increase the value of having a comprehensive financial plan, which is based on a clear set of assumptions regarding the external competitive environment. As any of these assumptions are proved to be false, the plan can be modified appropriately; indeed, contingency plans can be already developed for the most likely alternative scenarios.

THE PLANNING PROCESS

As already mentioned in Chapter 4 and indicated clearly in Figure 7.1, financial planning operates on two different timescales. These are sometimes separately referred to as strategic (i.e. long term) and operational or tactical (i.e. short term) planning, but this attempts to draw too great a distinction between these long and short-term timescales. Changes in strategy have to be incorporated in the short-term planning process even if achieving financial results from these changes will take some time, and will therefore only be seen towards the end of the long-term planning horizon. In fact, the short-term impact of the strategic change may be detrimental to both profitability and cash generation. For example, a key medium-term objective for one particular service may be to achieve market leadership while this market is still growing. This may require a significant increase in marketing expenditure in the short term. The increased cash outflow will depress profitability in the short term as it will normally be expensed immediately through the profit and loss account.

Of course, the financial justification for the higher rate of marketing support will have been based on the improved long-term return which *should* be achieved from the increase in market share. This potential financial benefit is dependent upon a large number of assumptions (such as the continued rate of growth in the market, its ultimate size, the duration of the maturity stage, the competitive responses to this marketing initiative, the ability of the company to maintain this increased market share, the profitability of the service during this overall period). Consequently, the planning process has to take account of the risks and uncertainties surrounding these forecasts and this can most easily be achieved by the use of sensitivity analysis. This technique indicates how sensitive the financial evaluation is to changes in the key underlying assumptions, but its application by many companies is unfortunately very mechanistic because the same level of volatility (e.g. plus or minus 10 per cent) is applied to each element included in the forecast. Not surprisingly, this process shows that the financial outcome appears to be most dependent upon the largest contributory factors, but these may, in reality, be subject to much lower ranges of possible outcomes than many of the other elements. The key objective of any sensitivity analysis is to highlight those assumptions and forecasts which can have the greatest impact on the eventual outcome of the decision. Thus the ranges used in the sensitivity analysis for each element should be individually selected to reflect the potential volatility of that element, rather than applying a general level to all elements.

One way of doing this is by applying probability estimates to the possible outcomes for each element of the forecast. This is, in fact, the normal way of arriving at the original 'expected value' which is used for the base case financial evaluation, but its use in sensitivity analyses yields several additional benefits. The type of probability distribution indicates the degree of risk surrounding the base evaluation which is using this probability based expected value, as shown in Figure 7.2. A low probability of a very high return with a strong probability of total loss should be viewed as a much higher risk project than an almost certain return which is equal to the same expected value.

In many long-term investment projects, the eventual success of the project is dependent on the successful achievement of several stages, each of which can be assigned a probability distribution to describe its set of potential outcomes. Where overall success of the project requires successful completion of each such stage in a particular sequence, the successive stages

Element A			Element B		
Value of Outcome	Probability of Outcome	Expected Value	Value of Outcome	Probability of Outcome	Expected Value
1000	10%	100	80	25%	20
	90%	–	100	50%	50
			120	25%	30
	100%	100		100%	100

Elements A & B (two required assumptions or forecasts in the planning process) have the same expected values, but the ranges of their outcomes have dramatically different profiles. Element A may have a value of 1000 or NIL, while element B is only expected to vary between 80 and 120 at the extreme (i.e. very close to its expected value of 100)

Figure 7.2 Use of probability estimates

can be assigned a cumulative sequential probability factor, which more accurately describes the likelihood of an ultimately successful outcome. This type of application is now being used by an increasing number of companies both financially to evaluate such complex projects prior to commencing expenditure and to control the projects once they are underway.

However, this potential volatility estimate also highlights where the business should concentrate its efforts during the planning process. Even a small increase in the probability of success of the higher risk element could have a significant impact on its expected value, as shown in Figure 7.3.

This potential for improvement means that the business should concentrate its efforts on refining its widest ranging estimates and on improving the chances of success for those areas which can make the greatest contribution to the overall business. Planning should not be viewed as a passive process, which records the current estimates of the future, but as a dynamic vehicle for improving these existing estimates. The focus for all competitive strategies has already been stated as the development and maintenance of a sustainable competitive advantage. The planning process, with its essential emphasis on the external business environment, is therefore a good illustration of the previously described related focus of strategic management accounting on 'accounting for competitive advantage'. This requires the planning process to be developed around the major strategic thrusts of the business (e.g. existing customer led strategies or existing service led strategies), which will also determine the main areas of interest of the preceding financial analysis.

Element A			Element B		
Value of Outcome	Probability of Outcome	Expected Value	Value of Outcome	Probability of Outcome	Expected Value
1000	10%	100	1000	20%	200
–	90%	–	–	80%	–
	100%	100		100%	200

A 10% increase in the probability of success to 20% results in the doubling of the expected value of the element, although the remaining 80% probability of total loss means that this element still has a high risk profile.

Figure 7.3 Revising initial probability estimates

LONG-TERM PLANNING

Such an emphasis is of particular importance in the long-term planning processes of many service businesses because the key strategic thrust of the business may hinge around the creation or exploitation of an intangible asset. As has already been discussed, a common characteristic of service companies is that they do not require significant investment in the more tangible assets which represent the major investments made by many manu-facturing industries. However, this does not mean that the normal long-term financial evaluation techniques, particularly discounted cash flow, are not relevant. The financial justification of cash outflows today must be carried out by comparison to the present value of the benefits expected to arise as a direct consequence of this expenditure. Thus, there is a vital need to produce expected future cash flows for service businesses even though the main items of expenditure are on intangible items, such as brand development or channels of distribution.

These future cash flows must be brought back to their equivalent present values by the application of an appropriate discount rate, which reflects both the time value of money and the risk factor associated with the future cash flow. While this technique is covered in all the basic texts on financial management, it still seems to suffer from some very serious practical short-comings in the way in which it is applied, and particularly in the way in which the discount rate is established. As just mentioned, the objective of discounted cash flow (DCF) analysis is to enable the expected benefits to be directly compared to the required up-front expenditure. Financial decisions are based on the future cash flows which are directly affected by the deci-sion (hence known as differential cash flows), and only these items should form part of the financial evaluation. This means that great care must be taken in ensuring that the potential impact of any major decision is properly assessed but, if the range of possible outcomes is very wide, this introduces the problem of which value should be included in the evaluation. If the values relevant to Element A in Figure 7.2 are used, the problem can be clearly illustrated. The successful outcome would produce a value of 1000, but there is only a 10 per cent probability of such an outcome with the result that its expected value is only 100.

If the expected value of 100 is included in the financial evaluation, the application of the probability factor weightings has already taken into account the high risk of total loss which is associated with this activity. Hence a relatively low discount factor should be used to reflect the incorporation of the *expected value* of the outcome in the DCF calculation. Alternatively, many companies would include the financial results of a successful outcome of Element A (i.e. 1000) and it is now essential that a high discount factor is applied to this future value to reflect the low probability of it being received. Either of these techniques will give an acceptable decision if properly applied, but quite frequently the wrong combinations are used together. Clearly, if the high, but unlikely value of outcome is used with a low risk weighted discount factor, the present value of the outcome will appear highly attractive. Conversely, and probably more commonly in practice, the expected value of the outcome is discounted by a very high discount rate which means that the associated high risk has been taken into account twice. This is a contributory factor to a number of companies finding it very difficult to justify financially high risk investments.

Similarly, there seems to be a wide degree of confusion regarding the way to handle inflation in DCF analysis. There are two ways in which to produce forecast project cash flows; either including inflation or excluding inflation. As indicated in Figure 7.4, if inflation is included in the forecast cash flows, a discount rate which also takes account of inflation should be used. Similarly, if the cash flows are projected in real values, i.e. excluding any inflation, the appropriate discount rate should only include the company's real required rate of return. However, this latter method does not mean that the company can ignore inflation in its long-term planning process (which would obviously be a major attraction), because the real cash flows must reflect the net impact of inflation (i.e. the relative effect which inflation can have on the current levels of cash flows). For example, any fixed cash flow items (such as certain lease payments) decrease in real terms if there is a positive rate of inflation, while some costs may increase faster than inflation (such as wages in many service companies) and thus must be shown as increasing in real terms. If the company ignores these net effects when using real cash flows and real discount rates, it is making the very unrealistic assumption that all sales revenues and costs increase exactly at the rate of

FUTURE CASH FLOWS

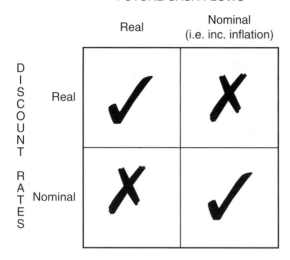

Applying a real discount factor to cash flows which include inflation will make the returns appear very attractive. Conversely, trying to take inflation out of cash flows which do not contain it will depress their present values unnecessarily

Figure 7.4 Impact of inflation on DCF analysis

inflation and that the impact on the investment in working capital is also exactly neutral.

The objective of DCF analysis is to evaluate whether the proposed strategic initiatives of the company create any added value. This is only achieved if the present value of the expected returns exceeds the required investment, i.e. a positive net present value is achieved in the DCF evaluation. Hence, the heavy emphasis which is placed on this analytical technique in the long-term financial planning process, which should, itself, be focused on creating and developing the competitive advantages that can create such positive added value for the business. However, as was emphasised in Chapter 3, most sustainable competitive advantages require considerable initial investment to develop and some of this investment is likely to be in removing existing constraints within the business.

One of the important roles of the long-term planning system is therefore to indicate where there are internal constraints which are restricting the future development of the business. Once identified, the long-term plan should try to eliminate the critical constraints by the allocation of resources to those areas where they will add most value. If it is impossible, even in the timeframe of the long-term plan, to remove completely the constraint, the strategy of business should seek to minimise the impact of the constraint on the long-term financial performance of the business. This is a major difference between long-term planning and the shorter term planning process, which is discussed in the next section of this chapter, because in short-term planning it is often impossible to remove or minimise existing major constraints. Hence they become a major given element in the planning environment, in much the same way as many parts of the external business environment cannot be changed in the short term.

However, a similarly important role of long-term planning is to forecast likely changes in the external environment, and to make appropriate modifications in its competitive strategy to take advantage of the opportunities and to minimise the impact of the potential threats. Thus, a classic but extreme marketing example is often cited, particularly by Professor Theodore Levitt, that the strategic problem of the US railroad industry was that it regarded itself as being in the railroad industry rather than in transportation. Consequently, it failed to identify and respond to the development and launch of other more customer oriented modes of transport. There is, of course, a large question mark as to whether, in this particular example, the existing competitive advantages of the railroad companies were readily transferable to these newer forms of transportation.

Much more recent and relevant examples of the need for service companies to reflect very fundamental changes in their competitive environments can be cited in the industries which have been subjected to changes in their regulatory framework. The forced break-up of the very dominant telecommunications supplier in the USA in an attempt to stimulate a greater degree of competition, at a time of great technological change in the industry, created a major opportunity for existing and new companies in this sector. At the same time, it also created several regional, but still very large and powerful companies which were quite quick to develop aggressive international growth strategies themselves.

When these regulatory changes are accompanied by a complete change in the ownership structure of the companies in the industry, the impact on the long-term planning process can be even more dramatic. In the UK, Cable & Wireless was privatised while it was still predominantly an overseas telecommunication systems operator (in particular, Hong Kong), but when British Telecom (now BT) was also privatised in 1984, it started to compete in its home market. Similarly, the UK gas and electricity industries have been subjected to both privatisation and differing degrees of deregulation which have opened these previously monopoly markets to potential new competitors. In all these cases, there are very high entry barriers in the form of the large scale investments needed to become a viable competitor, but the opportunity has been created by the change in the competitive environment.

Another industry with quite high barriers to entry is the private health-care sector, but a key element in its long-term planning process is, once again, the external business environment. In this case, the critical elements are the level of government spending in this area and the method of financial control and performance evaluation used within the nationalised part of the health-care industry. If government resources are constrained, the results may be a decline in the level of service provided, with a consequent increase in the demand for private health-care as waiting lists for operations increase, etc. However, if the government was to attempt to make its hospitals and district health services operate on a more business-like footing, these large centres might be prepared to sell at 'market prices' certain specialised services where they have excess capacity. This type of profit oriented behaviour by a nationalised 'not-for-profit' health service could have a significant impact on the financial return which would be achieved from certain types of investment by the private health-care companies. Yet again, a careful analysis of the likely changes in the competitive environment, including the development of unexpected new competitors, is a critical element in the long-term planning process.

In a rapidly maturing industry, the planning system may be looking for new areas in which the company can try to maintain its previous high rates of growth. An example of such an industry is electrical retailing in any of the major developed economies around the world. Most consumers in these markets now have the basic set of consumer electronic products (e.g. television, video, hi-fi, washing machine, cooker and even microwave and dishwasher) with the results that the market is dominated by replacement purchases. The growth is now created by product innovations by the electrical manufacturers which are desperate to stimulate sales of their products (e.g. digital audio tape, mini compact discs, satellite TV dishes and high definition television). A major problem of this type of product innovation strategy is that it tends to lead to shorter and shorter product life-cycles, as each new product is replaced by new technology on an increasingly faster basis. Indeed, some of these innovations may never attain significant sales volumes at all as they become technologically obsolete before they have even become established. This means that it is critically important for major electrical retailers to understand the risk profiles of each new product innovation before committing themselves to buy large quantities of stock on a confirmed basis. If the retailer delays too long it may have lost a significant amount of market share to a more aggressive competitor, but if large purchases of stock are made and the new product fails to achieve a reasonable market share quite quickly, the retailer may lose substantial amounts of money.

This changing market place puts increased emphasis on technical product knowledge but, in the retail financial services industry, it can be argued that the major change in recent years has been to increase the level of competition for the same customers. Most retail financial service companies have steadily expanded their range of products which they offer to individual customers and they all find the same types of customers attractive (i.e. either high net worth individuals who need investment advisory services, or individuals with good credit ratings who want a broad range of financial services including the provision of credit). Almost inevitably this broadened product range, in a maturing market, has effectively led to attractive customers being fought over by a number of companies attempting to provide one-stop shopping for all of the individual's financial needs. One way of attempting to achieve a sustainable competitive advantage in this type of environment is to take control of part of the distribution channel. This was tried during the 1980s in the UK by a number of companies which invested heavily in acquiring chains of estate agents, who handle the vast majority of house purchases in the UK. The logic was that buying a house represents the major investment decision for most people and requires financing via a mortgage. Many individuals also wish to arrange life insurance at the same time and may combine the two by taking out an endowment based mortgage. Hence, by controlling the estate agencies which sell the houses, the financial institutions gain access to prospective new customers at an ideal time in their buying life-cycle.

Unfortunately, most of these major acquisition programmes moved the financial institutions not only into an industry which they did not understand but which also rapidly went into a severe downturn due to the collapse of UK house prices in 1989/90. What was clearly a long-term strategic move into a new channel of distribution has been reviewed by several of these companies on a short-term basis with the consequent decision to exit, even though this means selling off or closing down their estate agencies at significant losses when compared to their acquisition prices. At least it indicates that these businesses appreciate that an historic sunk cost is not relevant to their financial decision which must be based on the future cash flows from the business.

SHORT-TERM PLANNING

There are several significant variations between the long-term and the short-term plans of any company, which necessitate some major differences in the planning systems used at each stage. While the overriding objectives of the short-term planning system remain the same, the more limited ability of the company to change either its internal or external business environment has already been mentioned. A major reason for this lack of planning flexibility is, in addition to the shortage of time in which the required changes can be implemented, the much more significant proportion of costs which are committed for the short-term planning horizon, which is typically the forth-coming financial year.

Financial planning is about making decisions and decisions concern the exercise of choice, but the company cannot exercise choice if the costs are already committed for the duration of the decision time period. Therefore, one of the most important factors for financial planning is the separation of costs between those where the company still has a large degree of choice (called discretionary) and those where the commitment has already been made. As previously discussed the financial control system should similarly focus on those discretionary costs, because control can only realistically be exercised before the company has committed itself. Unfortunately, this basic issue has still not been fully recognised by many companies.

Another important aspect of costs is the nature of their behaviour as levels of activity change. Fixed costs are unaffected by changes in the level of activity, while variable costs vary in proportion to the change. Clearly, timescale has a significant impact on this behaviour as, in the very long term, all costs will tend to vary with changes in output while, in the very short term, most costs cannot be changed even if the level of activity varies. Consequently, a greater proportion of costs will appear to be fixed in the short-term plan than in the long-term planning process. This combination of more committed, fixed costs severely restricts the decision-making ability of the company in the short-term budgeting process.

In the long-term planning discussion, the use of the DCF technique was emphasised without any undue concerns about the potential conflict between profit and cash flow. This is because they are automatically reconciled in the long term as, over the life of any project, the total profit generated by the project must equal the total net cash flow from the project. However, the application of normal accounting procedures will mean that there may be no such reconciliation in the short term and, indeed, the two measures may move in opposite directions. While it is perfectly correct to emphasise future cash flows as the basis for all economic decisions, most companies use some measure of profit as their method of assessing short term performance. Therefore, the impact in the short term on profitability is normally seen as an important element in the budgeting process.

Given the common high level of committed fixed costs, this focus on short-term profit movements has led to two important elements in many budgeting systems. First, the budgeting process itself is a circular iteration around the business, until an acceptable compromise result has been achieved. Whereas, in the long-term planning process many identified constraints could be removed by allocating additional resources, this is a much less practicable proposition in the short-term planning timeframe.

Consequently, as shown in Figure 7.5, the process has to be reviewed and the earlier desired level of activity curtailed if insufficient resources, including money, are available within the business. For example, in a long-term strategic plan, if a very financially attractive new business opportunity was identified it should normally be possible to include, in the long-term plan, the required fund raising activity so as to allow the company to take advantage of this value adding opportunity.

Although in Figure 7.5, as is the case for most companies, the budgeting process starts with the sales forecast, this is not essential. In fact, it may prolong the required number of iterations around the business, if sales are not the critical constraint on the short-term level of activity of the business. Thus, for certain extractive industries the short-term rate of production from the mine might constrain the level of sales which can be achieved by the company. Similarly some service companies may be constrained by a specific factor and therefore the budgeting process should start by identifying this key limiting factor, as this will determine the level of sales rather than the other way round. For example, a very popular restaurant, which is always fully booked well in advance, may be constrained by the number of available tables and the total number of meals which can be served. Of course, in the long term it may be possible to expand the capacity of the restaurant without destroying its popularity, but in the budgeting period the most probable solution may be to use pricing as a means of restricting the demand; the implications of using pricing as a competitive strategy are discussed in the next chapter.

Similarly, a leisure centre may find itself constrained by the level of its available resources in the short term, even though it may be able to build more tennis or squash courts, add another swimming pool area, etc. The key issue for short-term planning is to identify the constraint which acts as the limiting factor on the business and to use this constraint as the driving force of the business. This can be achieved most easily by also utilising the relatively fixed cost nature of many of the costs in the short term. Thus, if contribution analysis is used (i.e. sales revenue minus variable costs) but focused on the limiting factor, a very good short-term financial planning model can be developed. Such a model concentrates on the contribution achieved for each unit of the limiting factor which is used up by any particular activity, e.g. specific service or individual customer, as appropriate. This concept of the contribution per unit of limiting factor can be used to re-allocate resources from areas with lower rates of contribution to those generating higher rates; as with all such mathematical re-allocation models, an optimal solution is achieved when all products achieve the same rate of contribution per unit of limiting factor.

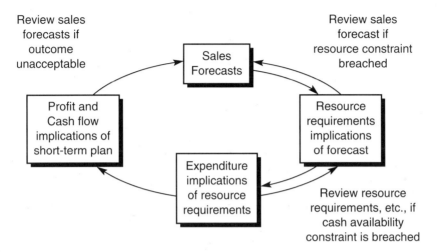

Figure 7.5 Circular budgeting process

Applying this concept to particular service companies can, in some cases, be relatively straightforward. Thus, for a software or consultancy business, the short-term limiting factor may be a particular type of skilled person. This means that the planning (and, subsequently, the financial control system) system should focus on the contribution produced per day of these people's time, and the productive utilisation of these limited resources should be maximised. Of course over time, the significance of this constraint may disappear or diminish and the planning and control system must monitor this; remember, it should be an objective of the long-term planning process to remove such an obvious internal constraint. If the constraints are likely to change within the short-term planning time horizon, it is important that the business has the flexibility to switch to focusing on the new critical limiting factor. This can be achieved by a good system which incorporates a flexible budget and a forecast in addition to the more formal budget or short-term plan. The budget is based on the best estimates at the time it is prepared but, as with all financial plans, it is likely that some of these assumptions and relationships will be wrong. Therefore the plan must be capable of being changed to reflect the most up-to-date assessment of the internal and exter-nal situation facing the business. The flexed budget is normally used to adjust for changes in the volume of activity from those predicted in the budget, but other relationships are maintained as per the original budget. This is unhelpfully restrictive from a financial decision making viewpoint and consequently most businesses now produce a regular rolling forecast which represents its best, most up-to-date estimate of its future performance.

It should therefore also focus on the most up-to-date estimate of the critical limiting factor which is constraining the business.

CONCLUSION

Financial planning, both short and long term is justified because it helps the financial management and control process of the business. It may be helpful to summarise, in a more structured way, how these benefits are achieved within the business. The main benefits can be summarised as co-ordination, communication and control.

Co-ordination is both a benefit and an essential feature of any financial planning process, because it is absolutely vital that the plan is internally consistent (e.g. that the sales budget can actually be delivered by the available level of internal resources). This can be achieved by carefully co-ordinating the individual plans of the various parts of the business so as to ensure that they are mutually compatible and are all aimed at achieving the overall corporate objectives.

A key element of achieving such good co-ordination is clear communication across the organisation. This communication must obviously cover the overall corporate objectives, towards which the individual plans must also be aiming. However, it must go much further in making each part of the business fully aware of the plans of, at least, those other parts of the business with which it must directly inter-relate. Ideally, the communication process will enable all segments of the business to understand fully what the plans of all the other areas are. Such a full process of communication requires a great deal of involvement of a wide range of managers in the planning process. Close involvement, combined with good communication and co-ordination, can have a very positive impact on the motivation of employees and managers within the company. This positive impact can be worth all the cost and effort of the planning process on its own.

If the plan has been well co-ordinated and properly communicated, it can subsequently be used as a reference base against which actual achievements can be measured and decisions taken as the year unfolds. The individual areas of the business can similarly use their own budgets but this creates a final prerequisite of the ideal financial planning system. In order for the final plan to be used as a basis for the subsequent review of managerial performance, it is important that it is agreed with the managers rather than imposed upon them from above. As already discussed, managers should only be held responsible for things that they control and this must, to some degree, include the targets against which they are assessed.

8 USING PRICING AS A COMPETITIVE STRATEGY

INTRODUCTION

Pricing is an important element in any company's competitive strategy as it is the most direct way in which the relative value of its product is communicated to its potential customers. Thus, developing a strategy of being the low cost producer of any given service does not create a competitive advantage which is visible to the customer. This is achieved by translating the lower cost-base into a relatively lower external selling price but, as discussed in Chapters 3 and 4, this raises the question of how the benefit of the cost advantage is shared between the company and its customers.

However, this indicates that the selection of pricing policies is just as important to companies pursuing a low cost strategy as it is to businesses trying to establish a differentiated position in their market. Indeed, it can be argued that a truly differentiated position makes the relative price of the service less relevant, as it becomes impossible for customers to carry out meaningful price comparisons. The pricing level of such a service is still very important, in practice, to the perceived added value which is delivered by the service.

No investment banking (or merchant banking, as it is known in the UK) service would be regarded as cheap by the average person, but the services are priced according to the level of added value which is created for the customer. In other words, the actual cost incurred in developing the particular idea and then delivering the service is of little relevance to the price which is charged. Of course, such prices are constrained by competitive pressures, so that a very high price can only be achieved for a unique investment banking product. As these products tend to have very short product life-cycles (because competitors use reverse engineering techniques to analyse and copy their key features), competitive pressure tends to lead to a rapidly declining price. A good example of this would be the very sophisticated debt to equity swap structures which were developed following the debt crises in Latin America and Eastern Europe. The first few deals of this kind generated fees of several million US dollars each. Now the product has become almost a routine commodity type transaction, with most of the profit being generated by trading in the offshore debt markets to source the outstanding country paper required for the swap transaction.

ALIGNING PRICING STRATEGY AND COMPETITIVE POSITION

The key issue for any pricing strategy is, therefore, that it must be very closely aligned with both the overall competitive strategy and the specific current competitive position. A competitive strategy, which is designed to create a differentiated position in the market, is not necessarily helped by a move to a significant price premium against competitors, before the attributes of the differentiated position have been clearly established in the minds of the target customers.

The need for such close alignment is particularly important in the case of service companies due to the common characteristic of the non-storability of service products. As discussed in Chapter 2, many businesses, such as hairdressing, operate a very flexible pricing policy which is designed to take account of the fluctuations in demand during their working week. The objective is to maximise the contribution generated from their limited resources at peak demand times and to try to avoid having spare resources during periods of lower demand. Ideally this is achieved by creating an incentive for some customers, who are flexible in the timing of their demand, to alter their time of purchase to the less crowded periods. This strategy has been implemented in a slightly modified form by some major retailers in order to encourage some shoppers into the stores at relatively slack times; e.g. special offers are given on certain weekday mornings and free transportation is even provided for some customers at certain times.

However, certain service industries with particularly perishable products have taken this flexible approach to pricing strategy much further. Retailers selling fresh produce (such as fresh fruit and vegetables, bread and cakes) discount their selling prices progressively as the available shelf life expires; the logical argument being that almost any sales revenue is better than having to throw the product away. Unfortunately, this logical pricing policy could create future problems once customers start to understand how selling prices move over time. If a large proportion of customers delay their purchases until selling prices are discounted, the retailer will find that an increasing proportion of its sales of perishable products are being made at these reduced prices, thus destroying the profit levels achieved by this area of the business. In the airline industry, this has led to a completely different type of ticket, the stand-by air fare.

The cost structure of the scheduled airline industry is almost totally fixed for any given flight and the product itself is immediately and totally perishable once the aeroplane has taken off. Therefore, it is clearly in the interests of the airline to try to avoid having empty seats on any scheduled flight, but it equally does not want to develop a reputation of regularly reducing its ticket prices just prior to the aeroplane's departure. The way to balance these conflicting pressures was to create a stand-by ticket which is sold at a much reduced price because it does not guarantee travel on any specific flight. Thus, a stand-by ticket holder is only allowed onto the aeroplane if there are available spare seats but if, right up to the last minutes before take-off, full fare paying passengers arrive to fill the plane the stand-by passengers have to wait for a later flight. These stand-by tickets are clearly attractive to cost conscious travellers who are not constrained by the exact time of their arrival at their next destination. The need to create such a product was increased by the problem of the airline industry in that it seemingly cannot impose cancellation charges on full paying passengers who fail to show up for their particular flight. Although a flight may appear fully booked, there is a probability that not all passengers will actually turn up; hence obtaining some replacement revenue from stand-by passengers is of great interest to the airlines. The more annoying (from the perspective of the travelling passenger) way of coping with this problem is for the airline deliberately to overbook the available seats on the flight, based on an expectation of a proportion of 'no-shows'.

This practice is also used by many hotel chains for exactly the same reason, but, in this industry, some companies have instituted a confirmed guaranteed reservation, which secures the room and requires the customer to pay whether or not the room is actually used. The hotel industry has a similarly high fixed cost structure and an instantly perishable product so that, not surprisingly, both industries have been extremely innovative in their use of flexible pricing policies. One interesting element is an attempt to smooth out the occupancy of many hotels over the weekend by offering dramatically reduced accommodation rates for stays which include Saturday night. The logic being that these additional customers will use many of the other revenue generating areas within the hotel (such as restaurants, bars, leisure facilities), and the overall contribution achieved will make the additional business financially worthwhile. What is less immediately obvious is why many airlines offer similar discounts on return air tickets which span a Saturday night?

An alternative response to this type of storability problem is to try to develop a pricing strategy which creates a queue of customers who are prepared to wait to buy the service at the particular offered price. Such a backlog of waiting customers (which, in the case of personal services, is often a physical queue) is, in effect, a method of storing the service because the demand is being created and stored until it can be satisfied. This type of pricing strategy clearly has its own associated risks because customers may become tired of waiting for the service and either go elsewhere or do without the service altogether. As already mentioned, if a flexible pricing strategy is being used to control demand at certain times only, the ideal response is for the customer to move their time of purchase to a less popular period when they would not need to queue.

IMPACT OF COST STRUCTURE ON PRICING STRATEGY

The nature of the cost-base of particular service sectors has already been shown to have a significant impact on their pricing strategies, but when this cost structure is allied to the risk profile of the business, the potential importance of innovative pricing strategies is increased dramatically. An airline not only has a high fixed cost structure but is also a relatively high risk business due to its dependence on a single sector of demand. To some degree, the airline tries to reduce this risk by spreading its operations geographically (even during the recession in the USA and Europe, air travel in the Far East was quite buoyant) and by also broadening its range of customers (by segmenting the aeroplane into first class, business class, full-fare economy and several categories of discount travellers). As a consequence of this potentially disastrous combination of high business risk and high financial risk (the high level of operational gearing), a sound risk-reducing pricing strategy would be to try to ensure that total sales revenue for each scheduled flight at least covered the specific costs of that flight. In the scheduled airline business, such a totally guaranteed strategy is not possible, but it is used in the chartered segment of the industry because the individual flight can be cancelled if its sales revenue does not cover its costs; the normal phrase used is 'consolidation with another flight', rather than announcing a cancellation. For scheduled airlines, the response has been a very heavy investment in marketing information and predictive simulation models which are designed to forecast, as far in advance as possible, how full each forthcoming flight will be. If the rate of incoming bookings is felt to be unacceptable, the airline can use its flexible pricing policy to stimulate the level of demand for this flight. This pricing change may not be in the form of a direct price reduction but may be given as 'buy one first class ticket and receive another one free', or 'receive a free economy ticket for future use', etc.

However, one industry has relatively recently tried to take this risk reduction strategy one stage further with interesting results. Golf clubs have for a long time tended to recover their core annual operating costs, which are largely fixed, by charging their members an annual subscription. The payment of this membership fee entitles the member to unlimited use of the golf course, unless a restricted type of membership (such as five-day membership) has been granted when the unlimited use is appropriately restricted. Additional facilities provided by the golf club are often funded by their specific sales revenues, so that the steward is paid for by the profits from the bar and restaurant, and the resident professional by teaching fees, shop sales and visiting golfers' green fees. Such a segmented pricing strategy has now been implemented, but on a much more sophisticated basis, by several multi-sport leisure centres.

This type of leisure centre, which may provide indoor tennis, squash, badminton, a gymnasium, a swimming pool and sauna and solarium facilities, has a very high level of fixed costs. Equally, it has a number of peripheral facilities which can be self-funding as in the golf club example, such as bar and restaurant and coaching facilities. Historically these centres charged a relatively low annual membership fee and then charged for each facility on a usage basis. The problem caused by this pricing strategy is that it acts as a disincentive to members to use the facilities, while the costs of providing the facilities are almost all fixed (there is a minor incremental cost in lighting the squash courts, etc., but the temperature in the swimming pool is unlikely to be increased because someone decides to go for a swim). This problem is exacerbated if existing members fail to renew their membership because they have not adequately used the facilities, which may be perceived to be expensive on an hourly basis.

The innovative alternative pricing strategy is to offer a range of alternative memberships ranging from the ultimate 'gold star' category which allows this type of member to use any of the facilities at any time without any additional payment. This type of unlimited free use membership can be made available on a single sport basis as well, for the dedicated enthusiast of only one pastime. The pricing levels established should be set so as to seem attractive to a heavy user of the facilities, but the attraction to the leisure company is in the increase in its guaranteed flow of sales revenue, from which it can defray its high level of fixed costs. In some such businesses it has been possible to sell sufficient of these guaranteed revenue producing memberships to cover all the fixed costs, so that profitability is generated from the 'pay as you use' members and casual visitors. The attraction of the higher cost memberships can be made even greater if these members are given preferential booking rights, e.g. they can book facilities two weeks ahead while other categories can only make reservations one week in advance.

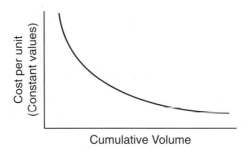

Figure 8.1 Learning curves

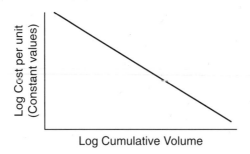

Figure 8.2 Learning curves: using log–log axes

MARKET DEVELOPMENT PRICING STRATEGIES

One of the most important periods for aligning the pricing strategy with the overall competitive strategy is during the rapid growth stage of the product's life-cycle. The company will be trying to ensure that the high rate of growth is maintained for as long as possible so that the market matures at the maximum size but, during this period, it is also critical that the share of this rapidly expanding market is increased to its optimum level (i.e. the maximum share which can be financially justified). This means that the pricing strategy must be developed with these objectives in mind, although pricing may be used as a major tool in the achievement of only one segment of the overall strategy. An initially low level of pricing may be established in order to encourage trial usage by new customers, with the joint objective of expanding the size of the total market and of increasing market share.

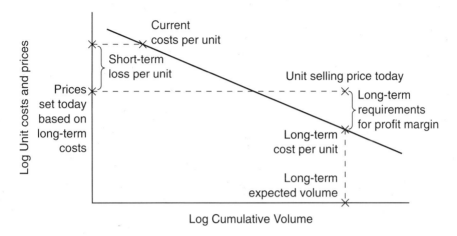

Figure 8.3 Use of experience curves in setting pricing strategies

In some service industries this apparently low price level may be established by using the predicted long-run cost levels for the business, based on an assumption of a successful sustained period of growth in demand. This can be done where the costs are subject to a learning process through which costs are expected to reduce with increased cumulative output. This is diagrammatically shown in Figure 8.1 as a declining cost curve, but more normally the relationship is depicted as a straight line by converting both axes to a logarithmic basis, as is done in Figure 8.2. These learning curves were first used extensively in the aerospace industries in the 1930s but, like many other financial techniques, they also have applications in several service businesses, such as computer software and consultancy. In addition to cost reductions achieved by employees learning how to design and deliver the service more efficiently, this technique has been expanded to include any economies of scale which result from increased levels of activity, as well as cost savings following from the introduction of any technology which can be justified as levels of output grow. This more comprehensive picture of the potential for cost reductions over time is normally described as the experience curve and its potential use in developing a pricing strategy is shown in Figure 8.3.

A low price per unit can be established today based on the expected long-run costs per unit which should be incurred by the company given its sales volume forecast. Although this low selling price may be below the short-term cost per unit, this loss can be regarded as a marketing investment both in helping to make the market grow to its maximum potential, and in developing a potentially significant sustainable cost advantage over competitors,

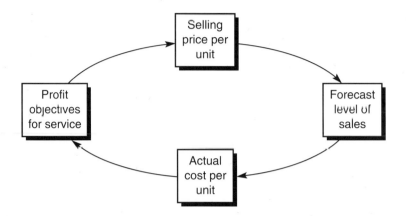

Figure 8.4 Pricing in an experience curve environment – an iterative process

who will be stuck higher up the experience curve as the industry matures. The critical issue is that the selling price established now will achieve an acceptable profit margin when the volume reaches its long-term level; as should now be clear, this is something of an iterative process because the current selling price will, in an experience curve environment, have an influence on the sales volume and hence on the long-term cost structure of the product. This is diagrammatically illustrated in Figure 8.4.

This type of low-pricing strategy may be used in the absence of any future cost reductions in an attempt to gain early market share, even though this may be achieved, in the short-term, at a loss or at an unrealistically low level of profit. The strategy may be based on creating a high degree of customer loyalty which will be retained even when prices are raised in the future, as they will need to be to restore long-term profitability. Unfortunately, as most industries mature, its customers tend to become more knowledgeable about the product and hence less willing to pay unnecessary and unwarranted price premiums; i.e. they become more price conscious and potentially less loyal unless some genuinely perceived added value has been created to retain their loyalty. A much more logical application of this type of strategy can be applied when the costs of acquiring a new customer are very high, such as in the advertising industry, because it then becomes much more critical to achieve a high level of customer retention. In many such cases, these long-standing customers are much less expensive to service, not least from an administrative point of view; they know how the ordering and invoicing system works, all their customer information such as delivery points, bank details, payment terms, contract terms, etc., are already in the supplier's computer system. This represents a cost saving not from volume but from the duration of dealing with the customer and a sensible way of retaining the customer is to share this benefit through a price reduction, not a long-term price increase.

Such a price reduction will build greater customer loyalty, not least because it increases, still further, the costs of acquiring this customer from the competitor's perspective, while reducing the financial attraction of doing so. If the cost saving is shared, the profitability of the customer should improve over time despite the reduction in selling prices.

Another way of trying to apply a low, penetration style of pricing is in an attempt to force out existing competitors which, if no new entrants subsequently come into the industry, could result in an increase in long-term selling prices. Once again, this aggressive pricing strategy is unlikely to work unless the industry has very low exit barriers (so that existing competitors are likely to leave in response to a short-term reduction in prices) but very high entry barriers (so that new entrants do not come into the industry when price levels eventually rise to attractive levels). Such a combination of low exit and high entry barriers is conceptually inconsistent.

The completely opposite pricing strategy is to set a high initial price for the service (this is often known as a skimming strategy) and can most easily be implemented by the early entrants in an industry which has very high entry barriers. The problem with such a pricing strategy is that the high prices will at best defer and at worst curtail completely the development of the overall demand for the product, thus limiting the long-term potential sales volume. However, in a market where there is a very limited level of repeat purchase, such a strategy of high prices could be used by a company with an innovative level of service, or completely new product, since building customer loyalty will not be a main objective. Therefore some very specialised areas of investment banking may use such an aggressive pricing strategy, if the client is not expected to want to use the bank's services again. Similarly, some very specialised software houses and management consultancies could also use this high price strategy provided that their degree of differentiation from their competitors is sufficiently strong, so that customers will still use their services despite the high prices.

Obviously relatively few companies follow this type of strategy on a consistent basis because it restricts the company to a very small specialised niche within its overall potential market; unless the company wishes to attempt to cope with the complexities of managing mixed or complex pricing strategies.

PROBLEMS OF MANAGING COMPLEX PRICING STRATEGIES

In some service industries the particular competitive strategies selected by certain companies can result in a very complex set of pricing policies which are being implemented either over time or in different segments of the market. The software industry is a good illustration of how the change in pricing strategy can be forced on the companies in the industry by an increasing level of sophistication on the part of customers and by the entry of other indirectly related competitors.

Initially the tailored software industry developed using a pricing strategy based on 'time and materials'; in other words, the software house would charge the client a set daily rate for each grade of staff multiplied by the time actually spent on the project plus the external costs incurred by the software house. This meant that the software house only had to focus on keeping its professional staff fully occupied on chargeable work, while the customer was responsible for the total cost of the project. Transferring this high portion of the project risk to the client was broadly acceptable as long as the original project specifications were very vague and customer demands were likely to change regularly during the project.

Over time, customers came to know what they wanted quite specifically at the outset of the contract and their increasing level of technical knowledge allowed them to evaluate any necessary changes as the project developed. Also the degree of complexity in the actual computer technology meant that the project specification was now done in business not computer terms (i.e. a global bank dealing room system might specify the required response time for a telephone or computer contact between the New York and Tokyo based dealers; how this was to be achieved would be under the control of the software developer). This development within the industry resulted in customers requiring fixed price quotations for specified deliverables (i.e. not just the software but all the hardware and telecommunications as well, known normally as a 'turnkey contract') and this clearly transferred the risk back to the software company.

If the software company is to be successful in this new pricing environment, it clearly needs to acquire some new financial management and control skills. The first essential skill is the ability to estimate and cost the work involved in any major new project which will be done on a fixed price basis. The more innovative and unknown the work is, the greater the risk involved, and this must be allowed for when quoting a price for the contract. Once the contract has been tendered for and won, the company needs very good project management skills in order to control the costs incurred in implementing the project. Inevitably adjustments will have to be made to the original estimates, but compensating amendments must be made, if possible, elsewhere in the overall project. If the software company can adapt success- fully to this new pricing environment, it can achieve considerably enhanced profit margins to compensate for its increased risk profile. However, as many such companies have unfortunately discovered, a significant cost overrun on even one substantial fixed price software development contract can prove financially disastrous.

At the other end of the spectrum in terms of per unit value and contractual timescale lies supermarket retailing, but the complexity of its pricing strat- egy is at least equal to the software industry. As has already been described, key elements in the industry's main competitive strategy have been to develop customer loyalty and to increase the range of products sold to these increasingly loyal customers. The development of retailer brands has been one important element in the implementation of this strategy, but another part has been a sophisticated development of the pricing strategy used by some retailers. These retailers no longer look for a uniform level of prof- itability across their ranges of products, because specific target profit levels are set according to the positioning of the product group within the overall competitive strategy. Thus, some leading brands may be sold at very low margins, and hence very competitive prices, in order to attract customers into the store. The same low price, low contribution strategy is also estab- lished for certain basic commodity products which are felt to be particularly price sensitive. The strategic logic is that the customers will buy a much wider range of products once they are actually in the shop, so that the low margins on these focused products will be more than offset by the higher margins achieved on the rest of the product range. This type of mixed pricing strategy depends on customers not restricting their purchasing to the very low margin lines offered by the particular retailer. However, the essen- tial segmented profitability analysis is also made much more complex by this deliberate element of cross-subsidisation, and the financial management information system must be appropriately modified to take this into account.

SUMMARY

It is clear that there is a wide range of potential pricing strategies which can be used to enhance the success of differing competitive strategies, provided that the appropriate combinations are used together. However, it should also be obvious that the financial information required by the managers in the company will differ considerably depending on the type of pricing strategy which is selected. Yet again, the financial management system must be tailored to fit the specific competitive strategy of the business.

9 COST CONTROL AS A CRITICAL SUCCESS FACTOR

INTRODUCTION

This chapter considers the implications for the financial management system within a service business of looking at cost as a critical success factor. While cost levels are always important if the added value produced by the company is to be maximised, it is most common to find a very strong emphasis on cost control when the company is implementing a low-cost competitive strategy. This immediately highlights a key element in any cost monitoring and control system; a competitive advantage based on being the low-cost supplier is, by definition, a relative statement. Hence any costing analysis should not be totally inward looking; an apparently good internal performance on costs of maintaining them at last year's levels does not look as impressive if competitors have achieved a 10 per cent reduction on their cost levels of a year ago. If these competitors already had a cost advantage last year, a poor competitive position is deteriorating quite rapidly.

Another critical aspect of developing cost control as a critical success factor is that the system must focus managers' attention on those areas of cost which they can control, in time for this control to be exercised. This very clearly means that cost control systems must concentrate on the cost prior to any commitment being made by the company, i.e. when the company can still genuinely exercise its discretion as to whether or not to spend the money. Unfortunately, in many companies there is absolutely no reporting of commitments made by the company, the whole financial reporting system is focused on either expenditure (i.e. when the payment is actually made by the company) or, even more commonly, on expense (i.e. when the expenditure is actually written off in the company's profit and loss account). Managers can exercise no effective direct cost control over either expenditure levels or accounting expenses as these inevitably follow from *the commitment* by the company to purchase the particular goods or services.

A good example of this type of commitment control is in the advertising expenditure undertaken by a company. In order to guarantee the particular advertising gaps in the specified television programmes desired by the marketing department, it is often necessary to book the advertising well in advance of the actual dates when the adverts will be shown. It is also often possible to negotiate quite substantial discounts from the standard list prices if a large burst of advertising is booked at one time. However, from the company's perspective it is critical to register that the booking of this television advertising space commits the company to pay for the adverts in due course. Thus future payment will only be avoided normally by the payment of a negotiated cancellation charge, which may almost equal the original committed cost of the proposed advertising campaign. Cost controls must therefore be aimed at the commitment stage of the expenditure cycle, and not at the payment stage.

ADDED VALUE RATHER THAN COST MINIMISATION

Many cost control systems also suffer from a further major weakness in that they automatically regard any reduction in a cost level as a good thing. The important relationship is what has happened to the total value added which is produced by the business. If the cost reduction initiative has led to an even greater reduction in the sales revenue, the total value added has decreased; the obvious financial objective for any sensible cost reducing strategy is to increase added value rather than simply to minimise the level of costs.

Consequently a sensible place for a cost control system to start is by analysing the value chain of the business to try to identify where the total value added is generated; this concept, which is known as value engineering, has been quite widely applied for many years in manufacturing companies but, as with many other examples, has been largely ignored in the service sector. As a very broad generalisation, experience has indicated that the Pareto 80:20 rule can be applied to added value, as well as to many other aspects of business. In other words, 80 per cent of the total added value is normally generated by 20 per cent of the company's activities, and this means customers, products and *costs*. Conversely, this means that a large part of the cost-base adds almost no value and some of the activities carried out by the company may even make a negative contribution.

Clearly the cost control system needs to distinguish between those areas of expense which make a large positive contribution and those which add nothing at all. The total value added of the business may be significantly improved if the resources allocated to the most productive areas are actually increased, despite this representing an increase in the total cost-base. Also, instead of looking to reduce the costs incurred in certain very unproductive areas of activity, the company should question why any expenditure is incurred in this area at all. The guiding principle should be 'do without rather than do more cheaply'. A major problem for many service companies has been to give in to the temptation to automate certain areas of activity which were really completely unnecessary and totally unproductive. By automating the area, the annual cost may have been reduced but what was probably originally a variable cost has now been converted into a long-term committed fixed cost of the business, with a correspondingly unnecessary increase in the volatility and risk profile of the company.

There are, of course, some investments in automated technology which reduce operating costs and generate significant added value as well. A good example would be the large scale introduction of bar-code scanning in high volume retailing. This technology increases throughput through the retail check-outs and reduces errors at the same time. It can also provide much better stock control and sales information which can be used to improve the financial performance of the retailer. Automated teller machines can also be used to reduce costs in retail bank branches as they remove the need to cater for such large peak loads at the normal teller counters, but they also improve the service available to customers by effectively increasing the opening hours of the bank.

A potential problem for any business which is concentrating on cost control is how to incorporate this added value benefit into the financial evaluation of the investment and its expected cost savings. It is important that, as far as possible, the cost control system uses physical attributes as the main control measure rather than exclusively focusing on the financial savings.

IDENTIFYING CLEAR MEASURABLE OBJECTIVES

This use of physical attributes means that the objectives behind the expenditure become the main focus of the evaluation process, in an attempt to measure the effectiveness of the operation rather than just its efficiency. If the effectiveness with which the objectives have been achieved is not included, any under spending against budget may be regarded as a good performance. Consequently, the culture of the cost conscious organisation becomes one where to overspend is unforgivable whatever the circumstances. This type of culture can be very dysfunctional, as it can be very advantageous sometimes to overspend slightly in order to achieve a critical objective, which would not otherwise have been achieved.

The sensible way of avoiding this issue is to ensure that the specifics of the required 'deliverable service' and any additional key attributes are included in the objectives of the business or the department, as appropriate.

It is then possible to establish a monitoring procedure to make sure that any cost reduction proposals do not destroy the ability to achieve these objectives. Such a process is absolutely essential when any services are being considered for outsourcing, particularly if the outsourcing contract is to be placed on a fixed price basis. The new potential supplier obviously has a large financial incentive to keep its cost base to the minimum level which is compatible with supplying the required service. If the performance characteristics of this 'required service' have not been properly specified the contractor may be able, quite legally, to make a significant profit on the contract simply by reducing the actual level of service which is provided. This can be a particular problem in the case of third party services where the contracting-out business does not actually receive the service now being supplied by an outside contractor.

Contracting out of many services by central government and local authorities can present these types of problems, unless the required 'deliverable service' is clearly defined in the tender documentation and then closely monitored. However, this should not be taken to mean that the existing level of service, which is now being supplied, should automatically become the required 'deliverable service' of the future relationship. A central part of the whole cost control system must be to establish the appropriate level of required deliverable service. The outsourcing decision must then be based on a valid comparison between the internal costs which would be incurred to supply this level of service and the quotations from potential outside suppliers. Any doubts regarding the ability of an outside supplier to achieve the specified performance standards must be seen as increasing the risk associated with granting the contract to this supplier.

These physical attributes of the required service can go a long way towards establishing measures of the effectiveness of the particular service and enabling their subsequent monitoring, but a cost focused company also needs good controls over the efficiency of its operations.

USING STANDARD COSTS IN THE SERVICE SECTOR

As has already been stated, standard costing represents the best financial control over the efficiency with which inputs are turned into outputs in most organisations. Although it is widely used in many manufacturing organisations, its level of use in service companies is disappointingly low because it can be applied to any largely repetitive process where there is a predictable relationship between inputs and outputs. These engineering type cost relationships exist in a wide range of service businesses and are particularly

A contract catering company operates a standard costing system for one of its high volume pre-prepared meat dishes which is sold to a wide range of customers. The basic labour and food costings per batch are as follows:

Standard labour oost	=	Standard time i.e. 8 hours	X	Standard rate per hour i.e. £12.50	= £100
Standard food cost per batch	=	Standard units per batch i.e. 25 kilos	X	Standard price per kilo i.e. £4	= £100

Total Standard Cost per batch £200

Required volume in the next month is 1,000 batches

Note: It is possible to reduce raw material wastage in the preparation of this pre-prepared meal by spending more time on each batch of product. The labour time per batch would increase to 9 hours and the raw material units would reduce by 10% to 22.5 kilos.

Figure 9.1 Problems of standard costing

common where large clerical labour operations are found (e.g. financial services, programming within software companies, retailers, etc.).

The only requirements to establish a standard cost are therefore a standard usage level and a standard cost per unit, as was illustrated in Figure 1.4. The key element within standards for operational control is the comparison between the level of usage which *should* have taken place, according to the standard allowance per unit multiplied by the *actual* level of activity, and the actual level of usage. This control can most effectively be exercised over the physical resources involved (e.g. labour hours), because the engineering input–output relationship should enable an accurate prediction to be made of the physical resources which are expected to be used at any given level of activity. However, accounting involves placing values on these physical units. It is very difficult for managers to make a sensible evaluation of relative performance if given a management report showing only an over-usage of 100 hours of computer programming time, and an apparently partially offsetting under-usage of 20 hours of computer processing time, in developing and testing a particular computer software system. Standard costing is designed to help to make such a comparison quite straightforward by using a standard cost per unit for each resource, which turns the physical quantity into a standardised financial value.

This apparently helpful step can actually prove quite damaging as it can encourage managers to take uneconomic decisions from the business point of view. A simplified numerical example of standard costing and traditional variance analysis can make this much clearer. This example is based upon the standard costing system operated by a contract catering company for its pre-prepared meals but the logic could just as easily be applied in many other situations (e.g. the maintenance and servicing of aeroplanes during turnaround stops between flights, where the routine operations required include catering, cleaning, equipment checks, many of which are suitable for the application of standard costing).

The base data for the standard cost of a batch of one particular meat based meal is shown in Figure 9.1 and this indicates a total expected cost per month of £200,000 for 1,000 batches of this product. It is also known that it is possible to reduce the wastage in the preparation process if employees are given more time to prepare the food more carefully; this type of economic trade-off between labour's rate of working and wastage/error levels is very common. At the standard prices per unit of labour and raw material, this alternative method of preparation is not financially attractive, as can be seen from Figure 9.2. However, if the relative prices moved in the future, the situation could quite easily and rapidly be reversed. A sensible financial management system would not only indicate this change but would also

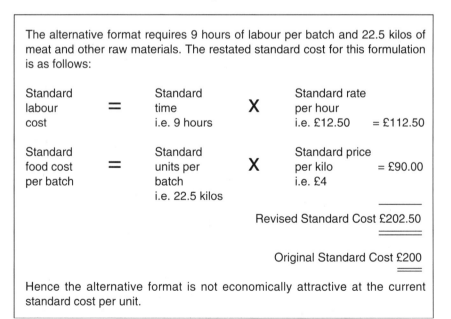

Figure 9.2 Initial evaluation of alternative methods of preparation

The actual labour cost per hour of £10 was lower than the standard, while the actual raw material price of £5 was higher than standard. The total labour hours used were 7,000 and the actual usage of raw materials was 28,000 kilos.

Overall the Actual costs incurred totalled	£210,000
while the expected standard costs were	£200,000
showing an increase in costs	£10,000

Figure 9.3 Actual results for the month

encourage managers to act on this new information if it could improve the performance of the business.

This is where the potential problem of the traditional method of analysing standard costs appears. There is no substantial danger as long as actual unit cost levels stay close to the standards established for this period: but, in many rapidly changing service industry environments, this may not be the case. Unfortunately for our catering company, its actual unit costs have moved quite significantly away from the standards of £12.50 per hour and £4 per kilo, as is shown in Figure 9.3. The net impact on the total expected costs is partially offset by the differences between the actual usage levels and the standard allowances generated from the physical input–output relationships; thus the total actual costs are £10,000 higher than those expected by the standard costs.

The traditional method of analysing standard costs calculates the variances (i.e. differences) between standard and actual in terms of its component elements, as this should facilitate management action. In the case of labour, these components are the variance due to the change in the labour rate per hour and the variance caused by the relative efficiency with which the labour worked. The labour rate variance is calculated by taking the difference in cost per hour and multiplying it by the actual number of hours which were paid for during the period. This reflects the extra cost or saving which was caused by the change in labour rate and, in this example, this calculation shows a saving of £17,500 in the month due to the £2.50 reduction in hourly cost and the 7,000 hours which were worked. In addition, the workforce achieved an improvement in productivity compared with that expected in the standard calculation, because the 1,000 batches were produced in 7,000 hours rather than the standard allowance of 8,000 hours (8 hours × 1,000 batches).

Labour variances
Rate variance:
(Standard rate – Actual rate) x Actual hours

i.e.	(£12.50 – £10)	x 7,000	£17,500

Efficiency variance:
(Standard allowance - Actual usage x Standard rate

i.e.	(8,000 – 7,000)	x £12.50	£12,500

TOTAL LABOUR VARIANCE – FAVOURABLE £30,000

Raw material variances
Price variance
(Standard cost – Actual cost) x Actual usage

i.e.	(£4 – £5)	x 28,000	£(28,000)

Efficiency variance:
(Standard allowance – Actual usage) x Standard cost

ie	(25,000 – 28,000)	x £4	£(12,000)

TOTAL MATERIAL VARIANCE – UNFAVOURABLE £40,000

NET UNFAVOURABLE VARIANCE £10,000

Figure 9.4 Traditional variance analysis techniques

The traditional variance calculation multiples this physical efficiency gain by the standard cost per hour because the total price/rate variance has already been taken into account in the earlier calculation. As shown in Figure 9.4, this gives a favourable efficiency variance of £12,500 which, when added to the favourable rate variance of £17,500, reconciles to the total variance in labour cost of £30,000 (a standard labour cost of £100,000 minus the actual labour cost of £70,000). One of the attractions of variance analysis and standard costing has been its self-reconciling nature.

A similar variance calculation is done for the raw materials but this time both computations show an adverse variance. The actual price per kilo is £1 above the standard and, with an actual usage of 28,000 kilos, this generates an adverse price variance of £28,000. This actual usage level is 3,000 kilos above the standard allowance of 25,000 kilos (25 kilos × 1,000 batches) and, when valued at the standard batch cost of £4, this results in an adverse usage variance of £12,000. Once again these variances combine to reconcile to the total variance on raw materials of £40,000 (standard cost of £100,000 minus an actual cost of £140,000). In total the variances on labour and raw materials can be reconciled to the actual overspend against standard of £10,000;

Standard preparation basis	Alternative preparation basis
8 hours @ £10 x 1,000 = £80,000	9 hours @ £10 x 1,000 = £90,000
25 kilos @ £5 x 1,000 = £125,000	22.5 kilos @ £5 x 1,000 = £112,500
TOTAL COSTS £205,000	£202,500

This shows that the increased cost of raw materials and the lower rate for labour makes it beneficial to change to the alternative method of preparation, whereas at the standard prices the change could not be cost justified.

Figure 9.5 Comparing alternatives at new actual prices, not standards

the variance analysis has 'explained' the total difference in cost in the decision support manner which is so important to all management accounting.

The operations manager would normally be complimented on the efficient use of labour but criticised for the excess use of raw materials; however, as mentioned earlier these results tend to go hand in hand. On a net basis, the manager has produced a net gain to the business of £500 (favourable labour efficiency of £12,500 less the adverse material usage of £12,000), so that it would appear that the faster working practices are financially justified. In most companies, operations managers would not be held responsible for the changes in cost levels because these changes are not under their control; hence the use of standard costs to calculate efficiency variances.

However, the changes in cost levels do make a significant difference to the economic performance of the business and, in particular, to the financial attractiveness of the alternative method of preparation, as seen in Figure 9.5. Despite the reduced labour unit cost, this method of working still results in a higher total labour cost, but this is more than offset by the reduced usage of the now more expensive raw material, net saving £500. This result seems to contradict the earlier variance analysis that indicated that it was financially worthwhile to save labour at the expense of using more raw materials. The use of standard prices in this traditional variance computation clearly overvalues the labour saving and under-records the real cost to the company of using more raw materials. A much better way of calculating the efficiency variances is to use the *actual* unit costs rather than the now outdated standard costs per unit. As can be seen in Figure 9.6, this method of calculation changes the previously reported net favourable efficiency variance of £500 into a net unfavourable variance of £5,000. The reporting of this more relevant variance should encourage managers to switch to the now more attractive method of

Original efficiency variances	Revised efficiency variances
Favourable labour	
1,000 hours @ £12.50 = £12,500	1,000 hours @ £10 = £10,000
Unfavourable raw material	Unfavourable raw material
3,000 kilos @ £4 = £(12,000)	3,000 kilos @ £5 = £(15,000)
Net Favourable £500	Net Adverse £(5,000)

Figure 9.6 Recalculating efficiency variances using actual cost per unit

preparation, which reflects the up-to-date costs which are being incurred by the business. Their own managerial efficiency is still reflected in the physical measures which are compared to produce the over- or under-usages of resources; the change is in how these physical difference measures are valued.

This numerical example has attempted to illustrate that standard costing can be of value to many service businesses, but that its value can be greatly enhanced if the way in which it is applied is placed in the context of the decisions and actions which can, and should, be taken by the managers. A good financial management system must encourage managers to act in the best interests of the company as a whole. For completeness, Figure 9.7 shows how the overall variance reconciliation can be maintained when this type of efficiency variance is calculated; however, it should be remembered that cost control is concerned with future decisions and actions rather than with neatly reconciling the historic financial results.

SUMMARY

Once again the importance of tailoring the financial management system to the needs of the company has been highlighted in this chapter, which has also indicated how some long-standing costing techniques can be applied in the service sector. The greatest challenge in cost monitoring and control is within a company which is trying to implement very different competitive strategies in different parts of its overall business (e.g. a low-cost strategy in one segment and a differentiated strategy in another). In some cases the conflicts created by this divergence, in terms of organisational cultures as well as financial management and control needs, have resulted in splitting

Labour variance

Rate variance
(Standard rate – Actual rate)   x Standard hours
i.e. (12.50   –   £10)   x 8,000   Favourable £20,000

Efficiency variance
(Standard allowance – Actual usage) x Actual Cost
ie   (8,000   –   7,000)   x £10   Favourable £10,000

                               Total Favourable Variance £30,000

Raw material variance

Price variance
(Standard cost – Actual cost)   x Standard usage
i.e. (£4   –   £5)   x 25,000 Unfavourable £25,000

Efficiency variance
(Standard allowance – Actual usage) x Actual Cost
i.e. (25,000   –   28,000) x £5   Unfavourable £15,000

                            Total Unfavourable Variance £40,000

Figure 9.7 Total variance reconciliation using actual cost based efficiency variances

the business into two parts (accountancy practices and their consulting arms, sophisticated computer software houses and their body-shopping programming operations).

10 MANAGING DYNAMIC GROWTH IN SERVICE BUSINESSES

INTRODUCTION

One of the critical long-term success factors for any company which is operating in a high growth environment is to achieve a good market share during this period of rapid growth, as was discussed in Part 2 and Chapter 6. However, there is a constraint on the rate of growth which can be sustained by the reinvestment of internally generated funds, and this rate of growth may not be adequate to achieve the desired market share. The maximum sustainable organic rate of growth is achieved by reinvesting all of the current profits of the company (i.e. paying no dividends in the short term). This means that the maximum rate of growth is controlled by the financial return which can be immediately generated on these reinvested profits. In some rapidly growing service industries (such as retailing), the short-term returns on reinvestments (in opening new stores or refurbishing existing locations) may not be very high but will increase significantly, and then stabilise, over time (as the new store becomes established). Thus, organic cash generation may limit the rate of expansion which the business can achieve, unless it brings in additional sources of funding from outside the company.

Another potential constraint on the internally generated rate of growth can be the company's ability to manage the problems which are inevitably created during periods of rapid growth. As was discussed in Chapter 4, any period of high growth is a time of high business risk due to the likelihood of significant short-term volatility in profits and cash generation. The changes taking place within the company, due to the dramatic expansion, can easily overstretch existing management, who do not have time to adapt to their rapidly altering environment. This can be particularly true in the personal services sector (such as hairdressing), because the senior managers in the originally successful business may have been heavily involved in developing, providing and marketing the particular personal service. Their managerial skills are not therefore necessarily appropriate to the demands of a much larger, rapidly growing business, in which their day-to-day involvement in the detailed operations is inevitably substantially reduced.

Where these rapid growth service businesses are heavily people based (such as computer software and consultancy), the rate of growth is limited by the problems of bringing in more and more people at the bottom of the normal organisational pyramid. The constraint is how quickly can these new recruits (at the graduate intake level, for example) be made productive and self-financing; in most such companies, there is a significant training cost which must be incurred before these employees become revenue generating.

These constraints on the rate of organic growth may make the company look for alternative ways to generate the desired high rates of growth and these alternatives are considered in this chapter. Another reason for considering dynamic methods of growth can be found in more mature industries where a company has not yet achieved an acceptable share of its market. The acquisition of one or more competitors could produce this much larger share of the market, and may be economically justified if there are substantial economies of scale and/or scope which could be achieved as a result of the acquisition.

FRANCHISING

One way of removing most of the growth constraints mentioned above is by developing the business as a franchised organisation, but this structure is not necessarily appropriate for all types of service business. The basic format is that the core business does not attempt to retain detailed operational control over its rapidly expanding network (hence franchising tends to be used in widely spread branch-based service businesses). Instead it brings in outside partners (its franchisees) to run the customer facing part of the business, but within strictly defined operational guidelines. Franchising is very widely used in the service sector and includes some leading retailers (Body Shop and Benetton), fast-food restaurants (McDonalds and Burger King), business services (photo-copying, printing and accounting), plumbing and drain clearing operations, as well as petrol stations (some of those operated under the major companies' logos are franchised), and milk delivery.

The advantages to the franchisor are that it reduces the cash funding demands of growth while allowing its senior managers to concentrate on fewer areas of the operation. As previously mentioned, it can be argued that it changes the real business of the franchisor quite significantly because it ceases to control the direct contact with the end customer. This necessitates a corresponding change in the financial management and control system because the franchisor must ensure that it receives accurate and timely information on how the market is developing.

The attractions to the incoming franchisee are that, in return normally for a signing on fee and an ongoing royalty based on sales revenue, it gains access to a much larger organisation which can provide good operational support and a well co-ordinated high profile marketing strategy. Of course the franchisee runs the risk that not only its investment in buying the franchise, but also the whole of its business may be put in jeopardy, if the main franchisor gets into financial trouble, as has happened on a number of occasions. This is because its marketing strategy, and hence its branding position, are inextricably linked into that of the overall business. It is possible that, if the franchisee has been operating successfully for some time before the franchisor collapses, it may have developed sufficient customer loyalty that it can continue in business without the branding and operational support of the franchise.

In fact this represents one of the major long-term threats to some franchised businesses. The franchisee regards the acquisition of the franchise as a fast learning curve way into the industry and, once well established, starts to question why it should continue to pay a substantial sales royalty to the franchisor. If the customer linkage is too closely attached to the particular operating unit, it may be possible for the franchisee to retain most of its customers even if it terminates the franchising arrangement. However, where the franchise has created a very strong brand image in the mind of the customer and the franchisor maintains strong control over the product sold in the outlets, this defection is less likely to be possible. Should individual customers also visit more than one outlet of the franchised business, this further reduces the risk to the franchisor. It should still place great emphasis on monitoring the level of added-value which it is creating for its franchisees, as this will greatly affect their motivation and commitment to the business.

ACQUISITIONS

Clearly the most obvious way of removing a perceived growth constraint is to buy an existing company and thus achieve external or dynamic growth in place of the internal organic type. However, this type of dynamic growth requires a large level of financing, as the businesses purchased must be paid for immediately whereas funding organic growth can often be phased as the growth is achieved. The critical issue with any acquisition led growth strategy is whether it creates any real value. In many cases, the research has demonstrated that acquisitions actually destroy value for the existing shareholders in the acquiring company, despite the acquisition of an existing, often growing earnings stream.

This additional stream of profits and ultimate cash inflows only adds value to the purchaser if the acquisition price paid for the business is less than the present value of the expected future cash flows which it will produce; in other words, it is bought for less than it is worth! There is no automatic reason for this to require the seller to have made a bad deal, because the business may genuinely be worth more to its new owners than it was in its previous condition. The concept of synergy where $2 + 2 = 5$ is a much discussed justification of acquisitions; experience suggests that it is much easier to discuss conceptually than it is to achieve in practice.

There is also a valid reason why a company may be prepared to pay what appears to be a small premium in order to acquire an existing business, rather than to invest a similar amount of money in accelerating the rate of organic growth of the company. The risks associated with the profitability and cash flows of an existing, established business are likely to be lower than for an aggressive organic growth based strategy, which is dependent either on increasing the market share of the business or on entering a new market altogether. If the business risk is reduced, it may be possible to introduce a higher level of financial risk into the funding structure of the acquisition. This means that some debt financing might be used to pay for the purchase and this lower cost funding might increase the return available on the remaining equity investments required. If the increased rate of return more than compensated for any increased risk perception caused by the financing structure, the acquisition might add value to the existing shareholders in the buying company.

It is still unlikely that the buying company would be able to finance the required equity payments, in a continuing acquisition led growth strategy out of retained profits. Consequently, new issues of shares are likely to be required and this can raise significant problems for many companies regarding dilution of control. In many large companies, the founders still retain a substantial element of control due to their shareholdings (e.g. the Sainsbury family still effectively control over 40 per cent of the supermarket chain bearing their name). However, if new equity funding is needed, these founder shareholders may not have the wealth outside the company to enable them to maintain their proportionate shareholding; this issue can result either in a slower rate of growth or the use of more innovative methods of financing which attempt to reduce the equity dilution element. A company can raise new funds by issuing new shares to its existing shareholders (known as a secondary public offering or a Rights Issue, in the UK) and it can then use these funds to pay for the acquisition or, of course, to fund a faster rate of organic growth. If the shares in the company are regarded as marketable (e.g. they are quoted on a public stock exchange),

A large publicly quoted Retailer (ALR) is acquiring a much smaller, but more rapidly growing retailer (RGR), and paying for the acquisition via a share swap. At present ALR's shares are quoted at £2 per share and the purchase cost is £20 million. ALR is making £50 million profit after tax and has 100 million issued shares prior to this deal. RGR is making a profit after tax of £1 million.

Before the deal, ALR's earnings per share are

$$\text{EPS} = \frac{\text{Profit after tax}}{\text{Number of shares}} = \frac{£50\text{m}}{100\text{m}} = 50\text{p}$$

In order to pay for the acquisition, ALR will need to issue 10 million new shares. This will result in a revised level of earnings per share after the deal:

$$\text{EPS} = \frac{\text{Combined Profit}}{\text{New Total of shares}} = \frac{£51}{110\text{m}} = 46.36\text{p}$$

Figure 10.1 Impact on earnings per share of an equity funded acquisition

the newly created shares can themselves be used as a more direct form of payment. This is achieved by a share swap whereby an appropriate number of new shares in the acquiror are exchanged for the existing shares in the target company. No cash directly changes hands but the shareholding structure in the acquiring company has changed and now includes the previous shareholders in the company which has been taken over.

The most important facet of both these methods of using new equity to finance an acquisition is, once again, whether the deal is perceived as creating added value for the shareholders, both original and new. The problem is that the number of issued shares has been increased and therefore, although the group's profits have also gone up (due to the consolidation of the acquired company's profits), the proportionate share of profits available to each share may have gone down. A key measure of financial performance for all publicly quoted companies is the earnings per share measure, as shown in Figure 10.1 (this is despite a number of conceptual shortcomings which can be attributed to this profits based computation). If the acquisition results in a decline in the earnings per share measure, the company will often reject the acquisition because it fears that the reaction of the stock market may be extremely negative. This can happen even if the deal makes significant financial sense and should, in the long term, create substantial value for the shareholders.

Such a short-term earnings focus makes it very difficult to acquire very high growth companies using equity financing, even though the high risk profile of these companies makes low risk equity financing the most attractive option. This has led to the development of a more creative way of structuring this type of deal, which also reduces some other associated risks. Unfortunately, as with most such innovations, it also introduces some new risks.

USING EARN-OUTS

When a service company is acquired, it is often critically important that the key managers are retained after the acquisition. This is particularly true in the case of a high growth company, where the purchase price will include a substantial premium to reflect expected future growth in profitability. Not only must the key managers be retained but they should also be motivated to deliver the high growth which has already effectively been paid for. If these key managers are also the owners of the target company, this retention and motivation can be a significant problem.

In order to overcome this type of problem, an acquisition financing structure was developed which linked the total purchase price to the subsequent profit performance of the acquired business; thus making this type of arrangement only attractive to owner-managers who feel they have some degree of control over this subsequent stream of profits. The effect of this structure is to make the sellers 'earn' the eventual price over the agreed period (known as the 'earn-out period') as they deliver the expected growth in profitability. Inevitably such an agreement transfers the risk related to this future growth to the sellers of the company because, if it fails to perform to expectations, the final selling price will be correspondingly lower. Logically risk and return should always be positively correlated. Therefore, the likely price which should be achieved, if the company performs to expectations, must be higher than that requested by the sellers as a fixed price today. If the company performs better than expected the sellers should receive a proportionately increased selling price. This 'upside' potential also has to compensate for the deferred receipt of at least part of the sales proceeds, because the normal earn-out structure pays a multiple of current profits now, followed by the same multiple of the growth in profits in each year of the earn-out period.

From the perspective of the acquiror, these motivation and risk transfer aspects are very attractive, but earn-outs can also enable companies to buy high growth businesses using equity financing without any short-term dilution in their own earnings per share (EPS). This is achieved because the multiple which needs to be applied to the earnings over an earn-out period

Global Advertising Group (GAG) wants to buy a much smaller but dramatically growing, owner-managed advertising company. It is very keen to retain the existing owner-managers and to motivate them to deliver the predicted spectacular growth in profits over the next three years. GAG's current position is a share price of £5 and profits after tax of £50 million, giving earnings per share of 50p on its issued shares total of 100 million.

The dramatic growth business is seeking a price of £30 million despite its current year's profits of only £1 million, because these are predicted to grow to £2 million, then £3 million and on to £5 million in three years' time.

If GAG issues new shares today to buy the other company there will be dilution in its EPS:

	Before	*After*	
EPS	50p	$\dfrac{£51m}{106m}$ =	48.11p

Figure 10.2 Buying a high growth company

can be made significantly lower than is required in a single point transaction. In the example in Figure 10.1, the sellers wanted £20 million for a company achieving profits after tax of £1 million, giving a Price/Earnings multiple of 20. It is this high P/E multiple which causes the dilution in the acquiror's earnings per share, but if an earn-out deal is used which incorporates the future growth in these profits within the final selling price, the multiple can be reduced so as to avoid the immediate dilution in EPS.

These features have made earn-out deals incredibly popular in several people based service industries and this type of acquisition structuring has been a major element of the growth strategies for many leading advertising agencies, software companies, and temporary employment agencies. A numerical example will help to illustrate how the structure actually works in practice.

The example is based around the acquisition of a high growth, owner-managed advertising agency by a much larger, more mature publicly quoted agency. As shown in Figure 10.2 if the deal is done immediately, the issue of an additional six million shares will result in dilution in EPS for the buyer. However, if the purchase is to be made on an earn-out basis, the sellers will require a higher expected price than the immediate £30 million they are seeking. This can be achieved, as demonstrated in Figure 10.3, by using an earn-out multiple of 8 which is applied to the profits achieved over the earn-out period. This compares to a multiple of 30 which would have been applied to the current level of profits under a traditional deal.

GAG offers to pay eight times the current profits and then eight times the growth in profits in each of the next three years. If the growth in profits is in line with expectations, the following payments will be received:

	Relevant level of profit		Multiplier	Payment
Immediate	£1m	×	8	£8m
End of Year 1	£1m	×	8	£8m
End of Year 2	£1m	×	8	£8m
End of Year 3	£2m	×	8	£16m
			TOTAL	£40m

Thus the sellers could receive £40 million (or more if Year 3 profits are even higher than £5 million) instead of their immediate requirement for £30 million. They should therefore be motivated to deliver the dramatic growth which is expected.

Figure 10.3 Motivating owner-managers through using an earn-out

The expected total selling price is now £40 million but this can vary significantly depending on the future performance of the business; hence the retention and motivation factors have been achieved. Also the reduction in the multiple has avoided the dilution in EPS which was shown in Figure 10.2. In fact, as shown in Figure 10.4, this deal would now contribute to a marginal increase in EPS during the earn-out period even though the acquiror is using equity to buy a higher growth company.

This overall result looks too good to be true in that it seems to reduce the risk and yet increase the return; it is too good to be true! The earn-out structure does remove some risks but by deferring a large part of the payment it is creating a future financing risk for the buyer. The company is not in reality acquiring the profits of the high growth target for a low multiple, because this lower multiple is also being applied to this growth as well. Hence, a lower growth company is being acquired for a lower earnings multiple. Indeed, the buyer is giving the seller a major financial incentive (in our example, the multiple of 8 is the size of the incentive) to bring forward, into the earn-out period, as much as possible of the future growth of the business. Further, there is no financial incentive for the sellers to spend money on ensuring the long-term sustainability of the profit figure produced at the end of the earn-out. These issues must be taken into account in the design and detailed specification of the earn-out formula.

Year	GAG's expected profits	Target's expected profits	Total profits	Total No. of shares	EPS (Incl. (Acqn.)	EPS (Excl. (Acqn.)
0	£50m	£1m	£51m	101.6m	50.2p	50p
1	£55m	£2m	£57m	103.0m	55.3p	55p
2	£60m	£3m	£63m	104.3m	60.4p	60p
3	£65m	£5m	£70m	106.5m	65.7p	65p

Notes:

(1)   It is assumed, for simplicity of calculation, that GAG's share price increases in line with its growth in profits (i.e. that it maintains its current P/E multiple of 10). In this case the number of shares required to fund the annual payment decreases slightly over time, as the share price rises.

(2)   The increase in EPS is quite small due to small scale of the acquisition but, without the earn-out, the impact would have been a decrease. Also the stock market rating of GAG is likely to improve as the growth in profits starts to be delivered.

Figure 10.4 Using an earn-out formula to produce growth in earnings per share

The use of an earn-out structure also means that the newly acquired business cannot be integrated into the rest of the group until the end of the earn-out period. If it is, how are the profits to be calculated for the earn-out computation? Thus it must be left as a self-contained entity even though its ownership has changed; by definition, this makes it very difficult to realise any synergy benefits from acquisitions which are done in this way.

However, the main risk that is associated with the earn-out process is what happens if, during the earn-out period, the performance of the seller is very good but the performance of the buyer is very bad. If the seller fails to perform, the result is quite simple. No additional payments are required, which is appropriate because the target company was not really a high growth business and did not deserve the high earnings multiple being sought by the sellers. However, if this target company outperforms expectations and delivers even better growth, the sellers are entitled to receive the correspondingly higher price. In our numerical example, the growth company could achieve £10 million profits in year 3 and is therefore expecting a final payment of £56 million (8 times the growth in year 3 profits which would be £7 million). Unfortunately, during this period the rest of the group has had a disastrous time and its profits have turned into a loss (excluding this particular acquisition) of £5 million. As a result its share price has collapsed to 2.5p, giving a market capitalisation of just over £25 million, compared to

£500 million at the time of doing the deal. How does GAG raise the £56 million it needs to meet the final payment when it has a market capitalisation of £25 million? Answers to this problem should be sent, on a postcard, to the advertising agencies, software companies, etc., which are trying to cope with this type of problem. Many large earn-outs were done in the late 1980s based on an apparent expectation that growth would continue forever, but the final payments are having to be financed in a lower growth, recessionary environment.

OTHER INNOVATIVE FINANCIAL INSTRUMENTS

Earn-outs are only appropriate for owner-managed people based businesses, but the idea of acquisition led growth strategies is not restricted to this sector. Consequently a range of other innovative financial instruments have been developed for use under different conditions but with similar aims and objectives from the buyer's perspective.

One of the most common situations is where the high growth target is itself publicly quoted but the acquiror still wishes to avoid any short-term dilution in earnings per share. This can often be achieved by issuing some form of a convertible loan stock or preference share which, if things go well, will subsequently convert into ordinary equity of the company. Billions of dollars, pounds sterling and trillions of yen have been raised by these types of instruments to fund acquisitions and organic growth strategies. As with earn-outs, when things go well these convertibles work beautifully but if things go wrong for the company, this type of financial structure can turn a problem into a major disaster. This is certainly the case in the advertising industry where major players were heavy users of both earn-outs and convertibles to finance their aggressive acquisition strategies of the 1980s.

Another major problem is caused by combining this use of very sophisticated corporate finance products in the company's financial strategy with a multitude of acquisitions. It becomes virtually impossible for any outsider, even a highly skilled financial analyst, to separate out any *real* growth from the creative accounting presentation of apparent growth in earnings per share, total profits, sales revenue, etc.

11 ASSET AND LIABILITY MANAGEMENT FOR SERVICE COMPANIES

INTRODUCTION

Most financial management and control systems tend to concentrate on the profit performance of the business, followed by the cash flow from operations (which is normally taken to be the profit of the business adjusted by adding the non-cash expenses such as depreciation). However, financial management is meant to encompass all aspects of financially managing a business and this includes the management of the assets and liabilities of the business, as well as the profits generated from these net assets. Interestingly, this aspect of financial management is particularly relevant to many service industries, even though service industries are often regarded as not requiring a high level of investment in assets.

The issues relating to the capital structure of the business have already been considered in terms of the relative risk profiles of the business and the appropriate sources of funding. Consequently this chapter concentrates on the asset mix involved in various types of service companies, and the ways in which sound financial management systems can make a significant contribution to the overall competitive strategy of the business.

FIXED ASSETS – TO BUY OR JUST USE

One of the main items of investment for many companies is in the fixed assets which are essential to their business. In the service sector, this is most clearly illustrated by the requirement for retailers to have stores in which to sell their products. Similarly, many other service businesses require premises from which to operate and software companies need computers on which to develop and test their new systems. However, although these fixed assets are essential to the business, it is the use of the asset which is essential and not its ownership.

In some cases, it may be difficult to separate the two elements because, in order to do so, it is necessary to find another party which is prepared to own the asset but allow the original company to continue to use it. The financial return clearly comes in the form of a rental income or lease charges but, as the owner is effectively lending money to the user, the risk associated with the transaction will determine the level of return which is required. Thus, for extremely specialised or unique assets, the perceived risk caused by the lack of alternative uses may make a leasing transaction unrealistic; it is difficult to envisage some of the major utility companies being able to lease some of their major fixed assets which include power stations, gas pipelines, reservoirs and sewage networks.

For many fixed assets, this alternative of using the asset without necessarily having to own it does exist and should therefore be properly financially evaluated as part of a comprehensive financial management and control system. As with most such financial alternatives, the arguments are not exclusively one side or the other and the optimum solution will normally only be identified within the context of the particular competitive strategy of the business. The example of retailers' stores is used to illustrate the various elements which need to be considered.

Many retailers have tended to own the freehold of their own stores wherever possible because this gave them the greatest level of operational flexibility. As owners they do not need to ask permission of an external landlord if they wish to refurbish the store or make any amendments to its internal layout; they still, of course, need permission from planning authorities to modify the outside of the store. The problem with this strategy is that it requires a large investment in freehold land and building, which can lock up a massive amount of capital. The operational saving which results from this strategy is the rent which would have had to be paid out if the store was leased or rented. This normally represents a very low annual return on the capital tied up in the freehold property, because the major financial justification for owning freehold land and buildings is because it is expected to achieve a significant capital appreciation over time. Hence the owner, which acts as a landlord, is prepared to rent the store out at a relatively low operating yield if it expects the value of the store to increase substantially. The effect of this is to make the comparison between two competing retailers quite complicated, if one has a strategy of owning its stores while the other rents all its locations. The owning retailer should show a higher profit level but a significantly lower return on investment, particularly if the fixed assets on its balance sheet reflect any revaluations to the increased market value.

The problem with the ownership strategy is that it is quite difficult to realise the capital gain, which has been achieved through the appreciation in property values, without destroying the existing retail business by selling an essential asset. The counter-problem with the renting strategy is that, if the retailing business is very successful, the value of the property is likely to increase because these retail premises are an attractive investment. The landlord is consequently likely to ask for a sizeable increase in the rent. In some markets, rentals for retail properties are actually directly linked to the sales revenue of the store; this does, at least, provide some reduction in operating costs for unsuccessful stores. Many of the retailers which have decided to own their stores have used this problem to argue that they end up paying the landlord for *their* success which increases the value of the *landlord's* freehold interest in the land and buildings. Hence they have decided to retain ownership, even though the increase in value cannot be easily realised because, in the long term, this strategy will keep down the operating costs (i.e. avoid very large rent increases) for their successful retailing business.

A more sophisticated strategy combines ownership with rental depending upon the perceived potential for capital gain in the particular retail property. In the case of a new supermarket out-of-town superstore development, the retailer may acquire the land and control the development itself, so that it owns the new store. It is allowed, in its published financial statements, to capitalise the interest expense incurred during this development phase, so that there is no adverse impact on its reported profits from this strategy. Most such new store developments show rapid growth in sales revenue during the first few years of opening as customers discover the new location and start to use the store on a regular basis. After this period, the sales growth dies away and reverts to the low level for the majority of well established superstores.

This means that there is likely to be a period of rapid capital appreciation if the new store location is successful, which obviously the retailer believes it will be. If the retailer retains ownership during this period, it can then realise the capital gain by entering into a sale and leaseback agreement with an external investor. The risk to the retailer is reduced by this time, because they do not expect to see any abnormal future growth in sales revenue from this particular store. Therefore there should be no abnormal movements in the value of the store either.

The reasons for the external investor (which is likely to be a property company or investment institution) buying the property on such a sale and leaseback deal is that they get a relatively guaranteed income stream from the retailer. The financial risk is directly linked to the credit rating of the retailer. The buyer also gets the long-term potential capital gain from the redevelopment of the site, once the current store development has reached the end of its useful life. Therefore the buyer will want to lock the retailer in to a long-term lease of the store but, since the retailer wants to be assured of the long-term *use* of the store, this is not a problem for the retailer.

As long as the retailer classifies trading in stores as part of its normal ongoing business, it is even able to include the capital gain generated on the sale as part of its operating profits. This is despite the fact that it is effectively paying a subsequent lease rental which is based on this sale value. An extreme alternative strategy may be adopted by a competing supermarket retailer. It could decide to take short term leases on large premises in the town centre. Many such opportunities occur when properties are scheduled for redevelopment after the original user has moved out. Consequently these locations are normally run down, but to a retailer following a low-cost strategy, they can provide a short-term, very cheap location from which to operate their discount retailing business. Once this lease expires, they move the short distance across the town centre to the next similar location, relying on the fact that their low selling prices will attract their customers to follow them.

OPERATING CASH FLOW

Another aspect of asset and liability management is also critical to many supermarket retailers, in that they run their businesses using a high level of *negative* working capital. This means that they buy goods on credit and both sell those goods and receive payment for them well before they have to pay their suppliers. Clearly this leaves the retailer in a net cash position in terms of the operating cash flow cycle illustrated in Figure 11.1. Some retailers use this cash to fund part of their investment in their freehold land and buildings (the stores), while the retailers occupying rented stores can deposit the cash in the money market and improve their profit margins by the interest income which this produces.

An even more interesting application of this operating cash flow cycle is in the advertising industry. Advertising agencies book the media advertising on behalf of their clients and they also normally make the payments on behalf of these clients. Their income is generated in the form of commissions on the advertising expenditure or as fees billed direct to their clients. This method of operation means that the cash flow passing through the business is very much greater than the sales revenue of the advertising agency. Consequently it becomes clear that a good system of financial control over this operating cash flow cycle can significantly enhance the total return from the business. (The same argument can be applied to almost any agency business. Thus this analysis also applies to insurance broking and travel agents, but the change to the advertising industry has been the most dramatic in

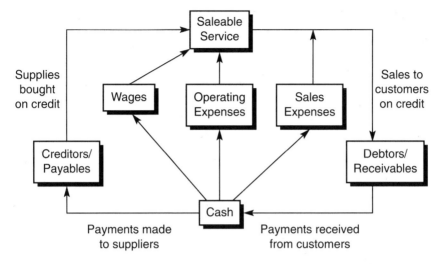

The key management element is to understand the length of time (in days normally) which it takes for cash to travel all the way around this operating cycle. A small improvement in this can make a significant difference to the financing needs of the company.

Figure 11.1 Operating cash flow cycle

recent years.) Historically, advertising agencies used to be controlled by creative managers or account executives, neither of whom were very interested in financial management and control systems.

However, Maurice Saatchi, of Saatchi & Saatchi, introduced a tight system of cash management in their new agency during the 1970s. This was developed by the incoming finance director, Martin Sorrell, and then carried on within WPP when he left Saatchi & Saatchi to become the chief executive in 1985. The key element in this financial control system is obviously to ensure that the company is not funding its clients by paying out for advertising before it has been paid by the client. If the situation can always be maintained slightly the other way round, the agency gains access to a substantial amount of funding itself. Both these companies consistently reported outstanding trade payable levels well above their outstanding trade receivables, indicating the continuing successful implementation of the strategy over a number of years.

Indeed, this type of financial strategy can be used as part of the financial evaluation of a potential acquisition target. If its current financial control system is not good enough to achieve this level of negative working capital, it is relatively straightforward to calculate, from the acquisition target's published financial statements, how much cash could be generated by moving the acquisition to the group's current operating standards. The scale of this cash generation can be staggering. For example, in 1987 WPP Group plc made a hostile acquisition bid for J. Walter Thompson, one of the best known names in the advertising industry. Using the published financial information for both companies, it was possible to identify a potential $150 million of cash which could be generated from JWT by moving its working capital management ratios to those achieved by WPP. The total cost of the acquisition was just over $550 million.

The software industry applies this concept of the operating cash flow cycle in yet another way, by requiring many of its customers to pay deposits before any work is started on the particular project. These payments are normally correctly classified on the published balance sheet of the software company under current liabilities because, if the project is never started for any reason, the software house may be liable to repay this deposit to the customer. Nevertheless, the software house has the use of the funds during this deposit holding period. Another aspect of their normal contractual relationship is that on major projects the client is billed as the work progresses; this is clearly vital to help the software house reduce what would otherwise be an extremely long operating cash flow cycle.

However, as discussed in Chapter 8, many software contracts are now structured as a fixed price deliverable, rather than on the traditional time and materials basis. Thus, notwithstanding the work done to date, the software house may not be entitled to keep the money already paid to it by the customer, if the contract is never properly completed in accordance with the project specification. As most software houses also take profit on these projects as the work progresses, the potential implications of a major problem can be very serious. It is not just a question of making a provision in the profit and loss account for the estimate of any cost overrun as soon as one becomes likely, but it may well be necessary as well to write back any profits which have already been taken into account on this project.

CREDIT RISK – IS IT WORTH IT?

A related aspect to this question of how to treat the outstanding receivable balance and progress payments received on contracts is the whole matter of whether it is financially sensible to take a credit risk. Most companies do this as an automatic part of their business by selling to customers on credit terms and they might quite correctly believe that, in their industry, there is no alternative as all their competitors do so. However, if a risk is undertaken, the level of return must be more than adequate to compensate for this

George has suffered a bad debt of £20,000. His wholesale business works on a gross margin of 5% and is left with a 1% net profit after overheads. Some of these are fixed and a financial analysis shows that the variable portion is equal to approximately 2% of sales revenue.

An additional £400,000 of sales @ 5% gross margin would earn £20,000 extra contribution. However, if the variable overheads are also taken into account, an extra sales revenue of £666,667 would be needed to generate £20,000 extra profit.

Figure 11.2 George's recovery of a bad debt

risk; this argument is used by a wide range of discount retailers for not extending credit to their customers.

The level of the potential problem can best be illustrated by using an example from an owner-managed wholesaler based in the north-west of England. The core part of the business was a cash-and-carry warehouse selling a wide range of products to smaller retailers in the surrounding region. This part of the company had sales revenue of around £10 million and operated on an average gross margin of approximately 5 per cent, with an overhead level which produced a net profit of only 1 per cent.

The owner-manager, George, felt that the business could generate a much improved bottom line if the sales volume could be improved, as additional sales would not automatically lead to a totally proportionate increase in overheads. One way of doing this was felt to be to sell to certain customers on a limited credit basis. This started on a test basis with some selected existing customers and a few specifically targeted new customers. The initial results were quite encouraging as some of the new credit accounts increased their buying from the wholesaler. Unfortunately, one of the fastest growing of these accounts then suddenly went into liquidation, leaving George with a bad debt of £20,000.

This financial loss was not enough to place George's company in jeopardy but, after analysing the numbers shown in Figure 11.2, which showed a sales increase of £666,667 to recover the £20,000 loss, it very quickly put an end to the credit sales experiment. The profit margin of the business is simply not large enough for it to accept the credit risk. If this situation is compared to a consultancy operation which has spare staff, its much larger gross profit margin would enable it to take a much more aggressive view of the credit risk involved in any new assignment. This is not to say that a sensible financial control system would not seek to minimise the risk involved. The rapid collection of all outstanding customer accounts is the best way to minimise the ongoing credit risk of losses through customer defaults.

SUMMARY

The use of sensibly tailored asset and liability management strategies can add significant value to the competitive strategies of most service companies. It is very important to remember that these different strategies can create major differences in the apparent financial performance of companies in the same industry. Therefore appropriate adjustments must be made before meaningful competitor comparisons can be carried out. In addition to adjusting the financial returns, the impact of these different asset and liability strategies on the risk profile of the businesses must be assessed.

Part 4

INFORMATION TECHNOLOGY IN THE SERVICE SECTOR

12 THE STRATEGIC USE OF INFORMATION TECHNOLOGY

INTRODUCTION

Information is power.

This punchy statement has been around a long time and has been well used in business since the days of the Duke of Wellington (according to the apocryphal story of getting news of the result of an important battle more quickly than anyone else). In the extremely competitive modern business environment the need for fast accurate information is greater than it has ever been; but in some areas this need has been outpaced by the revolution in technology which is now available to deliver such information. Therefore, in these areas, the challenge is for managers to learn how to harness the potential power of the *existing* level of technology, before it changes yet again. The next chapter deals with information technology in the context of the design and operation of financial management and control systems. In this chapter, the focus is on the ways in which information technology can be used to create a strategic competitive advantage for the business.

Not surprisingly, there are two generic types of competitive advantage which can be achieved by the strategic application of information technology. The cost base of the company can be reduced below that of competitors by the application of information technology, or the technology can be used to establish a differentiated strategy. In the case of information technology, this differentiation can be established in a variety of ways, most of which reflect the speed with which the information is made available. Thus this 'speed' can relate to the processing of data, making the processed information available, or even the speed of access to the available information. There are even examples where this increased speed can be achieved at a lower operational cost than the traditional methods of providing the information, as will be seen later in this chapter.

The increasing importance of information technology is reflected in the separation of a fourth hierarchy of industrial development, as was introduced in Chapter 1. This quaternary category covers companies providing information and expertise. These are often referred to as the 'knowledge' industries of the future, but most of them revolve around the ability of modern technology to process, almost instantaneously, vast quantities of data so as to transform it into usable information, which can also be communicated across vast distances. Despite the technological complexity involved, the resulting information must still be turned into a competitive advantage if it is to add value to the business and its stakeholders. This added value must, as usual, take the form of an above normal return on the investment required, after taking into account the level of risk involved in the project.

Many of these strategic information technology initiatives require the investment of very large sums of money over a considerable period of time, before it becomes clear whether any return will be achieved; let alone an above normal rate of return. Thus the risks associated with some of these strategies must be seen as very high, so that the required rate of return should also be set at a correspondingly high level in the financial evaluation process before committing funds to the project. A large part of the risk in many initiatives is associated with the technology itself and whether it will actually work in the required way. However other strategic uses of information technology involve innovative applications of existing, proven technologies, so that the associated level of risk may be considerably lower.

These different types of strategic initiatives can also be combined to create varying forms of competitive advantage, which must fit in with the main strategic thrust of the company. As already stated, one clear potential use of information technology is to reduce dramatically the cost base of the business but, in order to justify a large scale, relatively risky investment, such a cost advantage must be sustainable. In other words, the cost-reducing innovation should not be capable of being easily copied by competitors or, even worse, not just copied but improved upon because the competition can use the next generation of computer technology. If the new approach to information technology destroys, or dramatically reduces the effectiveness of, an existing barrier to entry into the industry, the innovative company can make it very difficult for existing competitors to adapt to this approach.

The financial services sector provides several illustrations of this method of using information technology. The launch of home banking is an attempt to provide retail banking services without the need for a network of branches to service customers' requirements. Transactions, and account information, are variously transmitted using telephone, television, computer links, post, etc., and cash needs are supplied by the large network of automated teller machines or other distribution channels. A similar development, which has shown very rapid growth, is direct insurance services where the customer deals directly with the insurance company, normally over the telephone.

Both of these new approaches attempt to reduce the need for the massive investment in branches, while providing a more direct, and hence added value, service to the customer.

Another way of doing this can also create an increased level of customer loyalty by supplying the customer with some supporting technology. This has now been done in a number of industries (including the travel business, which is considered later in the chapter), but was probably first used in the medical supply industry in the USA. The customer is provided with a computer terminal which is linked into the company's system. This terminal makes it easy for the customer to place orders, check stock availability, see the progress position on outstanding deliveries and monitor the position of their account. These benefits should make the customer more loyal to this supplier provided that the overall level of service is maintained at a competitive level.

PEOPLELESS PAYABLES

It is quite possible for this logic to be taken to its logical extreme by developing an information technology system which requires no human interference at all. The technology required for this in many of the accounting areas of business has existed for a number of years and yet progress has been relatively slow. This is particularly surprising as it is well known that the vast majority of errors are caused in the volume transaction processing areas of accounts payable, accounts receivable and payroll by the involvement of *people* rather than the system.

Some companies are now investing heavily in trying to reduce their cost levels in areas which are not perceived as adding value to the business. As mentioned in Chapter 9, the best way to achieve this is 'to do without the area completely, rather than making it smaller'. If this can be achieved while improving the efficiency and effectiveness of the function, the benefits should be very attractive. As an example of this type of opportunity, the area of accounts payable will be examined in order to establish what needs to be changed within a company to arrive at a 'peopleless payables' system, i.e. nobody employed in the accounts payable area.

Most companies now have computerised accounting systems but in many large companies there are still vast numbers of clerical employees, involved in reconciling orders to delivery notes, then to suppliers' invoices and then making payments against invoices or statements, etc., etc. If the system was properly designed and its operation is well controlled none of these functions should be necessary. The essence of good financial control is, as has been discussed several times before, to focus on the commitment stage of the buying cycle. This means that the financial control system must work with the buying manager before the order is actually raised, rather than within the accounts payable department.

It is therefore important that all the contractual details are agreed prior to commitment and these include prices, payment terms, delivery timetables and quality specifications. The company must also, of course, know who it is contracting with and these supplier details, including their bank account details for the subsequent payment, can be entered into the supplier master file at this stage. The details of the approved order can also be entered into an outstanding order file. These inputs can, and should, be controlled by the buying managers, because it is their responsibility to ensure that the correct information is held in the system.

The next stage is that the supplier fulfils the order, or part of it, by delivering the goods or carrying out the service. This event can also be entered into the system; in the case of physical deliveries, this can be done automatically by bar scanning the goods as they are received into the warehouse. The approval for accepting the delivery of the goods can automatically and immediately be given by the comparison of the outstanding order file and this proposed delivery. For the delivery of services, the occurrence of the event is entered by the manager receiving the service, but the comparison against the outstanding file is exactly the same.

As the delivery against an agreed order creates a legally binding contract, there is no need for the supplier to send an invoice, as long as all the required payment details are already held within the system. Thus the total payment due is calculated from the price per unit agreed in the order and the quantity delivered (this is required in the case of part deliveries). The agreed payment terms enable the due date for payment to be automatically computed by the system and this outstanding payment is held in the accounts payable file. On the due date, the required payment is automatically transferred to the supplier's bank account, details of which are held on the system's master file.

Of course this assumes that everything goes smoothly and there are no queries but, if there are queries, these can only be resolved by the people with real knowledge of the transaction. In most companies, the query solving function of the accounts payable department really only consists of receiving the query from the supplier and passing it to the department which can answer the problem; this merely causes delays and adds cost to the whole operation. As already stated, the technology to operate this type of system has existed for a number of years and yet relatively few companies have made good progress towards these available efficiency gains.

One reason is due to the perceived transfer of power away from the finance department because, at present in many companies, much of the data entry into these systems is done within the accounting area. However, control over inputting the data is not the same as controlling the expenditure of the money. The real focus of control must be moved to the point of commitment and this often occurs before the order actually gets entered into the system. Another reason for reluctance is in the area of the automatic payment to the supplier 'on the due date'. One of the most common ways in which finance managers try to manage the net asset position of the company is much cruder than those discussed in the previous chapter. It is simply by delaying payments to suppliers well beyond the terms of trade which were agreed at the time of placing the order. This practice is very difficult to reconcile with the very commonly stated strategic objectives of building long-term relationships with suppliers, requiring zero defects and just-in-time deliveries from these trusted partners in the business!

EPOS and EFTPOS

One area where automated payments systems have made very great advances is in the retail sector. The technology was first introduced to speed up the till check-out process by using bar-code scanning. This innovation also produces a significant improvement in the stock control system and in the detailed sales information available to the retailer. Details were now available not only on how much had been sold of each product but on the spread of sales according to the time of day. This additional sales information helps in scheduling deliveries to the store and deciding on stock levels and pricing strategies for highly perishable products.

Electronic point of sale (EPOS) systems progressively developed the capability to handle automatic payment mechanisms as well; thus acquiring the even longer acronym EFTPOS. This system automatically debits the customer's bank account, by referencing the account from their personalised account card, and credits the value of their purchases to the retailer's account. All of this happens while the customer is still at the store check-out and hence removes any credit risk from the retailer; if the customer has insufficient funds in their account, the transaction will not be completed. Unless an alternative method of payment can be offered, the goods purchased should not be allowed to leave the store. A similar technological development has been applied to the processing of credit card based transactions. Historically these were manually processed by the retailer and then sent to the credit card company for the physical transfer of the payment (much like a cheque payment) to the retailer. The delay was annoying to the retailer but the gap in validation of the transaction could be very expensive to the credit card company. The card could be stolen or the customer could already be over their allowed credit limit. By introducing automatic on-line validation at the time of the transaction, this problem should be greatly reduced.

The problem with all these technologically based advances in payment processing is that they do not provide any individual retailer with a sustainable competitive advantage. Indeed, to make the investment financially viable for the banks and the credit card companies, the technology must be made as widely available as possible. Thus the retailers have made very significant investments in technology which only really keeps them on a par with their competitors, rather than moving them substantially ahead. This has led to very heated discussions between the retailers and the banks as to which party should pay the costs of operating this automated payment system; both sides have been arguing that the major benefits accrue to the other side. So far the major beneficiaries, from the competitive advantage point of view, seem to have been the information technology companies which have been developing and implementing these innovative applications.

One way of applying these new technologies which can be said to have created a sustainable competitive advantage is in the development by the major retailers of an in-store charge or credit card. The idea is to create an increased degree of loyalty among existing customers by making it easier to buy from this particular retailer. The customer receives a single monthly bill for all the items purchased in this retailer's outlets. It is hoped that this deferral of the need to pay cash will also increase the value of the purchases made on each visit to the store. Although competitors can launch their own credit cards and therefore match these benefits as well, the operation of an in-store card provides a very good marketing data-base on the profile of the most loyal customers. By aiming specifically at these customers, the retailer can increase the prospects of success in expanding the range of products which are sold in the shops. As the attractive range of products sold by the retailer increases, the loyalty of the charge card carrying customer grows!

AIRLINE RESERVATION SYSTEMS

Another industry which is desperately keen to increase its customer loyalty is the scheduled airline industry. Scheduled airlines suffer an additional complication over the retailer because they do not sell direct to most of their customers; the airline booking is made through a travel agent. Thus the airline has to convince the travel agent to sell its flight in preference to those of its competitors or it must ensure that the traveller asks specifically for its company.

The end customer can be influenced by very strong retail branding of the airline or by a very low fare for the particular journey being considered. Regular travellers can be encouraged to be loyal to one airline by the offer of accumulating benefits depending on the total miles flown with the airline. The travel agent might be influenced by a higher level of commission on a particular airline's tickets or by particular attractive travel offers given to the travel agent's staff. However, all of these can be copied to some degree by competitors and none of them answer a key issue for many air travellers, particularly those flying on business.

A key factor in selecting an airline is the convenience of the actual flight schedule; how well does it fit in with the personal requirements of the traveller. The traveller may have a marginal preference for one airline but, if its flight arrives too late to make an important meeting or an onward connection, the more convenient flight will be booked. Thus flight schedules are important but, on most of the popular air routes around the world, there are several airlines with almost equivalent departure and arrival times. Also airline timetables for all bar the simplest journey are horrendously complicated.

This creates an opportunity for an integrated flight information and reservation system which could be provided to the travel agent by the airline. The technology involved is very complex and tremendously expensive because the system must be completely up-to-date in terms of flight timings and seat availability. It must also be accessible from anywhere in the world and must be available 24 hours per day, seven days per week, 52 weeks per year. The result is that it is not financially feasible for each airline to develop its own system and airlines have formed consortia to produce a limited number of these very large systems. They have given them very nice names, but the development and operating costs have been horrendous. Also the systems were originally developed on a regional basis, while the market has been moving to a more global structure. This change was reflected in an abortive merger attempt between Sabre (owned by American Airlines) and Amadeus (one of the two major European systems). In early 1993, Galileo (the other European consortium) announced its intention to merge with Covia-Apollo (a US based, consortium owned system). The combined system, to be called Galileo International, claims a 30 per cent share of the world airline reservation market.

These mergers, which are concentrating the control over the total market, indicate the scale of the risks involved in some of these strategic applications of information technology. If an airline invests heavily in one of the systems which does not end up with a viable market share, not only has the airline lost the money invested but also, and more importantly, its core airline business will now be competing at a severe disadvantage to many of its rivals.

RISK OF FAILURE

The scale of this risk can be amply demonstrated by the announcement in the second week of March 1993 of the cancellation of the Taurus project (another nice name). Taurus was supposed to make possible the 'paperless stock exchange of the future', which would ensure the London Stock Exchange's position as a leading international financial market.

The concept developed out of the stock market revolution in October 1986 when trading moved onto computer screens and away from the floor of the London Stock Exchange. It became very logical to automate the whole settlements system and then eventually to do away with the underlying share ownership certificates altogether. The entire trading transaction could be processed and recorded electronically and there would be no need for the delivery and reconciliation every day of thousands of pieces of paper.

Potentially the savings were tremendous and these were increased by the British government's promise to abolish stamp duty on share transactions when the new system came into operation. This was originally planned for 1990 but this was put back and then put back again. In early 1993 it was announced that implementation would not be before the middle of 1994, but even this was quickly overshadowed by an announcement of the abandonment of the project.

Clearly the Stock Exchange has spent a vast amount of money on the aborted development (estimates at the time of the abandonment announcement ranged from £75 million to over £100 million). This expenditure was, however, dwarfed by that incurred by the individual firms which were developing their own systems to interface with the actual Taurus system. The reasons given for the project's failure were the sheer complexity of the system, because many conflicting pressures were not adequately resolved in the design specification finalised in 1989.

CONCLUSION

The existing developments in information technology can easily lead to companies identifying potential new strategic advantages, either from the application of a particular technical breakthrough or by linking together several different aspects of the available technologies. There is a real danger that vast amounts of money are spent on these projects when the ultimate result, even if successful, may not yield a sustainable competitive advantage. Even more worrying, the project may get out of control and lead to spiralling costs which never do produce any benefits at all.

It is essential that the financial management and control system is capable of evaluating these projects before they start (including an assessment of the risks and the consequences of complete failure), and of monitoring and controlling them when they are underway.

13 THE OPERATIONAL USE OF INFORMATION TECHNOLOGY

INTRODUCTION

The requirements of the ideal financial management and control system can be stated very simply as 'providing all the financial decision support requirements of the business'. This can also be broken into three incredibly simple aspects; providing the right information to the right people at the right time. In this chapter an attempt is made to explain each of these aspects of designing and operating a financial management and control system for a service business. The logic of placing this topic under the above chapter heading is that these objectives of the ideal financial control system have only become at all attainable with the increasing processing power of information technology.

Indeed, it is now possible to argue that the design of many management accounting systems lags a long way behind the capabilities of the available technology. For example, most financial management systems are still predominantly focused on preparing regular routine operational reports, which are almost exclusively inward looking. As has been emphasised throughout the book, the key elements of financial management and control are to assist in the development and implementation of the competitive strategies of the business. The complications are that these strategic decisions require information on the external environment and are normally non-recurring in nature. Thus the design of the financial management and control system must change to accommodate this vitally important role, and it is here that the developments in information technology are so important.

The processing power of computers has increased even more rapidly than their costs have fallen, while the costs of not having the required financial information to support any major strategic decision have risen, due to the increasingly competitive business environment. As indicated in Figure 13.1, the cost curves have now crossed for most businesses. The opportunity cost of not having adequate decision support information outweighs the cost of designing and operating an appropriate financial management and control system.

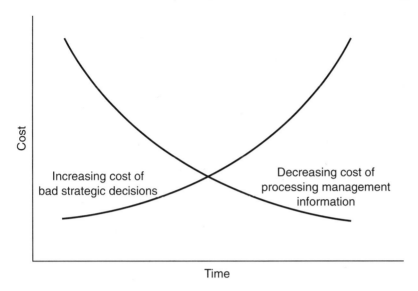

Figure 13.1 The changing cost relationship of management information

In order to develop a *strategic* decision support system, some form of financial data-base needs to be developed, because the type of information required cannot always be accurately specified a long way in advance of the particular strategic decision. Given the automated accounting systems which are in use within most companies, such a data-base is not an impractical proposition. Almost all of the required base data is already being fed into the system, but additional effort is needed to code it in such a way that it can be easily cross-referenced and speedily accessed to provide the required financial analysis for any specific decision. Obviously the most important element in designing a financial data-base is therefore in specifying the nature of the coding which is attached to each item of basic data. If the data is not adequately referenced, even the most sophisticated computer system cannot analyse it into usable information.

Much of the design effort should consequently be aimed at identifying the types of decision which are likely to face the company, and the sort of financial information which would be useful in these decision making processes. Another aspect of this analysis is the time requirements for these decisions because, if the decision would not have to be taken quickly anyway, there should be sufficient time to prepare the required analysis without accessing a comprehensive and expensive financial data-base.

THE RIGHT INFORMATION

The first essential element of a good financial management and control system is that it supplies managers with information, rather than raw unprocessed data. If the managers have to carry out further processing on the information supplied, then the system is not adequately tailored to their needs. This is a major criticism of many financial information systems; they seem to be designed by accountants for accountants, and not for the functional managers who will actually be using the information to support their decision making process. Thus it is obviously ludicrous to provide the senior marketing management team with a pile of sales invoices, or even a computer listing of all the sales invoices, when they are trying to decide how to refocus their marketing support during an unexpected downturn in overall sales. However, even if the sales history is analysed into appropriate segments of the business and this history is then properly summarised to include the required long-term trends and the shorter term fluctuations, the form of its final presentation may make a great difference to the ease with which the marketing managers can understand this financial information.

There is often a significant communication gap between the financial managers in a company and their colleagues in other functional areas. The primary responsibility for resolving this problem lies with the financial managers as they must supply the financial information in a readily comprehensible and meaningful way. Their major role in this area is one of decision support and this is why the financial information is being supplied. With the graphics and diagrammatic capabilities of modern computer systems, there is no need for financial information to remain restricted to long boring unintelligible columns of figures. A cynical view of some other functional managers is that their financial colleagues deliberately keep the presentations confusing, so as to maintain their power base within the business.

Another critical issue with regard to the type of financial information which is needed is that the main objective of the system is to assist in the *control* of the business. Control can only be exercised over the future, as all that can be done regarding the past is to explain what has happened and, if possible, why. Financial control can be broken into two phases. The first stage consists of monitoring how the financial plan is evolving and what, if anything, needs changing. The second stage involves taking decisions to make the changes which are indicated by the monitoring process. A system which stops at the end of the first stage does not add value to the business and therefore cannot, itself, be cost justified.

This raises a potentially significant problem for the financial control system if it is to be focused on decisions, as business decisions are financially evaluated using the future expected cash flows. In fact the fundamental business decisions which require financial analysis can be grouped as either entry/expansion decisions or maintenance/reduction/exit decisions. This further highlights the information dilemma as the entry type of decisions should be based on the incremental costs and benefits accruing from the decision. The exit style group of decisions require financial information on the avoidable costs, which could be saved if the decision is implemented, and the opportunity costs involved. Thus none of these categories of financial decisions is interested in the historic actual costs which *have been* incurred by the business, but this is what can most readily be produced by the financial information system.

Therefore a major task of the financial control system is to make extrapolations from the historic analysis so that rationally based financial predictions of future outcomes can be made. For this to be done effectively the historic data may need considerable modification to take out any abnormal, exceptional or extraordinary elements which have distorted the actual financial results. If they will not recur in the future they are not relevant to future decisions. The next stage is to adjust for any changes in the external environment which will make the future results of a forthcoming decision differ from the previous outcome. Clearly these types of adjustments mean that the financial information supplied to managers may not look at all like the simple financial explanation of the historic result on which it is based.

THE RIGHT PEOPLE

This point leads onto the issue of which managers this financial information is aimed at. One of the important benefits of modern information technology is that a multitude of tailored reports can be produced from the same financial data-base with a minimum of effort. Therefore managers should expect to receive the financial information which they require and they should not all have to compromise by receiving a single 'averaged' presentation which is not really suitable for any of them.

There will be a wide range of managers in any business who want to know in overall terms 'how the business is doing'. This objective can be achieved by supplying the relatively simple financial explanation of the actual historic results compared against the original plan and any subsequently updated forecast. These basic management accounts act as a kind of reconciliation between the plan and the actual, but they cannot be taken as an accurate guide to how the business will perform in the future.

This future performance will largely be determined by decisions taken now and these must be based on the tailored relevant forward looking information mentioned above. Therefore, the decision makers in the business require access to their own sources of financial information, as this information is not needed by other managers who are not involved in this decision. It is very easy to overload a manager with so much financial information that it becomes impossible for that manager to make proper use of any of this excess of riches. Consequently financial information should be separated into 'need to know' and 'nice to know' categories. It is 'nice to know' how the overall business is doing but each decision maker 'needs to know' the specific supporting information for the particular decisions they are facing.

Such a tailored approach to the supply of 'need to know' financial information means that the information flows are not hierarchically or even functionally driven within the organisation. Many decisions are taken by cross-functional teams at a particular level in the organisation and the information should be available to all those involved in the decision making process. Any arguments regarding the inability of certain members of the decision making team to understand the financial information should be taken as a criticism of the way in which the information has been presented. Other decisions are taken by multi-functional groups of managers who are at different levels in the organisation; for example, a pricing review for one particular range of services may involve the marketing manager for that product range, the sales director, the management accountant, and the appropriate operations manager/director. It would clearly be ridiculous if they were basing the decision on different levels of financial information due to their differing levels of seniority in the organisation structure, yet it is not unknown to find companies which still will not allow brand managers to know the product profitability of the range of services for which *they* are held responsible.

THE RIGHT TIME

Once it has been established what financial information should be supplied to which managers, the remaining question relates to the timing of the supply of this information. The simple answer is, as you might expect by now, the information should be supplied as frequently and as quickly as it is needed by the recipients. It is first important to register that the issue of timing has these two aspects, frequency and speed, and that they may be very differently affected by the particular type of decision.

A particular market research company has a policy of reviewing its pricing levels on an annual basis. The pricing committee will therefore require the appropriate, quite detailed financial information some reasonable period before the pricing decision is to be taken, so that due consideration can be given to it and any supplementary analyses can be requested. If, however, in the middle of the year, a major competitor unexpectedly announces an immediate, across the board, selling price *reduction* of 10 per cent, the board of directors are likely to require a very rapid, one-off pricing analysis for those products directly competing against this competitor. A review of all products may take place to see if any compensating adjustments can be made in other areas of the business.

In a more general way, the frequency of receiving financial information should be related to the frequency of taking control action. There is nothing mandatory about producing a full set of management accounts on a monthly basis, and many companies are now moving away from this standardised view of financial control. In a retail environment it is clearly important to reconcile sales inventories and takings on a very regular basis, while in banking very short-term cash reconciliations are a major factor of operational controls. However, in a software company involved in very long, large scale projects there is no logic in such short-term control systems, and even a monthly update may be unnecessarily frequent at certain stages of a project.

Thus financial information can be produced as appropriate with daily or hourly cash reconciliations, weekly sales statistics, monthly operating expense reports and inventory reconciliations, and a quarterly full set of management accounts. The important criterion is that there is no added value in producing financial information on a more frequent basis than that on which it can be used as a basis for decisions.

The same point applies to the speed with which the financial information is supplied. It must be supplied so that it can be used in the evaluation of the decision but it should not be supplied unnecessarily quickly. As already stated, there is normally a cost associated with increased speed and, unless there is an even greater benefit, this cost should not be incurred. This is a very important point because the developments in information technology have made it possible to produce sets of management accounts very quickly indeed. Unless these accounts are going to be used immediately as a basis for making decisions there is no logic in such an increase in the speed of production.

Indeed, some companies have taken this process to the absurd extreme of closing off their sales ledger *before* the end of the month, simply so that they can produce their management accounts more quickly after the end of the month. Some large groups make their overseas subsidiaries close off all their accounts a week, or even four weeks, before the end of the year so that the published financial statements can be released more quickly. They may be unnecessarily wrong but they are available very soon after the period has ended!

IMPLEMENTATION ISSUES

Most of the issues associated with actually operating financial management and control systems in service companies have been dealt with earlier in the book as this was its main thrust. However, it may be useful to draw together in this section some of the common implementation problems which are experienced in this area.

Many companies still confuse economic and managerial performance measures and this can have very damaging results. One of the obvious benefits of a good financial management and control system is that it does provide information on financial performance. However, these performance measures should be separated into those which indicate the relative economic performance of the business and those which reflect the performance of the managers in the business. As has already been illustrated, economic performance measures should take account of everything which affects the financial performance of the business. Thus external factors, such as a deep long-lasting recession, high interest rates and a sharp depreciation in the value of the company's home currency should all be included in the economic measurement of performance. This is so that decisions regarding the future allocation of resources both to the company and within the business can be based on the most accurate projection of future expectations.

However, there will be several factors in this 'warts and all' economic evaluation which cannot be regarded as being under the control of the management team. Equally a very good economic performance can be largely attributable to external factors and does not automatically reflect a good managerial performance. Managers should only be held responsible for those things over which they can exercise control, and this requires that managerial performance measures exclude a number of the exogenous factors included in the economic performance measures. It also means that the measures of managerial performance should change through the organisation as the span of influence and control alters. This results inevitably in quite a complex range of performance indicators which are used at different levels and for different purposes within a single company.

Another important aspect of financial performance measures is that they must be tailored to fit the objectives and competitive strategies of the business. This means that some of the measures should reflect the effectiveness with which the competitive strategy is being implemented and how success-fully this strategy is achieving the company's objectives. Unfortunately, most financial performance measures reflect the efficiency of the operations of the business and say nothing about the effectiveness. Even more damag-ingly, some of these efficiency measures (such as the simple comparison of actual expenditure to budget) can act as an incentive to managers to behave in a particularly ineffective manner; i.e. by giving them a disincentive to overspend even when this would significantly improve the effectiveness of this area's performance. Many of the most appropriate measures of manage-rial effectiveness are not financially based but this does not mean that they should be excluded from a financial control system. Indeed most managers actually exercise control over their usage of physical resources rather than the financial values of those physical resources.

The third main area of problem with financial management and control systems relates to how the business should be broken down. Most large businesses are split into divisions and these divisions are broken up by func-tional areas. This type of organisational structure may have little relevance to the way in which decisions are actually taken in the business. As financial information systems are designed to function primarily in a decision support mode, it is obvious that the system should follow the decision making struc-ture rather than the formal organisational hierarchy. However, it should also be clear by now that the decision taking process will change with the nature of the decision. This means that the financial management and control system must have sufficient flexibility to cope with these changing reporting requirements, without itself needing a fundamental redesign.

SUMMARY

Financial management and control systems should be aids to decision making, not historical reporting systems. Decisions are taken to assist the company in achieving its goals and objectives, but these have to be estab-lished and modified in the context of the external environment and the exist-ing competitive position of the company. Consequently, the financial infor-mation system should provide information which is relevant to the decisions which *need* to be taken.

This introduces a fundamental problem for the design of such an informa-tion system as many competitive strategy decisions are one-off non-repeat-able decisions. Therefore the information needs are also unique. Further, all decisions are evaluated using future information so that the information system must analyse the past data in ways which help to predict the future.

This involves adjusting the data for changed circumstances and removing exceptional and abnormal items which are not expected to recur.

This predictive financial information must be supplied to the relevant decision maker, in a format which makes it readily usable, and not simply to the most senior managers in the company. The financial management and control system must distinguish between the 'nice to know' information and the really important 'need to know' decision support report The 'need to know' information must be supplied in time for it to be used in the evaluation of the decision. It is important to remember that there is nearly always a cost involved in producing financial information more quickly; this cost may be financial or it may be in terms of the predictive accuracy which is achieved. Therefore, information should not be produced *more* quickly than it is needed. Equally, some degree of accuracy may have to be sacrificed if the financial information is to be supplied quickly enough; it is far better to be 'approximately right' than 'precisely wrong' because the information arrived too late.

Financial control is a learning process and therefore the current monitoring and analysis must be used to improve future decisions. This indicates that the analytical resources of the business must be concentrated on those areas where the learning process is likely to be of greatest value. Regular repetitive decisions should therefore be subjected to more rigorous post-event financial review, so that the learning points can be used to improve the future decisions. Subject to this review, they may not require a very deep financial analysis before each individual decision. Conversely, the one-off major strategic decisions require very careful financial analysis before the decision is taken, but the benefit of in-depth post-event financial reviews may be marginal; a sensible area of review may be the evaluation *process* if

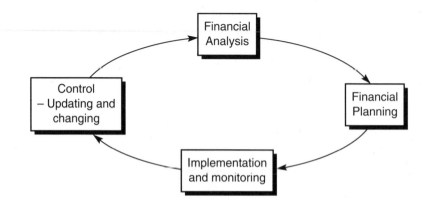

Figure 13.2 Financial control as a learning process

the decision went badly wrong. This type of differential analysis and review shows that the financial management and control system should itself be regarded as constantly developing and changing, as is the company in which it operates.

In other words, we end this part of the book as we started Part 1, with financial management as the iterative developing learning process which is shown in Figure 13.2.

Part 5

CASE STUDIES OF PARTICULAR SERVICE INDUSTRIES

OVERVIEW OF PART 5

This final part of the book uses an industry specific case study approach to try to draw together, in a very practical way, all the financial management and control issues raised in the earlier chapters. In each selected industry, the chapter attempts to show that alternative competitive strategies can be successfully implemented, but that these different strategies must be accompanied by the appropriately tailored financial information system. Equally, for each industry, there are certain common characteristics which require the implementation across the industry of specific financial techniques which may not be as relevant to service companies in other industries even though they are implementing a very similar competitive strategy. The end result is a need for a uniquely tailored financial system for each individual service company.

Quite deliberately, the structure of each chapter in this part is relatively standardised in order to facilitate any cross-referencing among them which may be desirable. However, the significant differences within the industries covered mean that this standard structure has not been rigidly adhered to. Thus each chapter begins with a background section describing the nature and the development of the industry; and highlights the particular parts of the industry which are covered in the chapter. Some of the main companies, involved in the industry are described in some detail so that the discussion can be directly related to these leading players, their strategic plans and implementation problems. However, given the global nature and complexity of each of these industries, it is only possible to select a very few companies for detailed consideration. Clearly the selection of illustrative companies and background issues from each industry has been made by reference to the significance of the related financial management and control matters.

The alternative competitive strategies which have been discussed in the background to this industry are then briefly reviewed with a main objective of drawing out the critical success factors associated with each such strategy. This then enables the main focus of the chapter, which is the financial management and control issues for each industry, to be summarised and linked to these areas of major importance to the companies involved. The last section of each chapter looks into the future at probable and possible developments in the industry, and raises issues and problems to which the financial managers may need to respond as new competitive challenges appear.

This brief overview indicates that most of the financial management and control issues contained in these case study chapters have already been discussed in the earlier appropriate section of the book. It is a deliberate part of the design of the book to draw these separate issues together in the context of a particular service industry. This is to illustrate how these techniques can be applied in practice.

BACKGROUND TO THE RETAILING INDUSTRY

It is even more important than normal to establish a working definition of an industry such as retailing, which everyone comes into contact with on a daily basis. This is because, without such a defined area of focus, people start to apply the techniques and issues into related but different service sectors. For the purposes of this chapter, retailing will be defined as 'the direct sale to the end user, normally from multi-location outlets, of products which have not been produced by the seller'. This definition is deliberately meant to exclude restaurants and direct selling to consumers by a vertically integrated manufacturer, even though some of both these types of company would regard themselves as retailers. The reason for the exclusion is that the main thrust of their competitive strategy may be significantly influenced by their other areas of interest, which could distort the impression of the issues affecting the critical success factors for a retailer.

The retailing industry, as restricted for our purposes, has gone through major changes in recent years in most major developed economies. In order to illustrate some of these changes, the supermarket industry in the UK is first considered before introducing some international companies which have had an impact on this market. Then a similar analysis is applied to a few companies in the fashion clothing retail sector.

J. Sainsbury plc is the largest retail grocer in the UK, in a sector which accounts for 30 per cent of total retail sales. Tesco is a very close second and there are three other chains of supermarkets which have large shares. In terms of profit margins and overall profitability, both of which have increased significantly, Sainsbury's has maintained or improved its superiority in each of the last ten years. The UK supermarket business contributes over 75 per cent of the group's operating profits and it is useful to consider how this business developed.

John James Sainsbury and his wife opened their first shop in 1869 in London selling butter, milk, eggs and subsequently cheese. The business expanded rapidly, as did their family of six sons and five daughters, and all the sons entered the business. By 1879 a number of branches were opened in a relatively small area, and Sainsbury decided it was time to go further afield and to 'design a better shop'; one that was easy to keep clean and could handle fresh food. This led to the introduction of the tiles and marble slabs which were to become synonymous with Sainsbury's for many years to come; the last of this style was closed in 1969.

By the time the founder died in 1928, the business had already introduced own label goods and the branch network had expanded to well over 150 shops. At the beginning of the Second World War, there were approximately 250 branches but the south-east of England still dominated in terms of branch locations. After the war, Sainsbury's imported the self-service idea from the USA and the 1950s saw new stores rapidly opening. In the 1960s Sainsbury's stood aloof from the rapid rise and even more rapid demise of trading stamps, but the rate of development accelerated again when Sir John (now Lord) Sainsbury became chairman in 1969.

In 1973 the company went public and a profit sharing and stock option scheme was introduced which has meant employees make up around 33 per cent of the group's shareholders, who total over 60,000. In 1979 the group experimented with computer check-outs and over £100 million has been spent in bringing EPOS into all its stores. The stores have got progressively larger and the group now opens no stores of less than 25,000 square feet. This policy has enabled selling space to almost double in ten years while the number of stores has only increased 20 per cent to around 300. As a consequence, almost half the total current selling space has been opened in the last five years; an amazing statistic in a company which is over 120 years old.

Sainsbury's is more dependent on own label products, or retailer brands, than its supermarket competitors with just over 50 per cent of sales by value being Sainsbury's own brand. In a typical superstore around 4,000 of the 10,000 product lines would be own label. Its competitive strategy has been to achieve comparable or better quality than equivalent branded items, as part of its overall marketing statement 'Good food costs less at Sainsbury's'. Thus the company is not necessarily regarded by its customers as the cheapest retailer but as offering good value for money. The company places great importance on maintaining this image and puts substantial marketing support behind its retail brand. This has resulted in a high degree of customer loyalty.

The rapid growth and correspondingly large investment in new store developments has made cash flow a key planning issue. The high family shareholding acted as a disincentive to raising new equity and the first post flotation equity offering was not made until 1991. This raised just under £500 million but also diluted the family interest from 47 per cent to around 43 per cent. Prior to this the group has used a number of alternative fund raising schemes. The company operates on significant negative working capital in that its total inventories and outstanding debtors are considerably less than its outstanding trade creditors, due to its very fast operating cycle of turning deliveries into cash, compared to its payments cycle for those deliveries.

Also, the group has entered into sale and leaseback deals, where the company sells the freehold interest in some of its stores but agrees to lease them back for most of their operating life, e.g. 35 years. Most of these deals have been done with British Land, which now owns around 50 Sainsbury supermarkets. This leaves around 60 per cent of the stores owned and 40 per cent rented. In addition, the group has raised corporate bonds and a form of convertible preference share, but it was probably the collapse of the UK commercial property market in early 1991 which led to the rights issue in June of that year, as it precluded any more sale and leaseback deals at financially attractive rates.

Although the group has continued to grow its mainstream supermarket business, it has also added three additional profit centres; Savacentre, Homebase and Shaw's. Savacentre was started as a joint venture with BhS (part of the Storehouse retailing group) to develop hypermarkets where Sainsbury's would be responsible for the packaged grocery sales and BhS for clothing. In March 1989 it was announced that Sainsbury's were to acquire the 50 per cent of Savacentre owned by BhS for £123 million and that they planned to invest another £200 million in doubling the size of the business.

Homebase is the DIY (Do-it-yourself) arm of the group and has grown rapidly since its launch in 1982. Due to Sainsbury's lack of product knowledge in this area, this business was also set up as a joint venture. In this case, a 25 per cent shareholding in Homebase is held by GB INNO BM (a leading Belgian DIY retailer), for whom this move would have been seen as a strategic thrust into a new market with an existing service. Thus, Sainsbury's moves into totally new product areas have been made using a risk reducing strategy of bringing in an expert partner.

A similarly risk averse culture can be seen in the group's international moves. Shaw's Supermarkets Inc is a New England, USA based retailing business which is now growing outside its regional base. It has been a wholly owned subsidiary from 1988, having been a joint venture since 1983 when Sainsbury's took a 21 per cent stake in the company. Shaw's was attractive to Sainsbury's as it had a similar competitive strategy and culture, having also been founded in 1869 and having a maxim of 'Every Day Low Price', which is not unlike 'Good food costs less'.

At the opposite end of the competitive strategy spectrum in the UK supermarket retailing industry is Kwik Save. Kwik Save Group plc is the sixth largest food retailer in the UK with a market share of around 3 per cent.

Although its total sales revenues are less than 25 per cent of Sainsbury's, it operates well over twice as many stores, which indicates one key difference between these two retailers; size of selling space, with Kwik Save's average store being well under 10,000 square feet. However Kwik Save's strategy is fundamentally at odds with most of its competitors.

The business was started in 1963 in the north-west of England on a logo of 'No Nonsense Food Stores', where the emphasis was entirely on price. Thus initially the group rented disused cinemas, etc., often on short leases, and had minimal store fittings and staffing levels together with a very restricted range of products, selling at very low prices. This strategy ensured a very high rate of stock turnover and low operating costs, which together compensated for the lower gross margins resulting from the discounted selling prices. The tightly focused range of suppliers increased Kwik Save's buying power, and the use of the very fast operating cycle enabled a significant level of negative working capital to be generated within the business. This cash could be invested to produce a flow of interest income to supplement the normal retailing margins.

Even today this strategy is still at the heart of Kwik Save and it specifically denies any desire to replicate 'the designer look stores of their competition'. However, it now believes that it is important to provide a 'pleasant shopping environment' with its main theme being 'simple and economic'. Thus, although price is still its main strategic thrust and it also often restricts its product range to the brand leader and possibly one other, the newer stores are larger, carry a larger product range and are less spartan with more staff. Kwik Save has not developed its own retailer brand, but it does have a number of exclusive brands, i.e. products supplied only to its stores but not branded as Kwik Save. This strategy is designed to guarantee high volumes to suppliers and to reduce Kwik Save's costs on quality control and product development. Inventory control is obviously critical and the company has always had sophisticated information systems in this area; but it was relatively late in introducing technology into the front of the store, although now 100 per cent of its stores have EPOS equipment.

The company has also changed its policy of not owning stores and now around half its stores are held on either a freehold or long leasehold basis. The group is also growing by acquisition and in February 1989 bought 53 Victor Value supermarkets from Iceland Frozen Foods. In 1990/91, it acquired 52 former Gateway Stores, seven stores from William Jackson and 18 R.T. Willis stores.

The group was expected to be adversely affected by the entry into the UK of other European discount retailers, most notably Aldi; but initial research indicates that these new competitors may have acted to expand the sector rather than to take significant share away from Kwik Save. However, Kwik Save has responded by reducing some of its prices still further.

OVERSEAS ENTRANTS

Aldi (which stands for Albrecht Discount) was founded in Germany by the Albrecht brothers, Theo and Karl. Although the business was actually started in the 1930s, and it had expanded during the 1950s using a traditional service counter format, it was not until 1962 that the first true Aldi discount store was opened in Dortmund. Until the 1980s the group expansion was mainly domestic but, as its share of the German market increased (over 2,000 stores and 30 per cent share of the discount grocery business), the focus of expansion became more international. Throughout this period all the expansion was by organic growth, without any acquisitions of existing businesses.

Aldi's strategy is very much low cost and low selling price. They operate spartan stores in relatively cheap locations, with displays on ceiling banners rather than on the individual products of the prices of the limited range of high selling lines. Aldi has a large share of its business in its own brands, but these are sold under individual brand names such as Albrecht coffee; some of these exclusive brands are among the brand leaders in their own markets. The range of products has expanded in recent years, away from the traditional area of 'dry groceries' and now includes fresh fruit and vegetables and some non-food ranges. Also more of the newer stores are larger and located away from the traditional town centres chosen in the past.

The effective saturation of the German discount market has led to some interesting strategic developments to maintain the growth of the business. Collaborative agreements have been reached with other retailers whereby Aldi either sub-lets space in its stores to non-competing retailers or takes space in the food halls of large multiple stores. Aldi's initial entry into the UK was also via a collaborative deal with Gateway under which the companies share three stores; Aldi selling a range of discount packaged foods and Gateway selling its fresh food lines. The company's objectives for net profit margins are probably lower than its main UK competitors.

Another developing strategy in European supermarket retailing can be illustrated by briefly considering the development of Carrefour, one of France's leading hypermarket chains. In June 1991 Carrefour surprised the French food retailing sector by acquiring a main rival Euromarche. Carrefour was launched in France in 1963, based on the American one-stop shopping principle of large out of town centres with easy car parking facilities and discount prices. Its hypermarkets are typically very large (more than

50,000 square feet) and operate on low margins, using their bulk buying power and economies of scale to keep prices down.

Carrefour is also an innovator, and has a strategy of trying to create customer loyalty rather than relying on casual passing shoppers. It was the first in France to introduce very low price own brands in the 1970s (now over 3,000 own label lines) and, in 1981, it launched its own direct debit/credit method of payment. It also introduced its own magazine which is mailed free each month to all registered customers. In 1991 the EFTPOS system was developed to accept the Smart Card, the electronic version of the charge and credit card.

The business developed rapidly through organic growth and some acquisitions, culminating with Euromarche in 1991, which gave the group a larger total sales revenue than Sainsbury's. In addition to its 130 hypermarkets, Carrefour also owns chains of discount stores and fresh produce shops around Paris, and has minority interests in several other retailers. It has also taken its retailing strategy to other countries, including 30 hypermarkets in Spain, 22 in Brazil, four in Argentina and one in Philadelphia, USA. Carrefour operates a decentralised strategy, which can be contrasted with the very centralised management of Sainsbury outlets, and its buying power has been enhanced by its membership of a European buying group, Deuro Buying AG.

LINKING SUPERMARKETS AND CLOTHING

A linkage between supermarket and clothing retailing can be achieved by considering the Marks & Spencer strategy. Marks & Spencer plc (M&S) is a leading UK retailer in both food and clothing with a very strongly identified image and a loyal customer base. M&S sells only own label, everything in the store is labelled 'St Michael', and the loyal customers perceive this as a guarantee of good quality at an acceptable price; this guarantee is effectively backed up by the M&S 'no quibble money back' offer for returned goods.

A key to the success of this own brand strategy has been a strong degree of control over quality from the wide range of suppliers used, as the suppliers are unknown to (and hence unblameable by) the consumers. M&S has a well established policy of having very close ties with its suppliers and of insisting on its own standards of cleanliness, employee welfare, etc., as well as demanding exacting quality and tight delivery schedules. A lot of the new product innovations are developed by the M&S team of researchers, so that the company can be likened to a vertically integrated manufacturing business which sub-contracts the ownership of its plant and machinery. M&S also likes to take a large proportion of each suppliers' output wherever possible, but this means that it cannot utilise the negative working capital strategy of other retailers. It pays its suppliers quite quickly because many of these suppliers are almost totally dependent on M & S for their operational cash flow.

In the UK, M&S has been very consciously exploiting its main intangible asset by extending the range of goods and services offered to its loyal customer base. Thus it launched its own credit card in the mid-1980s (it refuses to accept any other credit or charge cards); it now has over 2.5 million card holders and over 20 per cent of sales are made using the cards. It has also experimented with unsecured loans and has launched a range of unit trusts, which signed up over 50,000 investors in its month of launch. These innovations are in addition to extending the range of products offered both through the stores and in a mail order catalogue, which is available free to all cardholders.

The group has also moved internationally and now has sales in 30 countries. It has operated in Canada for a number of years but this has not been extremely successful and an exit strategy has been developed for part of these operations. In the middle of 1988 M&S acquired Brooks Brothers in the USA and, as part of the deal, negotiated preferential rights to retail space in new shopping malls developed by the sellers (which later went into bankruptcy), and which were suitable for food and clothing retailing. As part of this abortive strategy, M&S also acquired Kings Super Markets, a small east coast based food retailer with a similar market profile to M&S. Within Europe, the group has opened normal M&S stores with mixed results and has also moved into the Far East, including the use of franchising in some markets.

At the beginning of the 1990s, the continued record of success seemed to slip slightly, as financial results were static in nominal terms. In May 1991 it announced that its major US acquisition, Brooks Brothers, had been too expensive and was not performing as well as it should. The UK recession was also at this time putting pressure on its core business. Even though Sainsbury's was still turning in substantial growth in profits, the other UK clothing retailers were in very great financial trouble.

OTHER CLOTHING RETAILERS

The second largest clothing retailer in the UK (to M&S) is the Burton Group but its competitive strategy has developed in a very different way. Its stated aims are 'to meet the specialised needs of the largest and most profitable market sectors by developing a widespread but integrated portfolio of national, large and small space retail chains'. This strategy represented a dramatic shift away from its origins as a suit manufacturer which got into retailing to safeguard its access to the market. It was only in 1988 that Burton's sold its last three remaining manufacturing locations.

Growth has been organically generated by refocusing outlets at more specific target markets and by starting new brand identities, as well as by acquisition of other retail chains. At first these acquisitions were relatively small, but in 1985 the group acquired Debenhams plc, a large chain of department stores plus other businesses. At the same time Burton's took over a direct competitor, Collier's, and by the end of the 1980s the group operated a total of over 2,000 retail outlets.

At this time, the group was operating under ten distinct brandings, each one focussed at particular segments of the clothing market. In theory this allowed Burton's to attract a wider range of customers than its single branded competitors such as M&S. It also allowed Burton's a degree of flexibility in managing its property portfolio. If the composition of the customer traffic flow changed around any of its locations, it could consider locating another of its branded outlets into this particular store so as to take the best advantage of these demographic or structural shifts in local populations.

Burton's had moved into property management through the Burton Property Trust, which was involved in the building of five complete shopping centres with a total trading space of nearly 1 million square feet. Also, following the Debenhams acquisition, Burton's had expanded its credit card business. All these developments to its core strategy had been funded without issuing any new shares since the Debenhams purchase. Thus organic cash flow had been supplemented by borrowed funds and a lot of convertible loan stock had been issued.

This put the finances of the group under severe pressure when the UK economy faced rapidly increasing interest costs in 1988, and even more problems were experienced as the recession took hold in the early 1990s. The group's share price collapsed, the credit card business was sold, as was one of its business divisions, and the property business was put up for sale, despite the dramatic decline in the market value of its shopping centre developments. Two issues of new equity were subsequently raised at very low share prices to provide the group with sufficient capital to continue trading during the downturn. The group announced a unilateral decision to extend its payments terms to all its suppliers; traditionally payments to suppliers in the clothing industry have always been made very quickly (e.g. 7–14 days) and so this change in policy meant that their payments were still made more quickly than in much of the retailing industry.

Another fashion retailer which experienced massive problems during this period was Next plc; however, before it ran into problems, it went through a period of even more spectacular growth. Next was created in 1982 by a relatively stagnant clothing retailer, J. Hepworth & Son plc (which was a direct competitor of the traditional Burton's and Collier's businesses), but by 1986 Next had taken over its original parent. The focus of the business was originally on the segment of the 25–35 year old business woman market who wanted to buy fashionable clothes presented in a new shopping concept. It was immediately successful and the chain of shops grew rapidly; as did the range of Next 'concepts' which were aiming at different segments of the clothing market (e.g. Next for Men, Next Accessories). By 1986 the group had over 500 shops and this had been achieved by taking over other chains of retailers and converting the suitable locations into Next outlets.

In 1986 the group made a very large acquisition. It bought Grattans, a clothing mail order company, for around £300 million, as a base from which to launch its own up-market clothes catalogue, Next Directory. This was followed in 1987 by the acquisition of CES (Combined English Stores), which was a relatively diversified retailer with a total of 870 shops. Many of these were converted into Next outlets and some residual parts of the company were sold off, but Next now had acquired well over 1,000 outlets in approximately five years as a retailer.

This phenomenal growth required a vast amount of funding and the issued share capital of the company was almost trebled during this period. However, other types of funding were also used and the company issued two sizeable amounts of convertible unsecured loan stock. The rapid increase in interest rates in 1988 and the consequent slowdown in the UK economy would obviously have a dramatic impact on a high growth fashion focused retailer such as Next. Its share price collapsed even more spectacularly than Burton's and it also faced a severe liquidity problem due to the early redemption option (in 1992) held by its convertible bondholders. Next was able to avert this impending disaster by selling Grattans to Otto Versand (the large German mail order company) prior to the date of this redemption option, thus raising the cash required to buy back the bonds. However, the company has been severely constrained by its cash flow problems, and a key element in its recent strategy has been survival.

A similarly high profile and high growth retailer during this period was Body Shop International plc. Although Body Shop's share price was severely affected by its failure, in 1992, to announce significant growth in profits over the previous year, its business strategy has not been as adversely constrained. This is due to its strategy of franchising out its extensive range of retail outlets, including its international stores. Such a strategy reduces tremendously the required funding which has to be invested in developing this type of retail network. Consequently the short-term liquidity pressures on the company are reduced, but they are really transferred to the individual franchisees if the outlets suffer a significant downturn in trading volumes. It is therefore important that the franchisor ensures that these businesses adopt a suitably prudent financial strategy, which will enable them to withstand any foreseeable fluctuations in the future.

CRITICAL SUCCESS FACTORS

At first sight, the most obvious generic competitive strategy for the retailing industry would appear to be the low cost supplier route due to the low level of added value which the industry seems capable of generating. However, most of the retailers discussed in this chapter are putting the majority of their efforts into reducing the impact which price has on the customer's choice of retailer. Where low price is a key issue, it tends to be associated with the sale of highly branded goods, to which the retailer can itself add little value.

This indicates one of the critical success factors in reducing the importance of price and in developing customer loyalty; the creation of a powerful retailer brand. Most retailer brands cover a wider range of products than is normal for a successful consumer brand. Consequently, all of these products must have the same attributes if the positioning of the brand is not to be compromised. The retailer must be aware that the use of a retailer brand can be dangerous, as one bad product in the range can damage the whole image of the brand. Hence quality control is a key element in such a strategy. Another way of increasing customer loyalty is by additional added value services such as a store charge card.

Having achieved a degree of customer loyalty, the retailer often tries to grow by expanding the range of products sold to these loyal customers, particularly by using a retailer branding strategy. The alternative growth strategy for the retailer is to expand the number of shops and the market which it covers. In many sectors the trend is towards larger shops, which enable an increased range of goods to be stocked and achieves a degree of economies of scale at the store level.

A critical success factor for any retailer is to use its available resources in the optimum way and for most retailers the limiting factor is selling space. Therefore it needs to ensure that products are allocated selling and storage space in proportion to their relative profitabilities; this can be achieved by implementing a suitable system of direct product profitability (DPP).

However, the three most commonly stated critical success factors for retailing are location, location, location. If the shop is in the wrong place, there is very little that can be done about it. Thus retailers must take great care before committing resources to an investment in a new store location. Also because the required investment in stores is so large, the retailer may need to reduce its investment in the remaining net assets of the business. In the case of working capital this is often possible due to the common lack of extending credit to customers and the short operating cycle of turning stocks into cash. If the competitive strategy requires a significant net investment in working capital, the profit margin needs to be increased sufficiently to ensure that the investment receives a more than adequate risk adjusted rate of return.

FINANCIAL MANAGEMENT AND CONTROL ISSUES

The most obvious requirement is on cost information, particularly if the retailer is pursuing a price discounting strategy. However, this cost information must be related to the main constraints on the retailer and, if the retailer is constrained by available selling space, the production of DPP analyses is critically important to the decision making process of the company.

In some retailers, it is also useful to compare the profitability of different groups of customers (using a customer account profitability analysis), but in many cases it is not possible to collect the required base data on the retailer's customers. This is one of the reasons for having a company charge card because it can provide a very valuable customer marketing data-base.

The segmented profit analyses do not include the general shared overheads of the business, but these do need particularly tight control in the retail industry due to the low net profit margins which are achieved.

A key way of transforming a low net profit margin into an acceptable return on investment is by managing the net investment which is made in the business. This should be taken as trying to retain the use of the assets required by the business without having to finance them. With respect to the shops themselves the retailer has a choice between owning and renting, but the financial analysis must be done in the context of the long-term competitive strategy of the business as there is no absolute right or wrong answer. Similarly, many retailers operate with a net negative investment in working capital but the implications for the competitive strategy must be carefully considered. Can more than compensating savings be generated from having a much shorter payment cycle, in terms of faster delivery to the store, better quality of product and service, and faster response to any queries, etc.?

The financing requirements of growth can be reduced if franchising is used. Again, the overall impact must be brought into the equation, in terms of the loss of control over the direct consumer contact and the need to standardise the product range which can be sold.

The financial evaluation of store charge cards is another interesting area, particularly if a major element in the justification is through the enhanced level of customer loyalty which will be generated. This can be easily evaluated by calculating the increase in sales which would be needed to generate the required increase in return, and then testing this increase for reasonableness

LOOKING AHEAD

Many retailers got themselves into severe financial difficulties through the use of very innovative financial strategies to produce the required funding for their aggressive growth strategies of the 1980s. Although the spectacular rates of new store developments have now slowed, there are arguments that there will be an element of over-capacity in the retailing industry throughout the 1990s. This will continue to place a severe strain on the financially weaker retailers and will depress profit levels across the industry as a whole.

The trend towards concentration will continue as the weak fail and the strong look to get stronger by the creation of additional economies of scale and greater buying power. However, another trend may be to reduce the retailer's dependence on the store through the increased use of technology; thus high technology mail order is likely to take an increased share of the market.

At the other extreme, the vast warehouse based retailers will take a significant share of some markets, based on their ability to discount prices due to their lower cost bases. A particular trend is the warehouse 'club' concept as this also builds a degree of customer loyalty.

However, the most challenging prospect is caused by the existing level of customer loyalty and the desire of the major retailers to expand their product ranges even further. In some cases, their existing product ranges have meant that leading retailers have not actually competed with each other directly, even though they have a large number of shared customers. As each retailer moves more and more into new areas, this head-to-head competition becomes inevitable, e.g. as M&S increases its range of normal supermarket goods and Sainsbury's develops a range of clothing to replace the BhS range in its Savacentre outlets!

15 ADVERTISING

BACKGROUND

Although it is titled simply 'advertising', this chapter considers the financial management issues associated with the service industry which has developed to provide the whole range of marketing services for other companies and their products. Thus marketing expenditure is often broken into two segments, 'above the line', which covers mainly direct and indirect advertising, and 'below the line', which is used for promotional activities involving both the end customer and any intermediary channels of distribution.

The developments in these two sections of the industry diverged for a period, but the main thrusts of their competitive strategies now appear to be coming more into line once again. The traditional structure of the advertising services industry was based around a small creative team who set up their own agency on the back of a limited number of client accounts. If this business was successful, a constraint on the ultimate size of the business seemed to be the tendency for a few of this now expanded team to leave and set up their own advertising agency. This created an impression to the outsider that clients were primarily loyal to the account team handling their advertising and promotions, rather than to the advertising agency employing this creative team. It was also largely true that the main strategic thrust of these businesses was based on delivering a high quality service to the customer; thus there was a low emphasis, within most of these small agencies, on financial management and control.

This is very interesting because advertising is primarily a business-to-business service, where the client should be very interested in the financial justification of their marketing expenditure. If the advertising agency could show a good financial return from an increased level of activity, this would appear to be a sound economic argument for expanding its business with that client. However, such financial evaluations do not appear to have found a significant element in the marketing strategy of advertising agencies themselves.

During this period of development, a relatively small number of large, international agencies did develop, but even these tended to be built around either a limited number of very large international clients or a leading industry creative figure. Thus well known international names during the 1960s included J. Walter Thompson (JWT), Ogilvy & Mather (O & M) and Ted Bates, all of which were unsurprisingly US based. This position started to change in the 1970s and the rate of change accelerated dramatically in the 1980s, as a very few global agencies were created by a series of takeovers and mergers.

In August 1970, Charles and Maurice Saatchi launched their own advertising agency. Charles Saatchi, at 26, had already established a reputation as a brilliantly creative advertising copywriter, but the innovative element in the equation was Maurice. Aged 23, Maurice Saatchi had been working as an executive in the publishing industry and his expertise was much more on the finance and administration side of the business than in developing creative advertising. This additional skill at the very top of the organisation was to prove very important in the subsequent development of the business. The business was quickly successful and growth was rapid. The brothers were able to attract other small agencies to join them and so the initial growth was both organic and dynamic.

In 1975 they made their first major takeover of the larger and publicly quoted agency Garland–Compton (this brought them the prestigious Procter and Gamble account). It was also the stimulus for the company to become publicly quoted itself in 1976. This led to the recruitment of a financial director to assist Maurice in controlling and directing the embryonic empire. Martin Sorrell joined Saatchi & Saatchi in 1976 and was with the group during its spectacular growth over the following ten years.

The pace of acquisitions was intense and, as the group's share of the world advertising market grew it moved into other service areas such as consultancy. The acquisition strategy had two main themes; first, acquired businesses were left relatively alone from a creative stand-point but, as is critical with high growth people based businesses, the principals were motivated to maximise the growth of their businesses by making the final price dependent upon the profits over an earn-out period. Second, Saatchi & Saatchi developed a very strong central financial control system which concentrated on tight cash management, so as to maximise the benefit of potential cash flow timings from the client through the agency to the media supplier. Thus, if successfully implemented, the acquisitions could almost guarantee to generate growth in profits and earnings per share and not to use excessive cash in funding this growth in the early years after purchase. Another aspect of the financial strategy during this period was that Maurice Saatchi put considerable effort into demonstrating that the rate with which clients changed their advertising agency was much lower than most external observers had previously believed; this created a higher level of confidence in the company's ability to continue to generate existing levels of profits from these clients.

This consistent and rapid growth in EPS (twentyfold in ten years) not surprisingly gained Saatchi's a premium stock market rating against the advertising sector and a dramatically growing share price; in their first ten years as a publicly quoted company, the share outperformed the FT All Shares index by around 2,000 per cent. Annual growth in EPS of over 35 per cent was achieved for this decade despite the regular issues of equity which were used to fund the acquisitions; just between 1982 and 1987 the number of issued shares increased tenfold to over 150 million. The acquisition in 1986 of Ted Bates had made Saatchi and Saatchi the world's largest advertising agency and by 1988 the business employed 14,000 people in 57 countries, working for more than 250 of the world's top 500 corporations.

However, in 1985 Martin Sorrell had left to set up his own marketing services business. The original intention was not to compete directly with Saatchi's, but to focus on 'below the line' activities and other added value marketing services. The company chosen for this new strategy was interesting, because before 1985 Wire and Plastic Products plc was a steady but unspectacular company with a range of peripheral products in addition to its main line of supermarket trollies. In March 1985, Sorrell and a partner (Preston Rabl, who left the group in 1987) joined the board when the share price was just below 40p. The group changed its name to WPP Group plc and the Saatchis also took a stake in the company.

Rapid growth through acquisitions followed mainly using the earn-out formula and funding the annual payments through the issue of new equity. An added sophistication in some deals was to restrict the sale of the new shares issued to the owner-managers for a time period even after the earn-out itself had finished. By May 1987 the share price was over £10, giving the company a market capitalisation of £125 million. As with Saatchi & Saatchi, a key element in the implementation of this strategy was to strengthen the commercial management of the companies and to separate it away from the creative client service aspect of the business. Strategic decisions and financial management became centralised away from the operations centres. This separation was Martin Sorrell's area of influence as, like Maurice Saatchi, he was not a creative advertising copywriter.

In its first quarter results for 1987 JWT reported a loss and there were clearly senior management conflicts as some key personnel had left the organisation. The share price fell to around $30 from a previous trading level of between $50 and $60, with just under 10 million shares being in issue. WPP decided to bid for JWT despite having to offer over $560 million (approximately £375 million), which was three times its own market capitalisation at this time. A large rights issue (2 for 1) was used to pay for the acquisition, together with a substantial level of new borrowing.

As JWT was itself publicly quoted it was not possible to use an earn-out structure to finance this deal. In any case, the logic of this acquisition was much more akin to a large scale turnaround than the normal deals of acquiring a small high growth advertising business. Saatchi & Saatchi had similarly had to use a large rights issue (7 for 8 to raise over £400 million) in 1986 to fund the acquisition of the publicly quoted Ted Bates agency. The JWT deal was successfully completed in the summer of 1987, not that long before the stock market crash on October 19. The crash adversely affected the share prices of both WPP and Saatchis but it didn't reduce their appetite for acquisitions.

Indeed, despite having acquired JWT and needing to make it cash positive very quickly to service the large debt burden, WPP continued during 1987 and 1988 making acquisitions of below the line marketing services companies using earn-out structures. When the group announced its 1988 results, it had produced a 71 per cent increase in EPS over its 1987 level, helped considerably by restoring JWT's profit margin to normal industry levels.

During this period, Saatchi & Saatchi were broadening their horizons and were arguing that 'globalisation' and 'cross-fertilisation' between their communications businesses would become a key success factor for the 1990s. In 1987, this took the form of abortive approaches to both Midland Bank and Hill Samuel, the merchant bank, regarding acquisition or merger. Their rate of growth in EPS slowed to under 5 per cent in 1988, but the Annual General Meeting in *March* 1989 was the forum for the shock announcement by Maurice Saatchi that the 1989 results would be substantially lower than 1988. Saatchi & Saatchi was still expected to make around £100 million profit before tax in 1989, but the effect on investor confidence and on the share price was dramatic. In June 1988 Saatchi & Saatchi had raised £176.5 million in the form of redeemable convertible preference shares and the sharp decline in share prices made the conversion of these preference shares less likely; they also had an early redemption option in June 1993.

Following the Saatchi bombshell, WPP astonished the stock market in the opposite way by announcing in *May* 1989 that it was bidding for the publicly quoted agency Ogilvy & Mather. This deal would make WPP the largest advertising agency in the world, overtaking Saatchi & Saatchi. The negotiations surrounding the deal were very public and very volatile, but eventually in June 1989 WPP made an agreed final offer, valuing O & M at $864 million (around £550 million). This bid value was over twice the market capitalisation of WPP at the time, but the required financing was raised by the issue of over £200 million of convertible redeemable preference shares plus significant extra bank borrowings.

O & M was a very different acquisition from the JWT turnaround deal, as it was already showing profit margins approximately equal to the average for the industry and the potential for transforming its cash flow was not anything like as attractive; WPP had generated very significantly positive cash flow from JWT during its first year of ownership by instituting its strong cash flow control process. Despite this apparent lack of dramatic growth potential, WPP's 1989 financial results still showed EPS up by 34 per cent on the previous year. However, the stock market seemed relatively unimpressed and even a further 77 per cent increase in its 1990 interim pre-tax profits did not make the share price move up.

In November 1990 WPP announced its own profits warning regarding the growth in its full year profits for 1990 and its prospects for 1991. The share price collapsed spectacularly and the group had to enter into refinancing discussions with its bankers. During this period Saatchi & Saatchi had itself been through a financial drama. The sharp share price fall following its profits warning in March 1989 led to concern about the financing of both the probable redemption of its redeemable convertible preference shares in June 1993 and the continuing earn-out payments which had to be made by the group for acquisitions already done in previous years. WPP had similar outstanding earn-out payments and also had issued very large levels of redeemable convertible preference shares.

As a result of these problems, both groups have required fundamental changes to their capital structures, including significant modifications to their shareholder mix, as elements of the original financing have had to be converted into different categories of investment.

AN ALTERNATIVE COMPETITIVE STRATEGY

Another relatively large agency was set up in London in 1979 with the name Wight Collins Rutherford Scott. In 1983 it changed its name to the WCRS Group plc and it also became publicly listed. In the following years it grew organically and by acquisition, but some of these acquisitions moved it away from its origins as an advertising agency into PR consultancy and sports sponsorship. In 1988 WCRS was still expanding its advertising interests and bought a 20 per cent stake in Belier, Eurocom's French advertising consultancy, while Eurocom in turn bought 20 per cent of WCRS. By the end of 1989 Eurocom had increased its stake in WCRS's advertising business to 60 per cent, effectively taking control, and WCRS had wholly acquired Carat Espace, France's largest media buying company. Control of Carat Espace was acquired in two stages; a 50 per cent stake was purchased in 1988 and the rest in 1989 as part of a larger pan-European acquisition. Carat has become Europe's largest media planner and buyer with an estimated turnover in 1991 of US$5.6bn.

This change led to a fundamental reorganisation of the group. A new company, Aegis Group plc, was created to draw together the specialist media activities through separate operating divisions, i.e. Carat, API, one of the world's main sports sponsorship and event management groups, and the PR consultancy now known as Creamer Dickson International. Initially Aegis retained a 40 per cent shareholding in the revamped advertising business called Eurocom WCRS Della Femina Ball or EWDB (Della Femina Ball was a USA based acquisition by WCRS), but the management was controlled by Eurocom, which owned the remaining 60 per cent. Aegis's role is as a holding company, concentrating on corporate strategy, financial management and control, rather than being involved in the detailed operations of the individual business.

The strategic idea is to focus on providing specialist buying and advisory services for clients in the fields of advertising and other marketing services.

CRITICAL SUCCESS FACTORS

The advertising process can be broken into three main steps:

(a) developing a marketing strategy;
(b) creating advertising and promotional material to fit this strategy;
(c) planning and buying the required media space;

The planning and buying element is increasingly handled by independent agencies providing a brokerage service. One reason is that media buying is the only step which can show significant economies of scale, due to the volume buying power of the large scale specialist. A second reason is that the specialist service is normally backed up by the required research facilities, including computer based research tools. The world market for media space buying is estimated at over $150bn, with Europe being over $50bn. In Europe, over one-third of this expenditure is made through specialist buying agencies, with most of the rest being done by 'buying clubs', which are centralised buying units acting for a group of advertising agencies.

Aegis is the largest of its type of company in Europe and has an advantage in terms of experience and expertise. Saatchi & Saatchi has formed a media buying company, Zenith Media, and other major competitors will undoubtedly join this segment. Critical success factors for Aegis are maintaining and developing its current competitive advantages in terms of buying power, research expertise, and the quality of service which it provides to its clients.

There is a potential problem with this type of competitive strategy as it involves a mix of low cost and high quality factors. The buying power factor should give a price advantage over competitors and this low cost supplier strategy would logically be placed with a low cost strategy throughout the business. However, the emphasis on research, including forecasting viewing figures for television programmes, etc. seeks to improve the effectiveness of the client's advertising rather than just trying to improve the efficiency with which it is bought.

The strategies of the full service agencies are based upon providing a top quality creative advertising campaign for their customers. For those agencies which have gone global, a key element is the ability to cover the total needs of their equally international clients, i.e. global customers need global advertisers. This international aspect must be seen to add value to the client through better co-ordination of the total campaign, allied to in-depth knowledge of the needs of the local market. If this added value cannot be demonstrated, the client may decide to use the best agency in each local market; of course, if the client is very decentralised, the local management may decide to do this anyway. Also the trend towards international strategic alliances in place of totally owned subsidiaries may make it more difficult to sustain a very high level of client loyalty around the world. The logic of the 'one-stop shopping' strategy has largely been destroyed if only based on the convenience of the buying, rather than on any added value which is achieved.

An obvious critical success factor for a large, international advertising agency is to find a way of retaining and motivating the key creative people who, in the past, have tended to want to set up their own business. Where the development of the large business has involved a large number of acquisitions, the agency needed to find a sound method of managing the acquired businesses, without demotivating the existing management team, and of integrating the business within the larger group, as far as necessary and desirable.

In a way, both the overall competitive strategies discussed in this chapter are attempting to build a substantial entry barrier to the industry, which historically has been relatively simple to get into and even easier to leave.

FINANCIAL MANAGEMENT AND CONTROL ISSUES

The cost-base of most advertising agencies is largely fixed as it is comprised mainly of people and their related occupancy type costs. This means that a key issue for managing profitability is to ensure that these fixed costs are recovered, even during any economic downturn. An obvious way to increase long-term profits in this type of business is to increase the profit margin of the company, and standard levels can be established against the average achieved within the industry. Thus, managing the cost-bases is a critical issue but this must be done against valid effectiveness measures, rather than simply using efficiency type indicators such as comparing actual costs against budgets. One issue in this type of creative industry is how to balance the economic performance measures for each stand-alone area of the business with the managerial performance measures, which should be applied to the creative managers who are responsible for each such area.

However, undoubtedly a major element in the financial management of a modern advertising agency is the control of the cash flow, and the maintenance of a negative working capital balance within the business in terms of accounts receivable and accounts payable. This has enabled companies to maintain very high rates of growth over sustained periods, and where equity funding has been used, the financing problems of growth have been manageable. Equity funding is helped by the use of earn-out structures for acquisition pricing and these also help to retain and motivate the key owner-managers from the selling company. Managing the company during, and particularly after, the earn-out period requires particular financial skills as too great a level of interference can destroy the value of what has been purchased, whereas no involvement makes it difficult to see how any value can have been created by the purchase.

The separation of financial management and control from the operational side of the businesses has been a key feature of the successful competitive strategies in the advertising industry.

THE FUTURE

It will take the industry several years to recover from the problems caused by the financial excesses of the past. To a degree, it is now clear that the risks associated with some of the financial strategies implemented by these rapidly growing companies were too high, given the relatively high business risks also associated with these companies at this stage of their development. A combination of high debt levels and deferred payments on earn-outs and potentially redeemable preference shares could, if things go wrong as they have, create a liquidity crisis for the business; conversely, if things go very well as they did at first, the company may appear to be in a virtuous circle. Unfortunately, this may quickly turn into a vicious downward spiral when things go wrong.

It is likely that, as clients become more sophisticated in the way they internally financially justify their level of marketing expenditure, the advertising industry will develop into more specialised businesses. This may happen at both ends of the industry in that the large international businesses may focus on specific advertising related services in order to achieve the maximum economies of scale. However, the small local creative advertising specialist may also stage a significant return to prominence. If the media planning and buying is done by one large specialist and the global marketing strategy is done by another international player, the local advertising campaign can be developed by a small, focused creative house.

The requirements of each of these developments within the advertising industry, in terms of financial management and control systems, are clearly very different. Each will need its own tailored financial controls to suit the specific needs of its competitive strategy.

16 THE SOFTWARE INDUSTRY

BACKGROUND TO THE INDUSTRY

The software industry originally developed in two distinct segments but recent developments in technology have started to make these distinctions less significant. One type of software company concentrated on the development of packaged software products which, if successful, it hoped to sell in large volumes either to end users or to other software houses, or even to hardware suppliers. These packaged products could be further sub-divided into applications packages and operating systems packages. An operating systems package helps the computer to operate more efficiently and effectively or, in some cases, to work at all, while an applications package is aimed at a particular need of the user (e.g. a payroll or general ledger accounting package).

The other type of software house concentrates on designing customised systems solutions for specific customers and therefore tailors the actual software to the particular needs of each project, although many such tailored systems may incorporate one or more software packages. In recent years there have been a number of spin-off focused strategies which have been implemented, due to the rapidly changing demands within the information technology industry. These include the idea known as facilities management, under which a specialist company takes over the complete operational management for a client of all, or part, of its computer systems. This relieves the client's managers of day-to-day responsibility for a potentially critical, but technologically complex, area of business activity.

These different areas of the software industry are discussed in this chapter, but the main focus is on the way in which the specialist, customised systems houses have developed in recent years as they have seen the greatest degree of change in their industry. This is achieved by following one particular UK software company over more than ten years of its development during which it undergoes a dramatic transformation.

In 1981 CAP Group Ltd had to raise a considerable amount of external funding to be sure of staying in existence, due to the significant loss which had been incurred in an abortive software product development project. The company was not a new start-up having been formed in 1962, and it had originally grown as a traditional body-shop type of systems contractor; i.e.

selling its people's services at a daily rate largely for systems analysis and programming work. (CAP stood for Computer Analysts and Programmers.) Following the successful completion of the refinancing exercise, it focused its attention on its customer oriented software business, but the nature of much of this business was changing as the industry itself developed. Originally most software development contracts were done on a time and materials basis, which meant that the final price reflected the number of days worked on the contract at the appropriate charge-out rate for each grade of staff. However, there was a trend towards quoting a fixed price for a total systems solution; i.e. all the hardware and software required to perform a specified set of functions for the client. This changing method of doing business created a need for software houses to reorganise themselves and identify new key performance measures, as the risk associated with such projects was significantly increased.

Also, during the early 1980s there was a spate of software companies being floated onto the stock market, not least because their high growth prospects made them appear as attractive investments in what was then a very strong bull financial market. Software companies do not need masses of funding for the acquisition of essential fixed assets (they normally require only computers and office equipment), but the working capital involved in such a business can be very high depending on how the contracts are structured. The customer is always going to want to hold back some money until the actual system has been fully tested and, for many large software systems, the timescale of the project can be quite long. Also most software companies were run, during this period, by technical systems people, and consequently the financial management and control process was often not very sophisticated.

Thus, project managers were normally more interested in getting on with the project than in ensuring all the time-sheets, etc., were properly processed, so that the progress invoicing could be kept up to date. CAP's balance sheet illustrates this very clearly because, at the end of its 1984 financial year, it showed outstanding receivables of over £7 million on sales revenues of £26 million. Unlike many other service industries, this positive working capital investment cannot easily be offset by achieving an equally high level of outstanding accounts payables. These receivables are not capable of being factored or securitised in any way because, although they represent as usual the unpaid portions of invoiced work, this does not mean that the particular software contract has been completely finished. If the company does not survive to complete the full contract, the customer will normally refuse to pay the outstanding balance until the contract has been completed by another replacement software house. Their fees for completing the outstanding work will then be deducted from the total value of the contract before the balance is paid to the original company. This level of uncertainty regarding subsequent payment, if the contract goes wrong, makes it unsuitable as a source of security to a lender.

It is therefore very difficult for a software house to raise a significant amount of debt to finance its working capital needs, and these needs increase as its sales revenues grow. Also, the relatively high business risk involved in the software industry makes a high level of borrowing an unsuitable way to fund the business. Therefore, it was not surprising to find several software houses seeking stock market quotations in the early 1980s. Two of CAP's direct competitors, SDI (Systems Designers International) and Logica had obtained listings in this period, in 1982 and 1983 respectively, and both had share prices based on very high P/E multiples, reflecting the high growth expectations of their investors. This was undoubtedly a stimulus to CAP's own flotation which took place in 1985, but there were also a number of other significant factors at work.

First, the company's existing institutional shareholders, in particular those which invested at the time of the financial restructuring in 1981, were very interested in being able to realise at least part of the capital gain on their investment. The best way of achieving this is to make the shares as marketable as possible and this can be done by making them available to the very large selection of potential buyers which can be reached via a stock market flotation.

Second, the likely future growth strategy of the company would involve at least some acquisitions and these require funding. If the shares of the company are made publicly tradeable, the issue of new shares can be used as a valid form of payment, either by selling new shares to existing shareholders and using the ensuing inflow of funds to pay for the acquisition, or by issuing the shares directly to the seller in exchange for their existing shares in the target company.

Third, it is very important in such a people focused business to retain and motivate the key employees in the company. The software industry was famous for the high level of labour turnover among professional staff, but CAP had managed to achieve a much higher degree of staff retention. This had been done, at least in part, by encouraging employees to become shareholders in the company and, immediately prior to the flotation, the directors and other employees owned a substantial proportion of their own company. In many cases, this shareholding in CAP represented a major element of the wealth of the individual employees and some of them had borrowed the funds required to purchase the shares. It was therefore attractive to obtain a clearly known value for those shares, even though the employees would probably not want to sell their investment as a result of the flotation.

Following the successful flotation in July 1985, the company had to comply with the rules and regulations of the London Stock Exchange. In a people based business, this can create communication problems because employee shareholders must not use insider information to make unfair profits out of trading in their own company's shares. CAP had always operated an open system of communicating financial information to managers and senior employees; this financial policy had to be carefully reviewed as a result of the change in status.

It did not take the group long to start using the newly acquired marketability of its shares by making acquisitions of other software companies. Companies acquired in the period from 1985 to 1988 ranged from quite small owner-managed software houses, when an earn-out structure was sometimes used, to a publicly quoted company which was almost as large as CAP at the time of doing the deal. The result of these deals was that within three years of its flotation, CAP had doubled its issued number of shares but its sales revenue had increased to over £113 million (for the year ended 30 April 1988 compared to £36 million in the year ended 30 April 1985).

The other companies in the UK were also developing during this period. SDI and Logica had both been founded in 1969 by technical industry people. SDI grew through a series of acquisitions, including in the USA, while Logica's growth was mainly organic including setting up several overseas operations from scratch. In 1988 SDI merged with the BP systems subsidiary, Scicon, to form SD-Scicon. Another major UK company, Hoskyns, had been started in 1964 and in 1972 pioneered the concept of facilities management, which became its major activity. It had passed through several owners in the decade to 1988, when it was owned by Plessey. However, Plessey was itself then taken over by GEC-Siemens, which made Hoskyns available for sale because it did not fit with the new owners' strategy.

OVERSEAS BASED COMPETITORS

Another key aspect of the software industry during the 1980s was that it was also becoming much more global, not only in its products and customers, but also in the major companies comprising the industry. The major UK based companies had all added international activities to some degree and it was therefore not surprising to find overseas software houses looking very closely at the UK market.

The largest European software company was the French owned Cap Gemini Sogeti (CGS), which had grown rapidly through acquisitions and mergers. By the end of 1987, CGS generated half its sales revenue of £400 million outside France but it had no significant presence in the UK. It was well known to the CAP board that CGS had started building a significant stake in CAP during 1987. One of the problems of the significant increase in the total issued shares was that the employees now had a much smaller proportionate stake in the CAP group.

A close competitor of CGS in France was Sema Metra which was controlled by Banque Paribas and also had no real presence in the UK. CAP announced a merger with Sema Metra early in 1988, which created a company with sales revenues of £240 million and a workforce of around 6,500. This made it approximately the same size as the equally newly created SD-Scicon, but did not deter CGS as it bought a substantial number of the new shares (CAP issued another 48 million shares to the existing shareholders of Sema Metra) which came onto the market as a result of this deal. Shortly after the merger was completed the combined company changed its name to Sema.

Unfortunately for Sema, the euphoria of the merger did not last long because at the end of 1988 it was announced that the UK company had run into difficulties on some of its fixed price contracts. The profits for 1988 were virtually wiped out in the UK as a result of the required provisions on these overrunning projects. Not surprisingly there were some significant senior management changes within Sema as a result of these problems. CGS still did not seem deterred and, in fact, bought more shares in March 1989, increasing its shareholding to 22 per cent.

CGS, despite maintaining its sizeable stake in Sema, acquired control of Hoskyns in July 1990 from GEC-Siemens and SD-Scicon also lost its independence, being taken over by EDS in August 1991. EDS is the software subsidiary of General Motors which had been acquired from its creator Ross Perot in 1985.

Sema has continued to do deals and strike up strategic alliances including, in July 1991, a merger of its UK scientific divisions with the defence systems business directorate of BAe to form BAe Sema Ltd, a 50–50 joint venture company. CGS also continued to do deals, but this time the deal was the other way round. Daimler Benz, the German industrial giant, took a 34 per cent stake in Sogeti SA (CGS's holding company) with an option to take over majority control in 1996. The two companies decided to merge their software businesses, Debis (Daimler Benz Inter Services) and CGS, in a German joint venture company owned 51 per cent by Daimler Benz and 49 per cent by Sogeti.

CGS also announced towards the end of 1992 that it was changing its internal organisational structure to move away from its previously highly decentralised, almost loose federation of autonomous businesses to a more co-ordinated set of larger 'strategic business areas'. This change was designed to cope with the rapid growth to an annual turnover exceeding £1 billion and 21,000 staff. However, it was required to enable the group to deliver the well co-ordinated service required by its larger customers, who want to be able to harmonise their computer systems across the world. These software companies also have to respond to the aggressive competition on price which they are facing from computer hardware companies, who are being forced by the downturn in their traditional market to enter the software arena in a big way.

SOFTWARE PRODUCTS COMPANIES

As mentioned at the beginning of the chapter, there is another segment of the software industry which is focused on developing packaged software products. Some of these companies have become global on the back of a limited number of incredibly successful products. The most notable is Microsoft with its MS-DOS operating system for microcomputers which has become the industry standard. It has followed this with Windows and a range of applications programs for personal computers. Before Microsoft, Lotus created a very dominant position with its spreadsheet program, Lotus 1-2-3.

Other than the fact that they are technically in the same industry there is relatively little similarity between these products focused businesses and the tailored software companies discussed earlier in the chapter. The product development costs can be very large and normally have to be spent in full in advance of generating any sales revenues from the product. If the product works and gains acceptance in the market, the gross margin on the actual sales are normally very high, because the production costs for a computer disk and an instruction manual are very low. Thus one blockbuster product can create a vast stream of profits and cash flows, which can be used to try to produce the follow-up product.

This replacement product will probably be needed quite soon because the underlying technology changes so quickly in this industry and competitive product introductions can also affect sales dramatically. Consequently, the normal life-cycle for a packaged software product is very short, and this has important consequences for the competitive strategy of this type of company. It must be very aware of the changes in its market, both in terms of the technology and with respect to customer expectations. The time delay between final testing of the product and its launch into the market must be kept to a minimum. However, some companies have taken the risk of launching the product before it was fully tested; if software bugs are subsequently found, this can prove not only expensive but also disastrous in terms of market reputation.

The short life-cycle problem can, of course, be reduced or removed if the product acquires the status of an industry standard, as its life-cycle will become at least as long as the technology for which it adds value. In some cases, the hardware supplier or customer base may demand an updated version for subsequent generations of the technology as well which cements the success of the company owning the product.

CRITICAL SUCCESS FACTORS

The critical success factors of the product based software companies have just been discussed above. The tailored software systems companies have seen their critical success factors change as the pricing strategy within the industry has moved from a time and materials basis to the fixed price structure which is now much more common. Under the original regime a critical success factor was achieving an adequate utilisation level for professional staff at an acceptable fee rate. The first key level of utilisation is the break-even position of the company because, in any people based service business, the staff should be considered to be a fixed cost no matter what their contractual position. In this industry staff have a relatively short useful life in a technical sense, due to the rapid and dramatic changes in technology. Obviously, it is hoped that, by the time they are technically out of date, they have progressed to more general management roles within the company. In any case, this decay factor makes it essential to recruit new technical staff on an ongoing basis; it is difficult to see how any software house would be able to attract the cream of this year's university graduates if it had just had to lay off a large proportion of a recent previous year's intake. Any company with a very high proportion of fixed costs has a high risk profile and the vast majority of the costs in most software houses consist of salaries and other people related expenses.

Another critical success factor under the time and materials pricing system is the question of staff retention; this factor remains critical in the fixed price quotation environment. People are the key asset of any tailored software company (of course, in a product based company, a very successful product can become the key asset but such a product will have been developed by the key people at some time) and therefore they must be retained. To achieve this it is essential that career development paths are made available but there must be a range of career paths to suit the different needs and aspirations of the various types of individual attracted into the software industry.

With the changed pricing environment some new critical success factors need to be acquired because, while remaining very technologically complex and rapidly changing, the industry takes on many of the characteristics of any large scale project-based industry. Before a fixed price quotation is given to a customer in most industries, a sophisticated job costing system would normally be used to estimate the costs involved in carrying out the specifically required tasks. This is perfectly practical where this project is either a repetition of, or only a minor variation from, previous projects carried out by the business; in other words, where a financial data-base has been developed from which the required costing information can be developed. Unfortunately many sophisticated software solutions are very definitely one-off systems, which require that the estimating process is done on an even more rigorous basis due to the absence of readily available reliable historic data.

The software house needs to develop very good process analysis skills which enable it to break down the project into discrete tasks. Then the cost analysis can estimate the work involved in completing each of the tasks involved in the project. This is a sophisticated project management skill which was not really relevant to the industry's earlier way of doing business. Of course, the good news for the software industry is that these techniques utilise similar analytical skills to those which have always been necessary in their businesses, and so many software project managers have relatively little trouble adapting to their use.

However, it is one thing to quote a fixed price based on the best estimate of the costs involved, but it is still much more difficult to manage the project so as to deliver all the customer's expectations within the estimated cost. Thus another critical success factor for this type of software company is very good project management skills once the project has been won. Undoubtedly the original estimate will contain errors and some of these will be offsetting, but others will require the application of cost reduction/value engineering management techniques to the rest of the project, if the overall budget is to be achieved.

One way of achieving some cost savings may be in the grade of staff which is used on the job and this depends on how well the particular tasks to be performed can be specified. In the original estimate, this assessment would be less clear, but as the project unfolds it may be quite practical to define a particular section very tightly. Consequently, a lower grade of staff might be used than was originally expected. A similar aspect of managing the business in a time and materials environment is to re-allocate staff away from segments of the market where charge-out rates are depressed into those booming areas of demand where premium prices can be obtained.

Within these overall strategies there are some niche strategies which can be based on a strategic consultancy type problem solving role or can be focused at the operational level of the client's systems concerns. The critical success factor in almost all of these is in understanding the main areas of concern and perceived risk on the part of the potential customer. Most customers will be prepared to pay a premium price to get rid of something which they perceive as being a particularly high risk. Such an analysis is key to designing the type of facilities management contract which is appropriate to each customer. If the client's computer system operates real time systems which are critical to the business of the customer, the facilities management contract must effectively guarantee these systems against failure. The price charged can more than reflect the costs incurred in the essential back-up facilities, etc., provided that the perceived reduction in risk means that the contract still adds value to the client. It is important to remember that much of added value tends to come from the different perceptions of risk which the two parties to a transaction have.

FINANCIAL MANAGEMENT AND CONTROL ISSUES

The main implications for financial management and control systems are quite straightforward given the critical success factors for the different types of competitive strategy. The tailored software house is geared around a portfolio of projects and therefore the project should form the focus of the financial information system. Normally these projects can be grouped by market segment (i.e. type of customer, etc.) or nature of problem, or both. A good grouping of projects enhances the value of post-project appraisals as a means of improving future forecasts.

Managers require forecasting and estimating support for project quotations and a good project costing analytical system. This system must include an ongoing estimate of the costs to complete the project so that potential future profitability can be monitored and an early warning given of any impending problems. Utilisation ratios by type of labour are still of value but these should be analysed in terms of the way employee resources are actually managed and not the projects which the employees are working on.

In order to focus clearly and separately on these two key areas of project profitabilities and labour utilisation and recovery levels, many such software companies are now organised on a matrix basis. This means that some managers are held responsible for the labour resources of the business and these available resources are then sold internally, often using a transfer pricing system, to the individual projects, as agreed with the manager responsible for the project. Such a system makes the project manager responsible for the efficient use of the labour while it is being charged to the project, but the project is not charged for time when the labour is not needed, provided that this was made clear when the labour was requested, or bought.

One area of common interest to almost all software companies is the need to manage working capital carefully because it can very quickly absorb vast amounts of funding. The main problem in this industry is caused by the level of outstanding receivables, as these cannot be offset by a correspondingly long period before suppliers are paid (the largest element within suppliers is the company's own work-force). This problem should be addressed by the financial management and control system, and can be if measures are introduced which focus not only on the days receivables which are outstanding, but also on the level of work-in-progress which has not yet been invoiced. These measures should be made a specific element in the managerial performance assessment of the project managers. They can control the efficiency of their own invoicing process and as they are in the closest contact with the client on a regular basis, they can chase up the payment of overdue invoices, including resolving any outstanding queries.

Clearly, the main areas of concern for financial management in the software product companies relate to the control of product development expenditure and the analysis of relative product profitabilities. In order for the financial forecasts to be of any value, the financial information must be very closely linked into the marketing data-base of the company, particularly regarding forecasts of the total market potential for new products and the probable continuing economic lives for existing products.

PROSPECTS FOR THE FUTURE

Many of the current changes which are dramatically affecting the industry are likely to continue for some time yet. It is clear that, while several sections of the software industry have now reached the mature stage of their life-cycle, they have not yet reached a stable industrial structure.

Software projects seem to be getting bigger and more complex, which makes their associated risks also larger. If software companies continue to do them on a fixed price basis, it is very likely that more spectacular problems will be seen in the future. This may well include the financial failure of some large software houses, because the impact of even one major cost overrun could become cataclysmic.

The vertical integration moves into the software industry are likely to continue but are likely to take the form of strategic alliances, not outright acquisitions, due to the problems associated with managing these complex, people based service companies once they have been acquired. The other partners to these joint ventures will include customers, computer manufacturers, and telecommunications companies (as they perceive the need to have a closer involvement in a critical success factor for their own industry).

The challenges for financial management and control in the future are, therefore, to avoid the risks of collapse due to taking on very large projects, to devise appropriate financial performance measures as the industry matures, and to design sound ways of financially managing the large number of joint ventures which will be developed in the software industry.

BACKGROUND TO THE INDUSTRY

The airline industry has developed rapidly but its rate of change has itself accelerated dramatically in recent years, as the whole structure of the industry has been challenged and attacked both from within and by changes in its external environment. The development of the industry almost needs to be considered as separate elements but the recent changes are blurring some of these original distinctions; airlines originally grew on an international basis or focused on their domestic market, if this was large enough, and flew primarily either scheduled services or chartered flights.

Obviously some countries are physically not large enough to support more than a very limited domestic airline industry, and in these countries most airlines developed international strategies (e.g. most European and Far Eastern countries fit this model). However, in the USA and the old Soviet Union particularly, the massive potential size of the internal market offered a far greater growth opportunity in the early years of the industry than the international market did. Both types of markets were originally highly regulated with airlines needing to pass safety standards, etc., before being allowed to start operations. Even more importantly, in the international market, the individual routes and number of flights on those routes are still the subject of agreement between the respective governments.

This regulatory framework not only created very significant entry barriers to the financially attractive routes, but also encouraged almost all countries to develop their own airline, as this automatically became eligible for a high proportion of the available scheduled flights (often referred to in the industry as slots) into and out of their own country. Thus the size and prestige of the national flag carrier became, for many years, a country status issue; more recently, economic reality has tended to become a more important factor than merely the prestige of having a large, loss-making national airline. This change has been accelerated by the trend towards privatisation of some of these previously government owned national airlines (e.g. British Airways, Singapore International Airlines and Qantas, the Australian international flag carrier); it is interesting that the USA, which has never had a nationalised airline, did not develop a single dramatically dominant international airline.

However, the domestic US market received the greatest external shock-wave in the 1980s with the deregulation of air fares and the opening up of many established routes to new operators. Suddenly many of the previous entry barriers were dismantled and new airlines rapidly appeared. The ensuing price competition meant that many of them equally rapidly disappeared, and this highlighted a very important element in the competitive strategy of any airline.

A single flight normally forms only one element in what may be a complicated overall travel itinerary, even if it only involves a single journey. A potential passenger may want to travel from their home in a small village in the north-east of England to visit a relative living in a small town in Ohio, USA. In addition to the issue of assistance in getting to and from the airports at each end of the journey, the choice of airline for the Atlantic crossing will depend upon the ease of getting as close as possible to the final destination. This makes the routes covered by the airline important and the key to success is what is commonly known as having a hub and spoke, or gateway, system of routes. The logic is that all major airlines should be based at a major hub airport (e.g. for British Airways, this is London's Heathrow airport), through which masses of travellers pass in order to change flights on their way to their final destinations. This hub allows the airline to carry passengers relatively conveniently to a much greater range of destinations than could ever be achieved by even the most complex scheduling of direct flights. Thus many passengers wishing to fly to various parts of the USA will choose the airline to travel with depending on the frequency and directness of the linkages from their major US hub to their required final destination. Most European airlines have a limited access to the major hubs in the USA, which is a serious competitive disadvantage in gaining transatlantic passengers who have a need for onward connections from their first point of landing in the USA.

Similarly, a major perceived weakness in the international routes operated by Pan-Am and TWA (the two most established US based international airlines which both got into severe financial difficulties in the early 1990s) was that they had neither an adequate feeder network of domestic flights into their main departure points from the USA, nor a comprehensive set of linkages for onward travel after the inter-continental part of the journey. Therefore it was logical for some of the international routes to be purchased, when these two airlines went into bankruptcy, by other US airlines which had much stronger domestic hub and spoke flight networks within the USA. However these acquisitions, by American Airlines and United prompted very strong complaints by European airlines. They complained that, because they did not have a similar level of access into the domestic US air traffic network, they would be placed at a serious competitive disadvantage against these new entrants to some of their traditional routes.

The practical response, by some European airlines was to try to develop strategic alliances with predominantly US domestic carriers, which could provide the necessary spokes within the USA. These strategic alliances included proposals to acquire sizeable minority stakes in these airlines which, not surprisingly, caused a reciprocating level of protests from American Airlines, United and Delta, i.e. the major US international airlines. Many of these arguments reached government-to-government level and have resulted in much proposed amendment to, and renegotiation of, the rules regarding mutual route availability in the respective local markets (e.g. British Airways attempted acquisition of a significant minority stake in US Air was modified and re-reviewed several times, before it was cleared by the Clinton administration).

So far no mention has been made of the chartered airlines which were also developing during the industry's very rapid growth stage but in a quite different way. Air travel quite quickly became a major element in the growth of the long distance holiday industry, and this provided the main stimulus for the development of the chartered airline industry. It is therefore not too surprising that some of the major chartered airlines were owned by the major tour operators. However, in addition to providing internal services, most of these airlines attempted to spread their risk by selling seats in their planes to other tour operators as well.

The initial competitive strategies were mainly based on cost with the result that chartered airlines tended to use older planes but, as their customers became more experienced travellers, the required level of service had to be improved. Hence several chartered airlines started using newer aeroplanes and providing a faster more efficient type of service. Some of them (notably Air Europe which was part of ILG which also owned Intasun, the second largest UK tour operator) moved into running scheduled services as well as their traditional chartered operations, thus totally blurring the divisions within the airline industry.

RELATED INDUSTRIES

The airline industry cannot really be considered totally in isolation because of its very significant interrelationship with the aircraft manufacturing industry and the aircraft leasing industry. The production of commercial aeroplanes is a very long and highly risky business, which is now dominated by three major global players (Boeing and MacDonnel Douglas in the USA and the European consortium operating as Airbus Industrie). Obviously each manufacturer is desperately keen to win orders for its new aeroplanes as far ahead as possible so as to reduce its own risk profile. There is also an option position available on future orders which, in times of very strong demand, enables the airline to gain a position on the manufacturer's waiting list without being financially committed to take the aeroplane when it is actually produced.

The high cost of these aeroplanes would make them easily the major fixed asset of any airline, but what the airlines actually want is the ability to use the asset rather than the ownership of the aeroplane. Thus, in order to avoid the airlines having to buy the planes directly from the manufacturers, a large leasing industry has developed, which comprises the large banks plus a few very specialised aircraft leasing companies such as GPA, an Irish based company which grew very rapidly during the 1980s. Indeed it reached a position of almost dominating the future order books of the major aeroplane manufacturers, as it became responsible for buying around 10 per cent of the western world's production of commercial aeroplanes in the early 1990s; its publicly stated plans involved ordering $20 billion of aeroplanes in the decade up to the year 2000. In order to fund this, the company planned a public flotation in 1992 plus the raising of a large amount of additional bank financing. Concerns regarding the airline industry and GPA's own position led to the proposed flotation being aborted due to lack of investor demand for the shares, and the company then found itself facing severe refinancing pressures from its banks. This created a roll-on level of concern in the financial markets regarding the future of this type of leasing transaction.

ALTERNATIVE COMPETITIVE STRATEGIES

During the early years of the regulated industry, the main competitive advantage was access to a good range of routes and the provision of a better level of service (prices were also regulated in most markets during this period). Deregulation enabled development of new strategies including a low price strategy which was implemented first by Laker Airways (on the North Atlantic routes) and then by People Express (both internally within the USA and internationally, including the same North Atlantic routes). The dramatically reduced selling prices meant that these airlines needed both to reduce their operating costs as far as possible and achieve a very high load factor on the flight, due to the very high fixed cost structure of a scheduled airline.

Both these airlines collapsed eventually, but another new entrant (Virgin Atlantic) implemented a mixed pricing strategy including a very low price for most of its seats, but a business class equivalent fare for what it called a 'first class service' (this class of ticket was actually christened 'Upper

Class', presumably because initially these passengers travelled on the upper deck of the airline's jumbo jet). This mixed strategy was expanded by Virgin as it acquired more planes and also increased its range of international routes. Virgin also entered into long-term strategic alliances by bringing in Japanese companies as shareholders in the group.

At the other extreme to these low price strategies was the use by both British Airways and Air France of the supersonic Concorde, which provided the ultimate speed available for a very substantial premium price. In between these extremes, most airlines competed on levels of service but increasingly, due to the impact of deregulation on certain routes, also on price. However, in the indirect service market, the airlines were also competing for the loyalty of the actual traveller (who is, of course, in this indirect segment of services, not the person paying for the ticket), via all sorts of loyalty bonuses and special offers.

This range of alternative competitive strategies leads to the identification of a number of critical success factors for the airline industry.

CRITICAL SUCCESS FACTORS

One immediately obvious critical success factor for any airline is access to an attractive range of routes on which to fly. However, in addition to route availability, the actual flight schedule is also important in order to maximise the available flying time of the airline's most significant tangible asset, its aeroplanes. The other related element is the load factor which can be achieved on the particular route, with the agreed frequency of flights and at the specified timetabling.

Load factors are also affected by the pricing strategy of the airline and on the way in which the aeroplane is configured for this route (i.e. the mix of first class, business class and economy seats). Thus the ability to segment the market within an individual plane is a key element in an airline's competitive strategy. This can be done to some degree by branding the different classes of travel and this type of clearly segmented branding strategy was implemented by British Airways following its privatisation. The idea was to create a clear impression of what the first class passenger should expect on a BA flight. The objectives were to create a high level of customer satisfaction and hence loyalty, as well as a desire on the part of the business class passengers to upgrade their next flight to first class.

Thus, achieving a high degree of customer loyalty is a critical success factor, but this must be achieved in a cost-efficient manner; some of the frequent flyer programmes brought in by the US airlines proved incredibly expensive to operate and added to the financial problems of some airlines.

The cost base of a scheduled airline is basically fixed for any particular flight. It is critically important that sufficient revenue is generated from each flight at least to cover the specific costs of that flight. As the airline cannot significantly affect the costs, it must attempt to manage the total revenue which is generated from the flight. The airlines have developed sophisticated pricing mechanisms which are very appropriate to the highly perishable nature of their product. These include the physical segmentation of the actual aeroplane but this can provide the airline with a problem. It is quite easy, if their own class is full, to upgrade economy passengers into spare seats in business class, or business class passengers into first class seats that have not been booked; they are unlikely to object to being placed in a better environment than they are paying for. However, if first class is overbooked, it is not so easy to downgrade a passenger; the airline will have to compensate the passenger heavily and most airlines try to do this on a voluntary basis by making passengers an attractive offer to trade down on this flight.

The only reason that this type of problem occurs is that, in an attempt to fill each plane, the airlines overbook the available seats, based on an estimate of the passengers who will not physically show up despite being booked on the flight. A partial solution to this problem is to generate some income from any available seats and this is achieved by the introduction of the very low stand-by fare, where the passenger only travels if there is space on the plane. A better solution is for the airline to get a more accurate idea of how full the plane will be in time for it to take some action; a classic definition of a decision support system.

As this is so critical, the major airlines are investing large sums of money in developing sophisticated predictive models for seat occupancies. Using the historical data-base, the predictive model can estimate, a long time before the flight is scheduled to depart, how full the plane will turn out to be, depending on how sales are going so far. If it appears that the flight will have spare seats, the airline has the opportunity to instigate some promotional activity in an attempt to increase the final level of demand. Given that the marginal cost of an additional passenger is so low, there is very little difficulty in financially justifying the promotional expenditure.

Another critical success factor relates to the level of control over the channel of distribution through which the sales of airline tickets are made. Most bookings are made by a travel agent and hence it is critically important that the travel agent has the maximum incentive to book passengers on our particular airline, whenever there is a choice. This objective is being worked at by the development of the incredibly sophisticated, information technology based reservation systems. These enable the travel agent to check the seat availability on any suitable flights and to book the passenger directly onto the flight if seats are available; if the flight is full the passenger can be logged onto a waiting list in case there is a cancellation.

FINANCIAL MANAGEMENT AND CONTROL ISSUES

The airline industry is one where it is clearly necessary to produce financial information which is segmented in a number of different ways. Most costs are relatively fixed but the direct costs of providing the different classes of service must be regularly checked to ensure that the incremental revenue achieved more than covers the incremental costs. It is also important that costs are examined against their specific added value generation, even though this assessment may require a degree of subjectivity.

However, the main focus of the financial management and control system in this industry is on the segment profitability analyses. These can be done by route, by hub and by spoke, by class of passenger, by individual flight within a particular route, by groups of passengers, etc. What is vitally important to register immediately is that the direct costs which must be taken into account in these segmented analyses are each very different. In other words, these segmented profitability analyses are not designed to apportion the net profit of the airline across each of the categories. They should enable comparisons of the relative profitability of the different segments of the business to be carried out using the relevant, decision oriented financial information, and they must be designed and implemented accordingly.

The financial analysis system should also assist in the financial evaluation of the various promotional and other incentive schemes which are proposed by the company. This analysis can be greatly assisted by the development of a good historic data-base of the actual out-turns of previous expenditures. The financial evaluation of the very expensive information technology investments being made by the airlines are also important, as are the evaluations of the specialised financing schemes which are available for aircraft leasing. These financial evaluations must obviously take into account the risks associated with the particular project and with any alternatives against which it is being compared.

FUTURE DEVELOPMENTS

Deregulation in the US air travel market has led to a period of dramatic restructuring within the US airline industry. It is very likely that a similar level of restructuring will occur in the European industry when a similar level of deregulation occurs. Many airlines are currently trying to ensure their survival through this period of industry turbulence by entering into strategic alliances or by acquiring other airlines outright. This type of industry rationalisation and consolidation still has a long way to go.

The degree of market segmentation is likely to get greater as the airlines become more skilled at identifying and targeting specific sub-segments of the market, with particular needs and wants. For example, People Express identified and accessed a completely new type of passenger through their very low fares: the person who didn't fly before People Express made it possible.

The major constraint on air travel will become the take-off and landing slots at the major airports due to physical congestion. Hence there will be a need to use these as a critical constraint in the financial analysis of profitability; i.e. it might be useful to work out the contribution made per landing and take-off. This should mean that long flights and flights using very large aeroplanes would appear financially more attractive on this basis. Such an outcome might encourage airlines to increase their prices on those shorter flights using smaller planes to an even greater premium than they command already.

INDEX

accountancy firms, 50, 110

accounting for competitive advantage, 94, 112

activity based costing (ABC), 75

added value, 33

advertising industry, 41, 50, 79, 114, 140, 168, Ch 15

Aegis Group, 214

Air Europe, 120, 231

airlines, 15, 29, 82, 110, 136, 180, Ch 17

Air Tours, 120

Aldi, 200

alternative use value, 42

alternative way out, 106

American Airlines, 230

amusement arcades, 34

Ansoff matrix, 46

audit firms, 53

automated teller machines (ATMs), 17, 56, 146

avoidable costs, 83

banking, 17, 31

bank overdrafts, 104

bar code scanning, 146

barriers to entry, 37

barriers to exit, 41

Bates, Ted, 210

Battersea power station, 44

Benetton, 156

BET plc, 58

Body Shop, 27, 156, 205

bowling alleys, 34

break-even analysis, 107

British Airways, 120, 229

British Gas, 55, 109

British Telecom, 55, 126

budgeting, 70

Burger King, 50, 156

Burton Group, 203

business air travel, 29, 54

business risk, 66

business services, 28

Cable & Wireless, 126

CAP Gemini Sogeti, 221

CAP Group, 218

capital market line, 36

Carat Espace, 213

car dealerships, 38

car industry, 57

Carrefour, 201

cash 'n' carry warehouses, 112

charge cards, 113

chartered airlines, 110

cinemas, 34

clubs, 34

committed costs, 41, 75, 129, 144

communication, 132

competitive advantage, 34

computerised reservation systems, 54

computer maintenance companies, 40

computer industry, 39

computer services, 81

computer software, 40, 95, 109, 142, 170, Ch 16

consultancy, 114

contract caterer, 9, 28

contracting out, 32

contribution analysis, 130

contribution per unit of limiting factor, 130

control, 132

convertibles, 164

coordination, 132

corporate financial strategy, 12

corporate objectives, 69

cost/benefit analysis, 31

cost centre, 99

cost driver, 75

cost leadership strategy, 74

courier services, 97

critical success factor, 12

customer led strategy, 47
customer retention, 140

Dan-Air, 120
debt, 105
debt to equity, 133
deliverable service, 146
Delta, 231
differential cash flows, 123
differentiation of service, 44
direct product profitability (DPP), 49, 206
discotheques, 34
discounted cash flow (DCF), 100, 123
discretionary, 129
distributors, 112
do without, 146
dry cleaning, 45

earnings per share, 159
earn-out deals, 76
economic performance, 72, 190
economies of scale, 56, 76
EDS, 222
effectiveness measures, 72, 191
efficiency measures, 72, 191
electrical retailing, 127
electricity generating industry, 43
employment agencies, 58
engineered costs, 75, 147
entry barriers, 37
equity, 105
estate agents, 47, 128
Eurotunnel, 43
existing customer led strategy, 47
existing service led strategy, 49
exit barriers, 41
expected value, 121
expense centre, 72, 99
experience curve, 139
extractive industry, 21

facilities management, 32, 81, 219
fashion clothing retailers, 97
financial data base, 185
financial decisions, 87
financial risk, 66
financial services, 31, 47, 114, 127, 176
fixed costs, 41

flexible budgets, 131
focus strategy, 44
forecast, 131
free cash flow, 103
frequent flyer programmes, 29, 113
fresh produce, 134

gap analysis, 46
gateway, 230
GEC, 9
goals, 69
gold star membership, 137
golf clubs, 137
GPA, 232
Grand Metropolitan, 49

hairdressing, 16, 22, 26, 45
home banking, 54
home shopping, 54
Holiday Inn, 107
Hoskyns, 221
hotel accommodation, 30
hotel companies, 106, 115, 135
hub and spoke, 230

ILG Group, 120
incremental costs, 87
indoor tennis centres, 42
inflation, 124
in-store credit cards, 113, 180, 206
insurance broking, 51
insurance industry, 53
intangible assets, 61
internal rate of return (IRR), 103
investment, 61
investment banking, 133, 141

key limiting factor, 130
knowledge industries, 176
Kwik Save, 199

Laker Airways, 232
law of comparative advantage, 5
learning curves, 139
leasing, 42
legal profession, 115
leisure centres, 103, 137
Levitt, T, 126

Logica, 228
long term planning, 70
Lotus, 223
lowest cost supplier, 44

managerial performance, 72, 190
manufacturing industry, 21
market development strategy, 49
market penetration strategy, 46
Marks & Spencer, 28, 202
McDonalds, 49, 156
merchant banking, 134
Microsoft, 223
mission statement, 69
monopoly position, 43, 109
multi-screen cinemas, 34

national grid, 55
National Health Service, 89
need to know, 188
negative working capital, 42, 168, 199
Next plc, 204
nice to know, 188
not for profit, 127
nuclear industry, 44

off-centre retail parks, 42
Ogilvy & Mather, 210
opportunity cost, 41
organic growth, 156
Orient Express, 45
outsourcing, 58, 79, 147
Owners Abroad, 120
own lables, 48

package tour operators, 97
Pan Am, 230
Pareto rule, 145
penetration pricing, 74, 141
perishability, 15
personal service industries, 95
People Express, 232
pizza delivery service, 54
Porter, M, 44
Price/Earnings (P/E) multiple, 161
private health care, 126
private lables, 48
private health insurance, 53

privatisation, 43
probability estimates, 121
product development strategy, 47
product life cycles, 35, 65
professional staff, 109
profitability index (PI), 103
project costing, 226
public houses, 34
pubs, 34
Quantas, 229
QEII, 45
Quarternary stage, 7
queues, 73

replacement cost investment, 55
Residual Income (RI), 101
restaurants, 15, 51
retailer brands, 48, 113, 198, 206
retailing, 9, 15, 26, 42, 47, 166, 179, Ch 14
retail 'shed' concept, 42
Return on Investment (ROI), 8, 100
reverse engineering, 53
Rights Issues, 158
risk assessment process, 37
risk/return line, 35

Saatchi & Saatchi, 169, 210
Sainsbury, 158, 197
sale and leaseback, 107, 199
salvage value, 41
satellite TV stations, 34
scheduled airlines, 110
SDA, 220
SD-Scicon, 221
Sema Group, 222
sensitivity analysis, 121
sequential probability factors, 122
Singapore International Airlines, 229
slippage factor, 62
skimming pricing, 74, 140
software companies, 40, 95, 109, 142, 170, Ch 16
Sorrell, M, 169, 210
speed of response, 54
sport centres, 42
staff utilisation ratios, 109
stages of development, 3
stakeholders, 12

standard costing, 10, 76, 147
stand-by air fare, 134
Strategic Business Unit (SBU), 8
strategic management accounting, 12, 64
super-profit, 39, 49, 62
sustainable competitive advantage, 34
synergy, 158

Taurus, 182
telecommunications industry, 126
Tesco, 197
themed pubs, 35
third party maintenance companies, 40
Thompson, J Walter, 169, 210
time and materials basis, 13
travel agents, 54
travel industry, 113
turnkey contract, 142

TWA, 230

United, 230
utility companies, 109
value chain, 41, 48
value engineering, 145, 225
variance analysis, 150
vertical disintegration, 79
vertical integration, 28, 89
video rental shops, 34
Virgin Atlantic, 232

warehouse club, 208
water companies, 109
WCRS, 213
wholesalers, 112
Wimpy, 50
WPP Group, 169, 211